4th Biennial International Workshop on Balto-Slavic Natural Language Processing 2013

Sofia, Bulgaria
8 – 9 August 2013

ISBN: 978-1-62748-979-9

Printed from e-media with permission by:

Curran Associates, Inc.
57 Morehouse Lane
Red Hook, NY 12571

CURRAN ASSOCIATES INC. proceedings.com

Some format issues inherent in the e-media version may also appear in this print version.

Printed by Curran Associates, Inc. (2013)

Association for Computational Linguistics
209 N. Eighth Street
Stroudsburg, Pennsylvania 18360

Phone: 1-570-476-8006
Fax: 1-570-476-0860

acl@aclweb.org

Additional copies of this publication are available from:

Curran Associates, Inc.
57 Morehouse Lane
Red Hook, NY 12571 USA
Phone: 845-758-0400
Fax: 845-758-2634
Email: curran@proceedings.com
Web: www.proceedings.com

ACL 2013

The 4th Biennial International Workshop on Balto-Slavic Natural Language Processing

Workshop Proceedings

August 8-9, 2013
Sofia, Bulgaria

Preface

This volume contains the papers presented at BSNLP-2013: the Fourth in a series of Workshops on Balto-Slavic Natural Language Processing.

The motivation for convening the Workshops is clear. On one hand, the languages from the Balto-Slavic group play an important role due to their widespread use and diverse cultural heritage. The languages are spoken by over 400 million speakers worldwide. The recent political and economic developments in Central and Eastern Europe bring Balto-Slavic societies and their languages into new focus in terms of rapid technological advancement and expanding consumer markets. In the context of the European Union, the Balto-Slavic group today constitutes about one third of its official languages.

On the other hand, research on theoretical and applied NLP in many of the Balto-Slavic languages is still in its early stages. The advent of the Internet in the 1990's established the dominant role of English in science, popular culture, and other areas of on-line activity, which further weakened the presence of Balto-Slavic languages. Consequently, in comparison to English, there is a dire lack of resources, processing tools and applications for most of these languages, especially the smaller ones.

Despite this "minority" status, the Balto-Slavic languages offer a wealth of fascinating scientific and technical challenges for researchers to work on. The linguistic phenomena specific to Balto-Slavic languages—such as rich morphological inflection and relatively free word order—present highly intriguing and non-trivial problems for construction of NLP tools for these languages, and require richer morphological and syntactic resources to be exploited. In this direction, the invited talk by Kiril Simov on *"Ontologies and Linked Open Data for Acquisition and Exploitation of Language Resources"* presents methods for acquisition of language resources from different types of on-line and off-line data sources.

The goal of this Workshop was to bring together academic researchers and industry practitioners who work on NLP for Balto-Slavic languages. It is our hope that the Workshop would further stimulate research on NLP for these languages and foster the creation of tools for them. The Workshop gives the researchers a forum for exchange of ideas and experience, for discussion difficult-to-tackle problems, and for making new resources more widely-known. One fascinating aspect of this sub-family of languages is their structural similarity, as well as an easily recognisable lexical and inflectional inventory spanning the entire group, which—despite the lack of mutual intelligibility—creates a special environment in which researchers can fully appreciate the shared problems and solutions, and communicate in a natural way.

This Workshop continues the proud tradition established by previous BSNLP Workshops:

1. the First BSNLP Workshop, held in conjunction with ACL 2007 Conference in Prague;
2. the Second BSNLP Workshop, held in conjunction with IIS 2009: Intelligent Information Systems, in Kraków, Poland;
3. the Third BSNLP Workshop, held in conjunction with TSD 2011, 14th International Conference on Text, Speech and Dialogue in Plzeň, Czech Republic.

This year we received 31 submissions—a 50% increase over the First BSNLP Workshop in 2007. Of these, 16 were accepted for presentation (resulting in an acceptance rate of 51%). Compared to the previous BSNLP workshops, this year we have more papers about higher-level tasks, such as information extraction and sentiment analysis. This hopefully shows a trend towards building user-oriented applications for Balto-Slavic languages, in addition to working on lower-level NLP tools.

Three papers discuss approaches to sentiment analysis and opinion mining. Five are about classic information extraction tasks: three on named entity recognition and two on event extraction. Two papers are about WordNets for different Slavic languages. Two papers are about morphological processing and parsing. The rest of the papers cover different topics, including acquisition of resources, keyword extraction, and lexicon analysis.

The papers together cover nine different languages: 5 on Croatian, 4 on Russian, 2 each on Bulgarian, Polish and Slovene, and one each on Czech, Lithuanian and Serbian. We also accepted an interesting paper about named-entity recognition for Estonian—which, although it does not belong to the Balto-Slavic group, does belong to the Baltic area, and has morphological complexity at least matching that of the Baltic and Slavic languages.

It is our sincere hope that this work will help further stimulate the growth of this rich and exciting field.

BSNLP Organizers:
Jakub Piskorski (Polish Academy of Sciences)
Lidia Pivovarova (University of Helsinki)
Hristo Tanev (Joint Research Centre)
Roman Yangarber (University of Helsinki)

Organizers:

Jakub Piskorski, Polish Academy of Sciences
Lidia Pivovarova, University of Helsinki, and St.Petersburg State University, Russia
Hristo Tanev, Joint Research Centre of the European Commission, Ispra, Italy
Roman Yangarber, University of Helsinki, Finland

Program Committee:

Tania Avgustinova, University of Saarland, Germany
Kalina Bontcheva, University of Sheffield, UK
Pavel Braslavski, Kontur labs, and Ural Federal University, Russia
Boris Dobrov, Moscow State University, Russia
Tomaž Erjavec, Jozef Stefan Institute, Ljubljana, Slovenia
Katja Filippova, Google, Zurich, Switzerland
Radovan Garabik, Comenius University in Bratislava
Tatiana Gornostay, Tilde, Riga, Latvia
Maxim Gubin, Facebook Inc., Menlo Park CA
Mikhail Kopotev, University of Helsinki, Finalnd
Vladislav Kuboň, Charles University, Prague, Czech Republic
Olga Mitrofanova, St.Petersburg State University, Russia
Karel Pala, Masaryk University, Brno, Czech Republic
Maciej Piasecki, Wrocław University of Technology, Poland
Jakub Piskorski, Polish Academy of Sciences, Warsaw, Poland
Lidia Pivovarova, Univeristy of Helsinki/St.Petersburg State University, Russia
Adam Przepiórkowski, Polish Academy of Sciences, Warsaw, Poland
Agata Savary, Université François Rabelais, Tours, France
Kiril Simov, Bulgarian Academy of Sciences, Bulgaria
Joseph Steinberger, University of West Bohemia, Plzeň, Czech Republic
Pavel Straňák, Charles University in Prague, Czech Republic
Stan Szpakowicz, University of Ottawa, Canada
Marko Tadic, University of Zagreb, Croatia
Hristo Tanev, Joint Research Centre, Ispra, Italy
Roman Yangarber, University of Helsinki, Finalnd

Invited Speaker:

Kiril Simov, Bulgarian Academy of Sciences, Bulgaria

Table of Contents

Workshop Program

Thursday, August 8, 2013

9:00–9:15 Welcome Remarks

9:15–10:30 Invited Talk: *Ontologies and Linked Open Data for Acquisition and Exploitation of Language Resources*
Kiril Simov

10:30–11:00 Coffee Break

Session I: Opinion Mining and Sentiment Analysis

11:00–11:25 *A Comparison of Approaches for Sentiment Classification on Lithuanian Internet Comments*
Jurgita Kapočiutė-Dzikienė, Algis Krupavičius and Tomas Krilavičius

11:25–11:45 *Evaluating Sentiment Analysis Systems in Russian*
Ilia Chetviorkin and Natalia Loukachevitch

11:45–12:05 *Aspect-Oriented Opinion Mining from User Reviews in Croatian*
Goran Glavaš, Damir Korenčić and Jan Šnajder

Session II: Morphology, Syntax and Semantics

12:05–12:30 *Frequently Asked Questions Retrieval for Croatian Based on Semantic Textual Similarity*
Mladen Karan, Lovro Žmak and Jan Šnajder

12:30–14:00 Lunch

14:00–14:25 *Parsing Russian: a hybrid approach*
Dan Skatov, Sergey Liverko, Vladimir Okatiev and Dmitry Strebkov

14:25–14:45 *GPKEX: Genetically Programmed Keyphrase Extraction from Croatian Texts*
Marko Bekavac and Jan Šnajder

14:45–15:10 *Lemmatization and Morphosyntactic Tagging of Croatian and Serbian*
Željko Agić, Nikola Ljubešić and Danijela Merkler

Thursday, August 8, 2013 (continued)

Session III: Cross-lingual methods and Machine Translation

15:10–15:30 *Modernizing historical Slovene words with character-based SMT*
Yves Scherrer and Tomaž Erjavec

15:30–16:00 Coffee Break

16:00–16:25 *Improving English-Russian sentence alignment through POS tagging and Damerau-Levenshtein distance*
Andrey Kutuzov

16:25–16:50 *Identifying false friends between closely related languages*
Nikola Ljubešić and Darja Fišer

16:50–17:15 Discussion: Establishing BSNLP SIG

Friday, August 9, 2013

Session IV: Information Extraction

09:20–09:45 *Named Entity Recognition in Estonian*
Alexander Tkachenko, Timo Petmanson and Sven Laur

09:45–10:10 *On Named Entity Recognition in Targeted Twitter Streams in Polish.*
Jakub Piskorski and Maud Ehrmann

10:10–10:30 *Recognition of Named Entities Boundaries in Polish Texts*
Michał Marcińczuk and Jan Kocoń

10:30–11:00 Coffee Break

11:00–11:25 *Adapting the PULS event extraction framework to analyze Russian text*
Lidia Pivovarova, Mian Du and Roman Yangarber

11:25–11:50 *Semi-automatic Acquisition of Lexical Resources and Grammars for Event Extraction in Bulgarian and Czech*
Hristo Tanev and Josef Steinberger

Friday, August 9, 2013 (continued)

11:50–12:15 *Wordnet-Based Cross-Language Identification of Semantic Relations*
Ivelina Stoyanova, Svetla Koeva and Svetlozara Leseva

12:15–12:30 Concluding remarks

Invited Talk: Ontologies and Linked Open Data for Acquisition and Exploitation of Language Resources

Kiril Simov
Linguistic Modelling Deparment, IICT-BAS
Acad. G. Bonchev 25A, 1113 Sofia, Bulgaria
kivs@bultreebank.org

Recent developments in Natural Language Processing (NLP) are heading towards knowledge rich resources and technology. Integration of linguistically sound grammars, sophisticated machine learning settings and world knowledge background is possible given the availability of the appropriate resources: deep multilingual treebanks, representing detailed syntactic and semantic information; and vast quantities of world knowledge information encoded within ontologies and Linked Open Data datasets (LOD). Thus, the addition of world knowledge facts provides a substantial extension of the traditional semantic resources like WordNet, FrameNet and others. This extension comprises numerous types of Named Entities (Persons, Locations, Events, etc.), their properties (Person has a birthDate; birthPlace, etc.), relations between them (Person works for an Organization), events in which they participated (Person participated in war, etc.), and many other facts. This huge amount of structured knowledge can be considered the missing ingredient of the knowledge-based NLP of 80's and the beginning of 90's.

The integration of world knowledge within language technology is defined as an *ontology-to-text* relation comprising different language and world knowledge in a common model. We assume that the lexicon is based on the ontology, i.e. the word senses are represented by concepts, relations or instances. The problem of lexical gaps is solved by allowing the storage of not only lexica, but also free phrases. The gaps in the ontology (a missing concept for a word sense) are solved by appropriate extensions of the ontology. The mapping is partial in the sense that both elements (the lexicon and the ontology) are artefacts and thus — they are never complete. The integration of the interlinked ontology and lexicon with the grammar theory, on the other hand, requires some additional and non-trivial reasoning over the world knowledge. We will discuss phenomena like selectional constraints, metonymy, regular polysemy, bridging relations, which live in the intersective areas between world facts and their language reflection. Thus, the actual text annotation on the basis of ontology-to-text relation requires the explication of additional knowledge like co-occurrence of conceptual information, discourse structure, etc.

Such knowledge is mainly present in deeply processed language resources like HPSG-based (LFG-based) treebanks (RedWoods treebank, DeepBank, and others). The inherent characteristics of these language resources is their dynamic nature. They are constructed simultaneously with the development of a deep grammar in the corresponding linguistic formalism. The grammar is used to produce all potential analyses of the sentences within the treebank. The correct analyses are selected manually on the base of linguistic discriminators which would determine the correct linguistic production. The annotation process of the sentences provides feedback for the grammar writer to update the grammar. The life cycle of a dynamic language resource can be naturally supported by the semantic technology behind the ontology and LOD - modeling the grammatical knowledge as well as the annotation knowledge; supporting the annotation process; reclassification after changes within the grammar; querying the available resources; exploitation in real applications. The addition of a LOD component to the system would facilitate the exchange of language resources created in this way and would support the access to the existing resources on the web.

A Comparison of Approaches for Sentiment Classification on Lithuanian Internet Comments

Jurgita Kapočiūtė-Dzikienė
Kaunas University of Technology / K. Donelaičio 73, LT-44249 Kaunas, Lithuania
jurgita.k.dz@gmail.com

Algis Krupavičius
Kaunas University of Technology / K. Donelaičio 73, LT-44249 Kaunas, Lithuania
pvai@ktu.lt

Tomas Krilavičius
Baltic Institute of Advanced Technology / Saulėtekio 15, LT-10224 Vilnius, Lithuania
t.krilavicius@bpti.lt

Abstract

Despite many methods that effectively solve sentiment classification task for such widely used languages as English, there is no clear answer which methods are the most suitable for the languages that are substantially different. In this paper we attempt to solve Internet comments sentiment classification task for Lithuanian, using two classification approaches – knowledge-based and supervised machine learning. We explore an influence of sentiment word dictionaries based on the different parts-of-speech (adjectives, adverbs, nouns, and verbs) for knowledge-based method; different feature types (bag-of-words, lemmas, word n-grams, character n-grams) for machine learning methods; and pre-processing techniques (emoticons replacement with sentiment words, diacritics replacement, etc.) for both approaches. Despite that supervised machine learning methods (Support Vector Machine and Naïve Bayes Multinomial) significantly outperform proposed knowledge-based method all obtained results are above baseline. The best accuracy 0.679 was achieved with Naïve Bayes Multinomial and token unigrams plus bigrams, when pre-processing involved diacritics replacement.

1 Introduction

An automatic extraction of opinions from a text has become an area of growing interest in the recent years. Due to the user-generated content available on the Internet companies can measure the feedback about their products or services; sociologists can look at people's reaction about public events; psychologists can study general mind-state of communities with regard to various issues; etc. Thus sentiment classification helps solving many various tasks, ranging from a very general to the very specific, requiring special solutions. Majority of tasks consider the content in general by focusing on the subjectivity vs. objectivity or semantic orientation (positive vs. negative) detection of reviews, tweets, blogs, or Internet comments. Others are solving very specific tasks, e.g. early threats detection (Bouma et al., 2012), prediction of user's potentiality to send out offensive content (Chen et al., 2012), etc.

But even adaptation to the task is not always effective due to the variations and complexity of the language. Sentiments are not always expressed explicitly, while for the meanings hidden in the context additional world knowledge is necessary. Moreover, sentiments may involve sarcasm and be interpreted differently in various domains and contexts. Despite all the mentioned difficulties, sentiment classification task is rather easy for us, humans, but manual analysis is time consuming and requires a lot of human-resources. Due to this fact automatic sentiment classifiers are often selected instead.

Various classification techniques effectively solve sentiment classification task for such widely used languages as English, but there is no clear answer which method is the most suitable for Lithuanian. Our focus is at finding classification approach yielding the best results on Lithuanian Internet comments by classifying them into positive, negative and neutral categories.

2 Related Work

Due to the complexity of sentiment classification task, there is a vast variety of methods trying to tackle this problem (for review see Pang and Lee (2008)).

All methods used to solve sentiment classification task fall into the three main categories: knowledge-based, machine learning and hybrid.

In knowledge-based approaches sentiment is seen as the function of keywords (usually based on their count). Thus the main task is the construction of sentiment discriminatory-word lexicons with indicated class labels (positive or negative) and sometimes even with their intensiveness. Lexicons are constructed either manually (Taboada et al., 2011) or semi-automatically making use of such resources as WordNet (Hu and Liu, 2004); (Esuli and Sebastiani, 2006) or via word associations based on the heuristics evaluating word's occurrence alongside with the "seed" words in the text (Turney, 2002); (Turney and Littman, 2003).

Adjectives (or adjectival phrases) are considered as the most popular sentiment indicators, e.g. Benamara et al. (2007) claim that adjectives and adverbs (chosen based on the proposed adverb scoring technique) give much better results than adjectives alone; Taboada et al. (2011) show that such lexical items as nouns and verbs (not only adjectives and adverbs) can also carry important semantic polarity information.

Ding and Liu (2007) argue that semantic orientation is content dependent task and words alone are not sufficient sentiment indicators thus incorporate them into the set of linguistic rules used in classification; Choi and Cardie (2008) use heuristics based on the compositional semantics (considering the effect of interactions among the words) and achieve better results over the methods not incorporating it; Taboada et al. (2011) take into account valence shifters (intensifiers, downtoners, negation and irrealis markers) that influence the polarity of the neighboring words for English; Kuznetsova et al. (2013) – for Russian.

An alternative for the knowledge-based methods is machine learning that in turn can be grouped into supervised and clustering techniques. Clustering is rarely used due to the low accuracy, but the drawback of supervised machine learning (that we will further focus on) is that for model creation a training dataset (with manually pre-assigned sentiment class labels) is required.

The main issue for supervised machine learning techniques is proper selection of features. Nevertheless, the most basic approach remains bag-of-words interpretation. Pang et al. (2002) show that bag-of-words beat other feature types (based on token bigrams, parts-of-speech information and word position in the text) with Support Vector Machine (SVM) method. But on the contrary, Dave et al. (2003) report that token n-grams (up to trigrams) can improve the performance compared with simple unigrams; Cui et al. (2006) with higher order token n-grams (n = 3, 4, 5, 6) and Passive Aggressive classifier outperform unigrams and bigrams; Pak and Parubek (2011) with token bigrams and Naïve Bayes Multinomial method outperform both token unigrams and trigrams.

Dave et al. (2003) also report that stemming improves accuracy compared with the bag-of-words baseline, but other linguistic features (negation, collocations of words, etc.) on the contrary – hurt the performance. Raaijmakers and Kraaij (2008) use document-level character n-grams (n = 2, 3, 4, 5, 6) with SVM (geodesic kernel); Hartmann et al. (2011) claim that document-level character n-grams used, namely, with Naïve Bayes method are even better choice than token n-grams (because the probability of finding character n-gram is much higher and the relations between consecutive words are still considered).

Hybrid approaches combine both knowledge-based and machine learning methods thus achieving superior performance. As it is demonstrated by Mullen and Collier (2004) using SVM and combined token unigram features with those based on favorability measures (for phrases, adjectives and even knowledge of topic).

Sentiment classification results can be influenced by pre-processing as well. E.g. Kennedy and Inkpen (2006) claim that valence shifters and Mukherjee and Bhattacharyya (2012) show that discourse information incorporated into bag-of-words improve classification accuracy both for knowledge-based and SVM methods. But often pre-processing techniques (such as emoticons replacement, negation treatment and stop words removal) are selected without any considerations (e.g. see in (Pak and Paroubek, 2011)).

Both knowledge-based and supervised machine learning methods are domain-dependent (when classifier trained in one domain can barely beat the baseline in the other) and, moreover, domain-sensitive. E.g. Aue and Gamon (2005) with Naïve Bayes and SVM classifiers show that different types of features work better across different domains; therefore usually methods are built for the specific selected domain. Sometimes domain-dependent problem is circumvented by extracting related content with manually created rules (Wang et al., 2012) or via machine learning: i.e. by performing topicality classification at the first step and sentiment afterwards (Hurst and Nigam, 2004). Read and Carroll (2009) solve domain-depended problem by using special methodology to build the classifiers that are robust across the different domains.

Hence sentiment classification is domain and task dependent problem. Moreover, the performance of selected method can also depend on the language. E.g. Boiy and Moens (2009) demonstrate that the best accuracy with token unigrams (augmented with linguistics features) is obtained using Naïve Bayes Multinomial for English, SVM for Dutch and Maximum Entropy for French language. Besides, some solutions are proposed for multilingual texts as well, e.g. Cheng and Zhulyn (2012) show that generalized bigram model (especially suitable for the languages with a flexible word order) using Naïve Bayes and logistic regression classifiers can achieve high accuracy on different Germanic, Roman and East Asian languages.

We cannot provide any example of experiments based on sentiment classification for Lithuanian. Consequentially, this paper is the first attempt at finding an accurate sentiment classification approach (knowledge-based or machine learning) on Lithuanian Internet comments. Experiments will be performed with different pre-processing techniques, lexicons, and feature types.

3 The Lithuanian Language

In this section we discuss Lithuanian language properties focusing on those aspects (inflection morphology, word derivation system and word order in a sentence) that may be important in the sentiment classification task.

Lithuanian language has rich inflectional morphology, more complex than Latvian or Slavic languages (Savickienė et al., 2009). Adjectives are inflected by 7 cases, 2 (+1) genders, 2 numbers, 5 degrees of comparison, and have 2 pronominal forms; adverbs – by 5 degrees of comparison; nouns – by 7 cases, 2 (+1) genders and 2 numbers; verbs – by 3 moods, 4 tenses, 2 numbers, and 3 persons. Besides, verbs can have non-conjugative forms (participles, adverbial participles, verbal adverbs, and some forms of gerund) that can be inflected by tense, case, gender, number, and have an active or passive forms. Various inflection forms in Lithuanian language are expressed by the different endings (and suffixes), moreover, e.g. nouns have 12 different inflection paradigms; adjectives – 9.

Lithuanian language has rich word derivation system. 78 suffixes are used to derive diminutives and hypocoristic words (Ulvydas, 1965), that are especially frequent in spoken language; 25 prefixes are used for the nouns; 19 – for the verbs; and 3 (+4 in dialects) – for the adjectives and adjectival adverbs. Suffixes and prefixes change the meaning, e.g. suffix "-iaus-" change "geras" (*good*) to "geriausias" (*the best*) (by the way, the ending has to be adjusted to the new suffix, therefore "-as" is replaced by "-ias"); prefix "nu-" and reflexive participle "-si-" change "šnekėti" (*to talk*) to "nusišnekėti" (*to blunder out*). Prefixes in Lithuanian can also be used to derive phrasal verbs (e.g. from "eiti" (*to go*) to "įeiti" (*to go in*), "išeiti" (*to go out*), etc.) and negative words.

The particle "ne-" (*no, not*) or "nebe-" (*no longer*) giving to the words (adjectives, adjectival adverbs, adverbial adverbs, nouns, verbs and all their non-conjugative forms) an opposite meaning is attached to them as a prefix: "geras" (*good*) – "negeras" (*not good*); "skaisčiai" (*brightly*) – "nebeskaisčiai" (*no longer brightly*); "sėkmė" (*a fortune*) – "nesėkmė" (*a misfortune*); "bėgti" (*to run*) – "nebebėgti" (*no longer to run*); etc.

But if particle "ne", "nebe" or "nėra" (*no, not*) expresses contradiction, it is written separately (e.g. in "jis neblogas" (*he is not bad*) "ne" goes as the prefix, but in "jis ne blogas, o geras" (*he is not bad, but good*) "ne" goes separately.

The difference between English and Lithuanian is that a negative idea in English is expressed by only one negative word such as *nothing*, *nobody*, *never*, whereas in Lithuanian such sentence must contain two negated words, e.g. "niekas gerai nežaidžia" (*nobody plays well*) word-to-word translation is (*nobody well not plays*); "niekada nesakyk niekada" (*never say never*) word-to-word translation is (*never not say never*).

The word order in Lithuanian sentences is free, but it performs notional function, i.e. sentences are grammatically correct regardless of the word order, but the meaning (things that are highlighted) can differ. E.g. whereas in "tu esi labai geras" (*you are very good*) intensifier "labai" (*very*) is highlighted but in "tu esi geras labai" (*you are very good*) adjective "geras" (*good*) is highlighted, thus the first phrase gets higher positive intensiveness.

4 Methodology

4.1 Dataset

The dataset used in our sentiment classification task contains online Internet comments to articles crawled from the largest Lithuanian daily newspaper *Lietuvos rytas* (2013). These comments reflect people's opinions about the topical events in domestic and foreign politics, sport, etc.

All Internet comments were manually labeled as positive, negative or neutral. The decision about the class label was based on a mutual agreement of two human-experts. Efforts were made to focus solely on each comment, but known topic and previous posts could still influence experts' decision. Ambiguous comments were discarded thus leaving only single-labeled ones. Negative class strongly dominated the others. To maintain balanced class distribution the amount of comments (treated as instances in the classification process) belonging to the different classes was equalized by discarding redundant instances. See statistics of the dataset in Table 1.

Class label	**Number of instances**	**Number of tokens**	**Number of distinct tokens**
Positive	1,500	10,455	6,394
Negative	1,500	15,000	7,827
Neutral	1,500	13,165	4,039
Total	4,500	38,621	15,008

Table 1: Dataset statistics: the numbers were discarded; tokens (words) were transformed to lower-case.

The dataset contains texts representing informal Lithuanian language, i.e. texts are full of slang, foreign language insertions, and barbarisms. Besides, in the texts are a lot of typographical and grammatical errors. Moreover, Lithuanian language uses Latin script supplemented with diacritics, but in informal texts, diacritics (ą, č, ę, ė, į, š, ų, ū, ž) are very often replaced with matching Latin letters (a, c, e, e, i, s, u, u, z).

4.2 Classification methods

Sentiment classification task has never been solved for Lithuanian; therefore it is unclear which method could be the most suitable for the given dataset. Consequentially, in this research we will compare two different classification approaches – knowledge-based and machine learning – applying them on the informal texts.

The keystone of our knowledge-based approach is the lexicon that is applied to recognize sentiment words in the text. In our experiments we used two lexicons (see Table 2): manually labeled and automatically augmented one. Both lexicons are composed of 4 dictionaries: for adjectives, adverbs, nouns and verbs, respectively. Only lemmas (main words' forms containing ending and suffices/prefixes) are stored in the dictionaries.

The candidates for the first lexicon were extracted from 1 million running words taken from *Vytautas Magnus University Corpus* (Marcinkevičienė, 2000). These texts represent standard Lithuanian and were taken from six domains: fiction, legal texts, national newspapers, parliamentary transcripts, local newspapers, and popular periodicals. Words were transformed into their lemmas using Lithuanian part-of-speech tagger and lemmatizer *Lemuoklis* (Zinkevičius, 2000); (Daudaravičius et al., 2007) and transferred to the dictionaries containing appropriate parts-of-speech. Words in the first lexicon were manually labeled with their polarity values (-3/3 means that the word is strongly negative/positive; -2/2 – moderately negative/positive; -1/1 – weakly negative/positive; 0 – neutral). The decision was taken by mutual agreement of two human-experts that made efforts not to bind to the specific use cases, but consider only the most common sense of each word. The second lexicon was created by automatically augmenting the first one with the synonyms taken from *Lithuanian WordNet* (2013). Words from the manually labeled lexicon were used as the pre-selected "seeds" to search for the synonyms that automatically obtained the same polarity value and were added to the appropriate dictionaries.

Semantic orientation of each instance was determined by summing the polarity values of recognized sentiment words in the lemmatized texts. If total polarity value was positive (> 0), the instance was classified as positive; if negative (< 0) – as negative; if zero ($= 0$) – as neutral. E.g. "Filmas labai puikus" (*The film is great*) would be classified as positive, because *valueOf*("Filmas")=0 and *valueOf*("puikus")=3, thus $0 + 3 = 3 > 0$.

As the alternative for knowledge-based method we used two machine learning methods – i.e. Support Vector Machine (SVM), introduced by Cortes and Wapnik (1995) and Naïve Bayes Multinomial (NBM), introduced by Lewis and Gale (1994).

Polarity value	Adjectives	Adverbs	Verbs	Nouns	Total
-3	115 138	71 74	236 236	275 296	697 744
-2	151 175	120 122	333 337	719 775	1,323 1,409
-1	243 267	95 95	732 733	1,854 1,945	2,924 3,040
0	4,035 4,392	1,296 1,362	10,001 10,039	12,367 12,719	27,699 28,512
1	145 163	117 122	344 344	856 896	1,462 1,525
2	130 148	114 117	112 113	195 213	551 591
3	117 142	61 62	72 72	54 55	304 331
Total	4,936 5,425	1,874 1,954	11,830 11,874	16,320 16,899	

Table 2: Dictionaries statistics: the first value in each cell represents the number of items in manually labeled lexicon; the second – augmented with WordNet.

SVM is one of the most popular techniques for text classification, because it can cope with high dimensional feature spaces (e.g. 15,008 word features in our dataset); sparseness of feature vectors (e.g. among 15,008, each instance would have only ~3.34 non-zero word feature values); and instances do not sharing any common features (common for short texts, e.g. average length of instance in our dataset is ~8.58 words). Besides SVM does not perform aggressive feature selection which may result in a loss of information.

NBM method is also often used for text classification tasks (mostly due its simplicity): Naïve Bayes assumption of feature independence allows parameters of each feature to be learned separately. It performs especially well when the number of features is large. Besides, it is reported (e.g. by Pak and Parubek (2011)) that NBM can even outperform popular SVM in sentiment classification tasks.

In our experiments we used SMO kernel for SVM and NBM implementations in WEKA (Hall et al., 2009) machine learning toolkit, version 3.6[1]. All parameters were set to their default values.

4.3 Experimental setup

Before classification experiments tokens (i.e. words) in the dataset were pre-processed using different techniques. Knowledge-based method required lemmatization, whereas for machine learning methods lemmatization was optional. Despite that lemmatizer can solve disambiguation problems and achieve ~0.94 accuracy on normative Lithuanian texts (Rimkutė and Daudaravičius, 2007); it could not recognize even ~0.25 of words in our dataset.

Other optional pre-processing techniques involved emoticons replacement with appropriate sentiment words; Lithuanian diacritics replacements with appropriate Latin letters; and stop words removal.

Emoticons replacement demonstrated positive effect on English (Read, 2005) and triggered us to create such list for Lithuanian. The list contains 32 sentiment words (written in lemmas) with their appropriate and commonly used emoticon equivalents[2]. Thus, e.g. ":-)" would be replaced by "laimingas" (*happy*).

Words with replaced Lithuanian diacritics can neither be found in the dictionaries, nor recognized by the Lithuanian lemmatizer and therefore require special treatment. Whereas tools able to restore Lithuanian diacritics are not yet available, we have chosen opposite way by replacing all diacritics with matching Latin letters in the text, dictionaries and emoticons list and in such a way decreasing the number of unrecognized words (for knowledge-based method) and the sparseness of feature vector (for machine learning methods).

Stop words removal cannot affect the performance of knowledge-based method, but it can decrease the sparseness of the data for machine learning techniques. In our experiments we used stop words list with excluded interjections, because Spencer and Uchyigit (2012) showed that interjections are strong indicators of subjectivity.

Compulsory pre-processing steps included transformation of letters into lower-case, digits and punctuation removal. Statistics demonstrating the effect of different pre-processing techniques on the dataset are presented in Table 3.

Pre-processing was performed in such an order that previous steps could not harm following ones, thus lemmatization was performed before diacritics replacement, punctuation removal was performed after emoticons replacement, etc.

Knowledge-based method was evaluated using different combinations of dictionaries, whereas machine learning method – different types of features: *token unigrams* (the most common case);

[1]http://www.cs.waikato.ac.nz/ml/weka/.

[2]http://www.cool-smileys.com/text-emoticons.

token unigrams plus bigrams, i.e. token unigrams complemented with token bigrams (higher order n-grams sometimes outperform token unigrams); *token lemmas* (strongly recommended for highly-inflective languages); document-level *character 4-grams* (this type was reported as the best for Lithuanian topic classification by Kapočiūtė-Dzikienė et al. (2012)).

Class label	Tokens after lemma-tization	Tokens with emoti-cons	Tokens without stop-words	Tokens without diacrit-ics
Positive	10,386 3,177	10,664 4,027	8,982 3,941	10,455 3,724
Negative	14,928 6,475	15,107 7,811	11,945 7,716	15,000 7,457
Neutral	13,084 5,134	13,226 6,391	10,427 6,276	13,165 6,058
Total	38,398 11,669	38,997 14,966	31,354 14,923	38,621 13,983

Table 3: Pre-processed dataset statistics: the first value in each cell represents the number of all tokens, the second – distinct tokens. See Table 1 for unprocessed dataset statistics.

We expect the following statements to be confirmed experimentally: 1) emoticons replacement should increase the results since they usually reflect emotional state of the person; 2) diacritics replacement or lemmatization should improve the results by decreasing data sparseness and the number of unrecognized words; 3) all dictionaries should give better results for the knowledge-based method because contain more sentiment information; 4) machine learning methods should outperform knowledge-based approach because sentiments can be expressed in more complex ways.

5 Results

Accuracies (the number of correctly classified instances divided by all instances) of previously described experiments are summarized in Figure 1 – Figure 3.

Figure 1 summarizes the results obtained with the knowledge-based method. Figure 2 summarizes the results obtained with SVM method, Figure 3 – with NBM. 10-fold cross-validation was used in all experiments with machine learning methods.

6 Discussion

Since the balanced class distribution is maintained (see Table 1), both majority (probability to belong only to a major class) and random (the sum of squared probabilities of all classes) baselines are equal to 0.333. Figure 1 – Figure 3 show that obtained classification results are above the baseline.

The best results using knowledge-based method are achieved with *emoticons* and *diacritics replacement*, as expected (see Section 4.3), but emoticons replacement is more effective.

Augmented lexicon slightly outperforms manually labeled. Besides, *adjectives*, *nouns* and *verbs* improve the classification results for knowledge-based approach, but adverbs worsen it. Bad performance of adverbs contradicts our expectations. Analysis of erroneous cases revealed that very strong negative adverbs (used in slang) such as "baisiai" (*terribly*), "žiauriai" (*brutally*), etc. followed by the positive adjectives such as "geras" (*good*), "nuostabus" (*wonderful*) become positive intensifiers. Moreover, very often adverbs are found in the context does not expressing any sentiment at all, e.g. "gerai" (*well*) in "gerai pasakyta" (*well said*) should not be treated as positive word.

The results obtained with different machine learning methods – SVM and NBM are very contradictory and not always correspond to our expectations (see Section 4.3). In general the best feature type for SVM is either *token unigrams* or *token lemmas*; for NBM – *token unigrams plus bigrams*, but *token lemmas* is the second best result. Longer phrases (based on token bigrams) increase the sparseness of the data that seems to be harmful for SVM method, which does not perform aggressive feature selection. Whereas NBM is not as sensitive to it, *token unigrams plus bigrams* (carrying more sentiment information) give the best accuracy.

For both machine learning methods *token lemmas* are effective enough. The main problem is that Lithuanian lemmatizer could not recognize even a quarter of all words in the dataset, thus it can be assumed that this feature type could give even better results if lemmatizer would cope with informal Lithuanian language as well.

Results obtained by machine learning methods show that document-level *character 4-grams* (giving the best results for topic classification on Lithuanian texts) are not effective for sentiment classification. Character n-grams not only increase the sparseness, but result in a loss of important information about Lithuanian suffixes and prefixes. E.g. "gera" (*good*) and "negera" (*not*

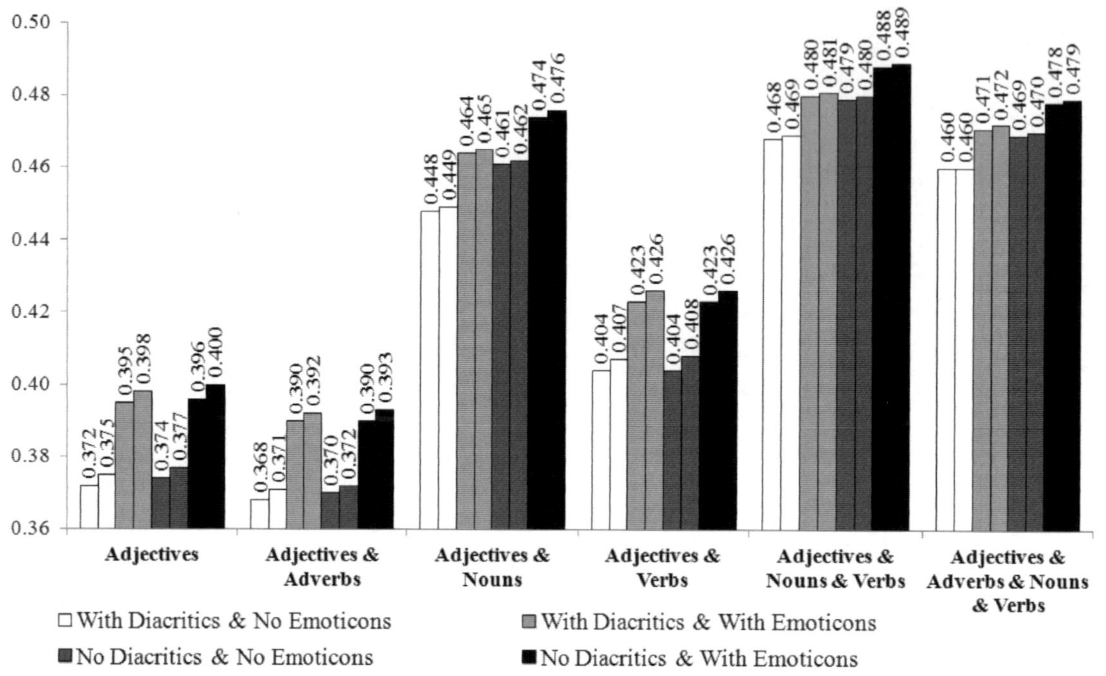

Figure 1: Accuracy of knowledge-based method, obtained using different lexicons and pre-processing techniques: groups of columns represent different combinations of dictionaries; shades of columns represent pre-processing techniques ("No Diacritics" stands for diacritics replacement, "With Diacritics" for no replacement, "With Emoticons" for emoticons replacement, "No Emoticons" for no replacement); the first column of the same shade represents results obtained using manually labeled lexicon, the second – augmented with WordNet.

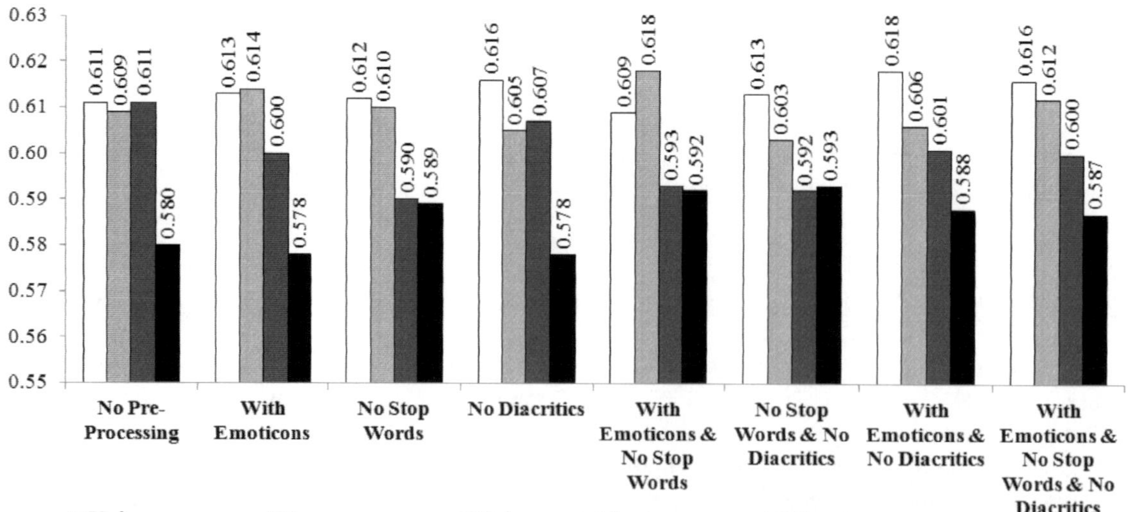

Figure 2: Accuracy of SVM method, obtained using different feature types and pre-processing techniques: groups of columns represent different pre-processing techniques ("With Emoticons" stands for emoticons replacement, "No Stop Words" for stop words removal, "No Diacritics" for diacritics replacement); shades of columns represent different feature types.

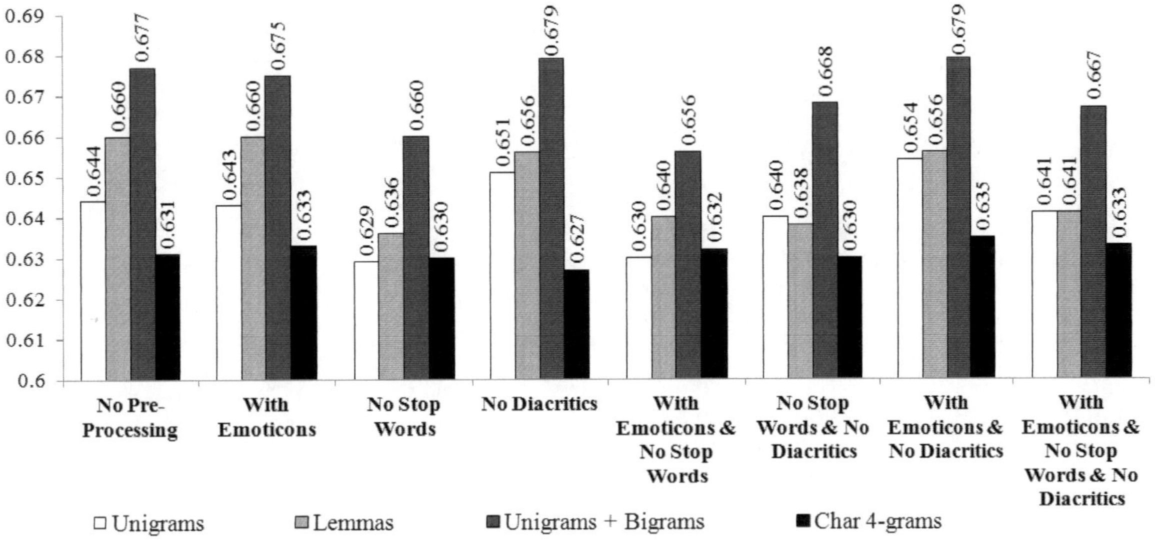

Figure 3: Accuracy of NBM, obtained using different feature types and pre-processing techniques.

good) contain the same 4 characters "gera", but prefix "ne-" reverses the polarity.

As presented in Figure 2 and Figure 3 emoticons and diacritics replacement positively affect classification results, but the effect is much weaker compared to the knowledge-based approach. In general, for SVM there is no single pre-processing technique that could significantly stand out from the rest, while for NBM diacritics replacement is the best one, stop words removal is the worst. It can be assumed that despite stop words seem unimportant; they still carry sentiment information, especially significant using token bigrams.

As expected (see Section 4.3), machine learning methods significantly outperform knowledge-based. One of the main reasons is that the lexicons are not adjusted to a specific domain. Our goal was not to achieve as high accuracy as possible, but to determine a real potential of such method on informal Lithuanian texts. The analysis of erroneous cases revealed that adjectives, nouns and verbs are not the only sentiment indicators, e.g. interjection "valio!" (*hurray!*) in "valio! Auksas!" (*hurray! Gold!*) can express positive sentiment also.

Besides, diacritics replacement is still a considerable problem: e.g. whereas lexicon contains "šaunus" (*cool*, in masculine gender); the same word with replaced diacritics in feminine gender "sauni" will neither be recognized by lemmatizer, nor found in the lexicon with replaced diacritics.

The best result with knowledge-based method exceeds baseline by 0.156; with machine learning – by 0.346, but they are still low compared to the results obtained on English texts. Analysis of erroneous cases revealed that classifiers mostly fail due to the language variations when sentiments are expressed implicitly and require special treatment considering informal Lithuanian language specifics.

7 Conclusion and perspectives

In this paper we are solving Internet comments sentiment classification task for Lithuanian, using two different approaches: knowledge-based and machine learning.

Adjectives, nouns and verbs (excluding adverbs) are the most important sentiment indicators for the knowledge-based approach that was significantly outperformed by the machine learning methods. The best accuracy 0.679 is obtained using Naïve Bayes Multinomial with token unigrams plus bigrams as features and diacritics replacement as pre-processing technique.

In the future research we are planning to perform detailed class-wise error analysis that could help to find the solutions decreasing the number of erroneous cases. Besides, it would be interesting to experiment with the implicitly expressed sentiments.

Acknowledgments

This research is funded by European Union Structural Funds Project "Postdoctoral Fellowship Implementation in Lithuania" (VP1-3.1-ŠMM-01).

References

Anthony Aue and Michael Gamon. 2005. Customizing sentiment classifiers to new domains: A case study. In *Proceedings of the International Conference on Recent Advances in Natural Language Processing (RANLP)*.

Farah Benamara, Carmine Cesarano, Antonio Picariello, Diego Reforgiato, and VS Subrahmanian. 2007. Sentiment analysis: Adjectives and adverbs are better than adjectives alone. In *Proceedings of International Conference on Weblogs and Social Media (ICWSM)*.

Erik Boiy and Marie-Francine Moens. 2009. A Machine Learning Approach to Sentiment Analysis in Multilingual Web Texts. *Information Retrieval*, 12(5):526–558.

Henri Bouma, Olga Rajadell, Daniël Worm, Corné Versloot, and Harry Wedemeijer. 2012. On the early detection of threats in the real world based on open-source information on the internet. In *Proceedings of International Conference of Information Technologies and Security*.

Ying Chen, Yilu Zhou, Sencun Zhu, and Heng Xu. 2012. Detecting Offensive Language in Social Media to Protect Adolescent Online Safety. In *Proceedings of the International Confernece on Social Computing (SocialCom 2012)*, pages 71–80.

Alex Cheng and Oles Zhulyn. 2012. A System for Multilingual Sentiment Learning On Large Data Sets. In *Proceedings of 24th International Conference on Computational Linguistics (COLING 2012)*, pages 577–592.

Yejin Choi and Claire Cardie. 2008. Learning with compositional semantics as structural inference for subsentential sentiment analysis. In *Proceedings of the Conference on Empirical Methods in Natural Language Processing*, pages 793–801.

Corinna Cortes and Vladimir Vapnik. 1995. Support-vector networks. *Machine Learning*, 20:273–297.

Hang Cui, Vibhu Mittal, and Mayur Datar. 2006. Comparative experiments on sentiment classification for online product reviews. In *Proceedings of the Twenty First National Conference on Artificial Intelligence (AAAI-2006)*, pages 1265–1270.

Vidas Daudaravičius, Erika Rimkutė, and Andrius Utka. 2007. Morphological annotation of the Lithuanian corpus. In *Proceedings of the Workshop on Balto-Slavonic Natural Language Processing: Information Extraction and Enabling Technologies (ACL'07)*, pages 94–99.

Kushal Dave, Steve Lawrence, and David M. Pennock. 2003. Mining the peanut gallery: opinion extraction and semantic classification of product reviews. In *Proceedings of the 12th international conference on World Wide Web (WWW'03)*, pages 519–528.

Xiaowen Ding and Bing Liu. 2007. The utility of linguistic rules in opinion mining. In *Proceedings of the 30th International ACM SIGIR Conference on Research and Development in Information Retrieval*, pages 811–812.

Andrea Esuli and Fabrizio Sebastiani. 2006. Sentiwordnet: A Publicly Available Lexical Resource for Opinion Mining. In *Proceedings of the 5th Conference on Language Resources and Evaluation (LREC 2006)*, pages 417–422.

Mark Hall, Eibe Frank, Geoffrey Holmes, Bernhard Pfahringer, Peter Reutemann, and Ian H. Witten. 2009. The WEKA Data Mining Software: An Update. *SIGKDD Explorations*, 11(1):10–18.

Tino Hartmann, Sebastian Klenk, Andre Burkovski, and Gunther Heidemann. 2011. Sentiment Detection with Character n-Grams. In *Proceedings of the Seventh International Conference on Data Mining (DMIN'11)*.

Minqing Hu and Bing Liu. 2004. Mining and summarizing customer reviews. In *Proceedings of the tenth ACM SIGKDD international conference on Knowledge discovery and data mining (KDD'04)*, pages 168–177.

Matthew F. Hurst and Kamal Nigam. 2004. Retrieving topical sentiments from online document collections. In *Proceedings of Document Recognition and Retrieval*, volume XI, pages 27–34.

Jurgita Kapočiūtė-Dzikienė, Frederik Vaassen, Walter Daelemans, and Algis Krupavičius. 2012. Improving Topic Classification for Highly Inflective Languages. In *Proceedings of 24th International Conference on Computational Linguistics (COLING 2012)*, pages 1393–1410.

Alistair Kennedy and Diana Inkpen. 2006. Sentiment classification of movie and product reviews using contextual valence shifters. *Computational Intelligence*, 22(2):110–125.

Ekaterina S. Kuznetsova, Natalia V. Loukachevitch, and Ilia I. Chetviorkin. 2013. Testing rules for a sentiment analysis system. In *Proceedings of International Conference Dialog*, pages 71–80.

David D. Lewis and William A. Gale. 1994. A sequential algorithm for training text classifiers. In *Proceedings of Seventeenth Annual International ACM-SIGIR Conference on Research and Development in Information Retrieval (SIGIR-94)*, pages 3–12.

Rūta Marcinkevičienė. 2000. Tekstynų lingvistika (teorija ir paktika) [Corpus linguistics (theory and practice)]. *Gudaitis, L. (ed.) Darbai ir dienos*, 24:7–63. (in Lithuanian).

Subhabrata Mukherjee and Pushpak Bhattacharyya. 2012. Sentiment Analysis in Twitter with Lightweight Discourse Analysis. In *Proceedings of 24th International Conference on Computational Linguistics (COLING 2012)*, pages 1847–1864.

Tony Mullen and Nigel Collier. 2004. Sentiment Analysis using Support Vector Machines with Diverse Information Sources. In *Proceedings of Empirical Methods in Natural Language Processing*, pages 412–418.

Alexander Pak and Patrick Paroubek. 2011. Twitter for Sentiment Analysis: When Language Resources are Not Available. In *Proceedings of Database and Expert Systems Applications (DEXA 2011)*, pages 111–115.

Bo Pang and Lillian Lee. 2008. Opinion Mining and Sentiment Analysis. *Foundation and Trends in Information Retrieval*, 2(1-2):1–135.

Bo Pang, Lillian Lee, and Shivakumar Vaithyanathan. 2002. Thumbs up? Sentiment classification using machine learning techniques. In *Proceedings of Conference on Empirical Methods in Natural Language Processing, EMNLP*, pages 79–86.

Stephan Raaijmakers and Wessel Kraaij. 2008. Polarity Classification of Blog TREC 2008 Data with a Geodesic Kernel. In *Proceedings of the Seventeenth Text Retrieval Conference (TREC 2008)*, volume 500–277.

Jonathon Read and John Carroll. 2009. Weakly supervised techniques for domain-independent sentiment classification. In *Proceedings of the 1st international CIKM workshop on Topic-sentiment analysis for mass opinion (TSA'09)*, pages 45–52.

Jonathon Read. 2005. Using Emoticons to Reduce Dependency in Machine Learning Techniques for Sentiment Classification. In *Proceedings of the 43th Annual Meeting on Association for Computational Linguistics (ACL'05) (Student Research Workshop)*, pages 43–48.

Erika Rimkutė and Vidas Daudaravičius. 2007. Morfologinis Dabartins lietuvių kalbos tekstyno anotavimas [Morphological annotation of the Lithuanian corpus]. *Kalbų studijos*, 11:30–35. (in Lithuanian).

Lietuvos Rytas. 2013. Lietuvos rytas. Internet daily newspaper, March. [http://www.lrytas.lt/] (in Lithuanian).

Ineta Savickienė, Vera Kempe, and Patricia J. Brooks. 2009. Acquisition of gender agreement in Lithuanian: exploring the effect of diminutive usage in an elicited production task. *Journal of Child Language*, 36(3):477–494.

James Spencer and Gulden Uchyigit. 2012. Sentimentor: Sentiment Analysis of Twitter Data. In *Proceedings of European Conference on Machine Learning and Principles and Practice of Knowledge Discovery in Databases*, pages 56–66.

Maite Taboada, Julian Brooke, Milan Tofiloski, Kimberly Voll, and Manfred Stede. 2011. Lexicon-Based Methods for Sentiment Analysis. *Computational Linguistics*, 37(2):267–307.

Peter D. Turney and Michael L. Littman. 2003. Measuring praise and criticism: Inference of semantic orientation from association. In *Proceedings of ACM Transactions on Information and System Security (TISSEC)*, pages 315–346.

Peter D. Turney. 2002. Thumbs up or thumbs down?: semantic orientation applied to unsupervised classification of reviews. In *Proceedings of the 40th Annual Meeting on Association for Computational Linguistics (ACL'02)*, pages 417–424.

Kazys Ulvydas, editor. 1965. *Fonetika ir morfologija (daiktavardis, būdvardis, skaitvardis, įvardis) [Phonetics and morphology (noun, adjective, numeral, pronoun)]*, volume 1. Mintis, Vilnius, Lithuania. (in Lithuanian).

Hao Wang, Dogan Can, Abe Kazemzadeh, François Bar, and Shrikanth Narayanan. 2012. A system for Real-time Twitter Sentiment Analysis of 2012 U.S. Presidential Election Cycle. In *Proceedings of the 50th Annual Meeting on Association for Computational Linguistics (ACL'12)(System Demonstrations)*, pages 115–120.

Lithuanian WordNet. 2013. Lietuvių kalbos WordNet, February. [http://korpus.sk/ltskwn_lt.html] (in Lithuanian).

Vytautas Zinkevičius. 2000. Lemuoklis – morfologinei analizei [Morphological analysis with Lemuoklis]. *Gudaitis, L. (ed.) Darbai ir dienos*, 24:246–273. (in Lithuanian).

Evaluating Sentiment Analysis Systems in Russian

Ilia Chetviorkin
Faculty of Computational
Mathematics and Cybernetics
Lomonosov Moscow State University
Moscow, Leninskiye Gory 1, Building 52
ilia2010@yandex.ru

Natalia Loukachevitch
Research Computing Center
Lomonosov Moscow State University
Moscow, Leninskiye Gory 1, Building 4
louk_nat@mail.ru

Abstract

In this paper we describe our experience in conducting the first open sentiment analysis evaluations in Russian in 2011-2012. These initiatives took part within Russian Information Retrieval Seminar (ROMIP), which is an annual TREC-like competition in Russian. Several test and train collections were created for such tasks as sentiment classification in blogs and newswire, opinion retrieval. The paper describes the state of the art in sentiment analysis in Russian, collection characteristics, track tasks and evaluation metrics.

1 Introduction

Sentiment analysis of natural language texts is one of the fast-developing technologies of natural language processing. Many lexical resources and tools were created for sentiment analysis in English. But lately a lot of research work was initiated for sentiment analysis in other languages (Mihalcea et al., 2007; Abdul-Mageed et al., 2011; Pérez-Rosas et al., 2012).

The development of sentiment analysis in Russian previously did not attract a lot of attention at international conferences. Besides, until recently, the interest to sentiment analysis within Russia was connected only with election campaigns. But now there is a considerable interest to sentiment analysis within Russia both from the research community and from the industry.

Therefore during the last years, two workshops on the evaluation of sentiment analysis systems were organized within the framework of Russian Information Retrieval Seminar ROMIP[1] . In many respects ROMIP seminars are similar to other international information retrieval events such as TREC and NTCIR, which have already conducted different sentiment analysis tracks. Besides, there are various shared tasks connected to the sentiment analysis like (Morante and Blanco, 2012; Pestian et al., 2012; Wu and Jin, 2010; Amigó et al., 2012).

In this paper we partly overview the sentiment analysis tasks proposed at ROMIP-2011 (Chetviorkin et al., 2012) and ROMIP-2012 (Chetviorkin and Loukachevich, 2013), the data prepared for evaluation (and therefore available for other interested researchers), and the results obtained by participants. In addition we summarize the results of two initiatives, compare them with the state of the art in English and describe some interesting issues connected to news-based sentiment analysis. We justify all our decisions about the conducted tracks based on the experience of the other researchers, who made the similar initiatives in English. ROMIP-2011 and ROMIP-2012 are unique events for Slavic languages and other European languages different from English.

The paper is structured as follows. In section 2 we review papers on Russian sentiment analysis, not related to the ROMIP evaluations. In section 3 we consider sentiment analysis evaluation tasks proposed during ROMIP-2011, 2012 and consider the main results obtained by participants.

2 Sentiment Analysis in Russian

In Russia studies devoted to sentiment analysis in Russian before 2011 are not very numerous.

In (Ermakov, 2009) a sentiment analysis system extracting opinions about cars from a Russian blog community (http://avto-ru.livejournal.com/) is presented. The approach is based on the detailed description of knowledge about car trade marks, their details and characteristics, semantic patterns of sentiment expressions. This paper is the first, to our knowledge, paper in Russia that reports evaluation results of the proposed approach: precision 84%, recall 20% (self-evaluation).

[1] http://romip.ru/en/index.html

In international research Russian sentiment analysis appears mainly in multilingual experiments.

In (Zagibalov et al., 2010) comparable corpora of reviews related to the same books in English and in Russian are described. These corpora allowed authors to study specific ways of sentiment expression in Russian and English.

In (Steinberger et al., 2011) construction of general sentiment vocabularies for several languages is described. They create two source sentiment vocabularies: English (2400 entries) and Spanish (1737 entries). Both lists are translated by Google translator to the target language. Only the overlapping entries from each translation are taken into further consideration. The set of target languages comprises six languages including Russian. The extracted Russian list of sentiment words contained 966 entries with accuracy of 94.9%.

In one of the recent papers not related to the ROMIP evaluations (Chetviorkin and Loukachevitch, 2012), the generation of the Russian sentiment vocabulary for the generalized domain of products and services is described. Authors constructed a new model based on multiple features for domain-specific sentiment vocabulary extraction, then applied this model to several domains, and at last combined these domain-specific vocabularies to generate Russian sentiment vocabulary for products and services – ProductSentiRus. Now the extracted list is publicly available[2].

3 Sentiment analysis tasks

The tasks of two Russian sentiment analysis evaluations ROMIP-2011 and ROMIP-2012 included:

- Sentiment classification of user reviews in three domains (movies, books, digital cameras) using several different sentiment scales,
- Sentiment classification of news-based opinions, which are fragments of direct or indirect speech extracted from news articles,
- Query-based retrieval of opinionated blog posts in three domains (movies, books, digital cameras).

In ROMIP-2011 sentiment evaluation there were 12 participants with more than 200 runs. In ROMIP-2012 17 teams sent more than 150 runs. The presentations describing approaches were organized as a section of International Conference on Computational Linguistics and Information Technologies "Dialog" (www.dialog-21.ru/en/).

3.1 Sentiment classification of reviews

The only task of ROMIP-2011 and one of the tasks of ROMIP-2012 was sentiment classification of users reviews in three domains: movies, books and digital cameras.

The training data for this task included movie and book collections with 15,718 and 24,159 reviews respectively from Imhonet service (imhonet.ru) and the digital camera review collection with 10,370 reviews from Yandex Market service (http://market.yandex.ru/). All reviews have the authors score on the ten-point scale or the five-point scale.

For testing, another collection of reviews without any authors' scores was created. The testing collection contained blog posts about the above-mentioned entities found with Yandex's Blog Search Engine (http://blog.yandex.ru). So in this track we tried to model a real-word task, when a classifier should be trained on available data, which can be quite different from the task data. The participants stressed that our track is more difficult than training and testing on the similar data, but agreed that this task setting is more realistic.

For each domain a list of search queries was manually compiled and for each query a set of blog posts was extracted. Finally, results obtained for all queries were merged and sent to the participants.

For the evaluation, annotators selected subjective posts related to three target domains, assessed the polarity of these posts and labeled them with three scores corresponding to different sentiment scales (two-class, three-class and five-class scales).

The participants systems had to classify the reviews to two, three or five classes according to sentiment. The primary measures for evaluation of two and three class tasks were accuracy and macro-F1 measure. Macro-measures (Manning et al., 2008) were used because the majority of user reviews in blogs are positive (more than 80%). Macro-averaging means a simple average over classes. The five-class task was additionally evaluated with Euclidean distance measure, which is the quadratic mean between the scores of the al-

[2]http://www.cir.ru/SentiLexicon/ProductSentiRus.txt

Domains	2-class		3-class		5-class	
	F1	Acc.	F1	Acc.	F1	Acc.
Movies	0.786	0.881	0.592	0.754	0.286	0.602
Books	0.747	0.938	0.577	0.771	0.291	0.622
Cameras	0.929	0.959	0.663	0.841	0.342	0.626

Table 1: Best results of blog review classification in ROMIP-2011

Domains	2-class		3-class		5-class	
	F1	Acc.	F1	Acc.	F1	Acc.
Movies	0.707	0.831	0.520	0.694	0.377	0.407
Books	0.715	0.884	0.560	0.752	0.402	0.480
Cameras	0.669	0.961	0.480	0.742	0.336	0.480

Table 2: Best results of blog review classification in ROMIP-2012

gorithm and the assessor scores.

Practically all the best approaches in the review classification tasks used SVM machine learning method (Kotelnikov and Klekovkina, 2012; Pak and Paroubek, 2012; Polyakov et al., 2012). Besides, the best methods usually combined SVM with other approaches including manual or automatic dictionaries or rule-based systems. The best achieved results according to macro-F1 measure and Accuracy within ROMIP 2011 are presented in Table 1 and within ROMIP 2012 in Table 2.

Observing the results of the open evaluation of sentiment analysis systems in Russian during two years we can make some conclusions about the state of the art performance and specific characteristics of the track.

The average level in 2-class classification task according to Accuracy is near 90%, near 75% for 3-class classification task and near 50% for 5-class task. Such results are consistent with the state of the art performance in English. However these figures are slightly overestimated due to the skewness of the testing collections. This fact is the consequence of using blogs as a test set. The majority of blog opinions about various objects is positive, but such a collection is a priori unlabeled, which leads to fair evaluation results.

3.2 Sentiment classification of opinionated quotations

The next task of ROMIP-2012 concerned sentiment classification of short (1-2 sentences on average) fragments of direct or indirect speech automatically extracted from news articles (further quotations). The somewhat similar task was conducted within the NTCIR-6, where one of the main tasks was extraction of opinion sentences from the news articles in three languages: English, Chinese and Japanese (Seki et al., 2007).

The topics of quotations could be quite different: from politics and economy to sports and arts. Therefore this task should be difficult enough for both knowledge-based and machine-learning approaches.

Assessors annotated quotations as positive, neutral, negative, or mixed. After the annotation the quotations with mixed sentiment were removed from the evaluation. So the participating systems should classify quotations to three classes. This task is similar to sentiment classification of political quotations (Awadallah et al., 2012; Balasubramanyan et al., 2012) to pro and contra positions. In (Awadallah et al., 2012) authors state that short quotations are difficult for classification because useful linguistic features tend to be sparse and the same quotation can have different polarities for different topics. In our case the task was even more difficult because of unlimited topics and three-class classification.

In ROMIP-2012 evaluation 4,260 quotations were prepared for training. For testing more than 120 thousand quotes were sent to participants, but real evaluation was made on the basis of 5,500 quotations randomly sampled and annotated from the testing set. An example of the quotation is as follows: Patriarch Kirill, says feminism is a "very dangerous" phenomenon offering an illusion of freedom to women, who he says should focus on their families and children.

In this task class distribution was rather balanced in comparison with the review classification task: 41% of quotes were negative, 32% of

RunID	Macro P	Macro R	Macro F1	Accuracy
xxx-4	0.626	0.616	0.621	0.616
xxx-11	0.606	0.579	0.592	0.571
xxx-15	0.563	0.560	0.562	0.582
Baseline	0.138	0.333	0.195	0.413

Table 3: Best results for the news quotation classification task in ROMIP 2012

RunID	Domain	P@1	P@5	P@10	NDCG@10
xxx-0	book	0.3	0.32	0.286	0.305
xxx-8	book	0.25	0.31	0.332	0.298
yyy-9	camera	0.402	0.313	0.302	0.305
yyy-1	camera	0.402	0.328	0.325	0.226
zzz-3	film	0.494	0.449	0.438	0.338
zzz-8	film	0. 494	0.448	0.444	0.332

Table 4: Best results in the task of retrieval of opinionated blog posts

quotes were positive and 27% of quotes were neutral. For evaluation again macro-measures and accuracy were applied.

The results of the participants are presented in Table 3. The baseline results correspond to classification of quotations according to the major class. In opposite to the review classification task, the leaders in the news-based classification were knowledge-based approaches. It is due to the absence of a large training collection appropriate for this task because of the broad scope of quotation topics.

The authors of the best approach in this task report that their knowledge-based system has a considerable vocabulary including 15 thousand negative expressions, 7 thousand positive expressions, around 120 so-called operators (intensifiers and invertors) and around 200 neutral stop expressions including sentiment words as their components. The system has a small number of rules for aggregating scores of sentiment word and operator sequences (Kuznetsova et al., 2013). The second and third results in this task were obtained by a rule-based system with comparably small sentiment dictionaries but a rich rule set based on syntactic analysis (Panicheva, 2013).

An interesting conclusion is that the size of sentiment dictionaries can be compensated with various syntactic rules, which allows handling the variety of situations in expressing sentiment.

The results of this task can be compared with one of the recent studies on lexicon-based methods for sentiment analysis in English (Taboada et al., 2011). The text fragments in the paper and in ROMIP evaluation are rather equal by style (news quotes versus opinionated news sentences). We cannot directly compare the results of analogous systems in Russian and English, because we worked with 3 class classification problem (positive, negative, neutral) versus 2 class task in the paper, but available figures are the following: the accuracy of sentiment analysis systems in Russian is near 61.6% in the three-class task versus 71.57% for the two-class task in English.

3.3 Query-based retrieval of opinionated blog posts

For several years TREC Blog tracks were connected with opinion finding and processing of blog data (Ounis et al., 2007; Macdonald et al., 2008; Ounis et al., 2008; Macdonald et al., 2010; Ounis et al., 2011). During the research cycles within these initiatives, the following sentiment analysis tasks were considered:

- Opinion finding (blog post) retrieval task,
- Polarised opinion finding (blog post) retrieval task.

The query-based retrieval of opinions from blogs was one of the basic tasks for the TREC Blog Track. Thus, we also decided to start with the similar task for Russian language. Here the participants had to find all relevant opinionated posts from the blog collection according to a specific query. Examples of queries include (translation from Russian):

- movie domain: *The Girl with the Dragon Tattoo; film "The dictator"*;
- book domain: *Agatha Cristie "Ten little niggers"; Dan Brown "The Code da Vinci"*;
- digital camera domain: *Canon EOS 1100D Kit; Canon PowerShot G12*.

Only one group participated in this task and therefore organizers implemented a simple approach to conduct the track. The approach to the sentiment post retrieval was based on computation of weighted sum of three components: TFIDF similarity of a query to the title of a blog post, TFIDF of a query to the text of the post and the share of sentiment words in the post. For computation of the latter component, aforementioned Russian sentiment list ProductSentiRus (see section 2) was used:

$$Weight = \alpha \cdot (\sum_{w \in q} tfidf + \sum_{w \in q} tfidf^{header}) +$$

$$+ (1 - \alpha) \cdot (SentiWeight)$$

The organizers experimented with different values of $\alpha = 0.2, 0.4, 0.5, 0.6, 0.8$. The best performance was obtained with $\alpha = 0.6$ for all subdomains of this task. To avoid underestimation of participant results, the evaluation was made only on the basis of labeled documents. For this task we used two measures: $P@n$ and $NDGN@n$. $Precision@n$ indicates the number of correct (relevant) objects in the first n objects in the result set and $NDCG@n$ measures the usefulness, or gain, of a document based on its position in the result list (Manning et al., 2008). The main measures of the performance in this task were $NDCG@10$ and $Precision@10$ (Table 4).

4 Conclusion

In this paper we reported the state of the art of Russian sentiment analysis. Our report is based on the results of two evaluations of sentiment analysis systems organized in 2011–2012 within the framework of Russian seminar on information retrieval ROMIP. We proposed user review classification tasks in a practical setting, when available data should be used for training a classifier intended for similar, but another data. Besides, one of the interesting and complicated tasks of ROMIP-2012 was sentiment classification of opinions extracted from news articles.

Acknowledgments

This work is partially supported by grant N11-07-00588-a.

References

Muhammad Abdul-Mageed, Mona Diab, and Mohammed Korayem. 2011. Subjectivity and sentiment analysis of modern standard arabic. In *Proceedings of the 49th Annual Meeting of the Association for Computational Linguistics: Human Language Technologies*, volume 2, pages 587–591.

Enrique Amigó, Adolfo Corujo, Julio Gonzalo, Edgar Meij, and Md Rijke. 2012. Overview of replab 2012: Evaluating online reputation management systems. In *CLEF 2012 Labs and Workshop Notebook Papers*, pages 1–24.

Rawia Awadallah, Maya Ramanath, and Gerhard Weikum. 2012. Polaricq: polarity classification of political quotations. In *Proceedings of the 21st ACM international conference on Information and knowledge management*, pages 1945–1949.

Ramnath Balasubramanyan, William W Cohen, Doug Pierce, and David P Redlawsk. 2012. Modeling polarizing topics: When do different political communities respond differently to the same news? In *the International AAAI Conference on Weblogs and Social Media (ICWSM)*.

Ilia Chetviorkin and Natalia Loukachevich. 2013. Sentiment analysis track at romip 2012. In *Proceedings of International Conference Dialog*, volume 2, pages 40–50.

Ilia Chetviorkin and Natalia Loukachevitch. 2012. Extraction of russian sentiment lexicon for product meta-domain. In *Proceedings of COLING 2012*, pages 593–610.

Ilia Chetviorkin, P Braslavskiy, and Natalia Loukachevich. 2012. Sentiment analysis track at romip 2011. In *Proceedings of International Conference Dialog*, volume 2, pages 1–14.

Alexander Ermakov. 2009. Knowledge extraction from text and its processing: Current state and prospects. *Information technologies*, (7):50–55.

Evgeniy Kotelnikov and Marina Klekovkina. 2012. Sentiment analysis of texts based on machine learning methods. In *Proceedings of International Conference Dialog*, volume 2, pages 27–36.

Ekaterina Kuznetsova, Natalia Loukachevitch, and Ilia Chetviorkin. 2013. Testing rules for sentiment analysis system. In *Proceedings of International Conference Dialog*, volume 2, pages 71–80.

Craig Macdonald, Iadh Ounis, and Ian Soboroff. 2008. Overview of the trec 2007 blog track. In *Proceedings of TREC*, volume 7.

Craig Macdonald, Iadh Ounis, and Ian Soboroff. 2010. Overview of the trec 2009 blog track. In *Proceedings of TREC*, volume 9.

Christopher D Manning, Prabhakar Raghavan, and Hinrich Schütze. 2008. *Introduction to information retrieval*, volume 1. Cambridge University Press Cambridge.

Rada Mihalcea, Carmen Banea, and Janyce Wiebe. 2007. Learning multilingual subjective language via cross-lingual projections. In *Proceedings of the Annual Meeting of the Association of Computational Linguistics*, volume 45, pages 976–983.

Roser Morante and Eduardo Blanco. 2012. * sem 2012 shared task: Resolving the scope and focus of negation. In *Proceedings of the First Joint Conference on Lexical and Computational Semantics*, pages 265–274.

Iadh Ounis, Maarten de Rijke, Craig Macdonald, Gilad Mishne, and Ian Soboroff. 2007. Overview of the trec 2006 blog track. In *Proceedings of TREC*, volume 6.

Iadh Ounis, Craig Macdonald, and Ian Soboroff. 2008. Overview of the trec-2008 blog track. Technical report, DTIC Document.

Iadh Ounis, Craig Macdonald, and Ian Soboroff. 2011. Overview of the trec 2010 blog track. In *Proceedings of TREC*, volume 10.

Alexander Pak and Patrick Paroubek. 2012. Language independent approach to sentiment analysis (limsi participation in romip11. In *Proceedings of International Conference Dialog*, volume 2, pages 37–50.

Polina Panicheva. 2013. Atex. a rule-based sentiment analysis system. processing texts in various topics. In *Proceedings of International Conference Dialog*, volume 2, pages 101–113.

Verónica Pérez-Rosas, Carmen Banea, and Rada Mihalcea. 2012. Learning sentiment lexicons in spanish. In *Proceedings of the Eight International Conference on Language Resources and Evaluation (LREC'12)*.

John P Pestian, Pawel Matykiewicz, Michelle Linn-Gust, Brett South, Ozlem Uzuner, Jan Wiebe, K Bretonnel Cohen, John Hurdle, and Christopher Brew. 2012. Sentiment analysis of suicide notes: A shared task. *Biomedical Informatics Insights*, 5(Suppl 1):3–16.

Pavel Polyakov, Maria Kalinina, and Vladimir Pleshko. 2012. Research on applicability of thematic classification methods to the problem of book review classification. In *Proceedings of International Conference Dialog*, volume 2, pages 51–59.

Yohei Seki, David Kirk Evans, Lun-Wei Ku, Hsin-Hsi Chen, Noriko Kando, and Chin-Yew Lin. 2007. Overview of opinion analysis pilot task at ntcir-6. In *Proceedings of NTCIR-6 Workshop Meeting*, pages 265–278.

Josef Steinberger, Mohamed Ebrahim, Maud Ehrmann, Ali Hurriyetoglu, Mijail Kabadjov, Polina Lenkova, Ralf Steinberger, Hristo Tanev, Silvia Vázquez, and Vanni Zavarella. 2011. Creating sentiment dictionaries via triangulation. *Decision Support Systems*, pages 28–36.

Maite Taboada, Julian Brooke, Milan Tofiloski, Kimberly Voll, and Manfred Stede. 2011. Lexicon-based methods for sentiment analysis. *Computational linguistics*, 37(2):267–307.

Yunfang Wu and Peng Jin. 2010. Semeval-2010 task 18: Disambiguating sentiment ambiguous adjectives. In *Proceedings of the 5th International Workshop on Semantic Evaluation*, pages 81–85.

Taras Zagibalov, Katerina Belyatskaya, and John Carroll. 2010. Comparable english-russian book review corpora for sentiment analysis. In *Computational Approaches to Subjectivity and Sentiment Analysis*, pages 67–72.

Aspect-Oriented Opinion Mining from User Reviews in Croatian

Goran Glavaš* **Damir Korenčić†** **Jan Šnajder***
*University of Zagreb, Faculty of Electrical Engineering and Computing
Unska 3, 10000 Zagreb, Croatia
†Ruđer Bošković Institute, Department of Electronics
Bijenička cesta 54, 10000 Zagreb, Croatia
{goran.glavas, jan.snajder}@fer.hr damir.korencic@irb.hr

Abstract

Aspect-oriented opinion mining aims to identify product aspects (features of products) about which opinion has been expressed in the text. We present an approach for aspect-oriented opinion mining from user reviews in Croatian. We propose methods for acquiring a domain-specific opinion lexicon, linking opinion clues to product aspects, and predicting polarity and rating of reviews. We show that a supervised approach to linking opinion clues to aspects is feasible, and that the extracted clues and aspects improve polarity and rating predictions.

1 Introduction

For companies, knowing what customers think of their products and services is essential. Opinion mining is being increasingly used to automatically recognize opinions about products in natural language texts. Numerous approaches to opinion mining have been proposed, ranging from domain-specific (Fahrni and Klenner, 2008; Qiu et al., 2009; Choi et al., 2009) to cross-domain approaches (Wilson et al., 2009; Taboada et al., 2011), and from lexicon-based methods (Popescu and Etzioni, 2007; Jijkoun et al., 2010; Taboada et al., 2011) to machine learning approaches (Boiy and Moens, 2009; Go et al., 2009).

While early attempts focused on classifying overall document opinion (Turney, 2002; Pang et al., 2002), more recent approaches identify opinions expressed about individual product aspects (Popescu and Etzioni, 2007; Fahrni and Klenner, 2008; Mukherjee and Liu, 2012). Identifying opinionated aspects allows for aspect-based comparison across reviews and enables opinion summarization for individual aspects. Furthermore, opinionated aspects may be useful for predicting overall review polarity and rating.

While many opinion mining systems and resources have been developed for major languages, there has been considerably less development for less prevalent languages, such as Croatian. In this paper we present a method for domain-specific, aspect-oriented opinion mining from user reviews in Croatian. We address two tasks: (1) identification of opinion expressed about individual product aspects and (2) predicting the overall opinion expressed by a review. We assume that solving the first task successfully will help improve the performance on the second task. We propose a simple semi-automated approach for acquiring domain-specific lexicon of opinion clues and prominent product aspects. We use supervised machine learning to detect the links between opinion clues (e.g., *excellent, horrible*) and product aspects (e.g., *pizza, delivery*). We conduct preliminary experiments on restaurant reviews and show that our method can successfully pair opinion clues with the targeted aspects. Furthermore, we show that the extracted clues and opinionated aspects help classify review polarity and predict user-assigned ratings.

2 Related Work

Aspect-based opinion mining typically consists of three subtasks: sentiment lexicon acquisition, aspect-clue pair identification, and overall review opinion prediction. Most approaches to domain-specific sentiment lexicon acquisition start from a manually compiled set of aspects and opinion clues and then expand it with words satisfying certain co-occurrence or syntactic criteria in a domain-specific corpus (Kanayama and Nasukawa, 2006; Popescu and Etzioni, 2007; Fahrni and Klenner, 2008; Mukherjee and Liu, 2012). Kobayashi et al. (2007) extract aspect-clue pairs from weblog posts using a supervised model with parts of dependency trees as features. Kelly et al. (2012) use a semi-supervised SVM model with syntactic features to classify the relations between entity-property pairs. Opinion classification of reviews has been approached using supervised text categorization techniques (Pang et al., 2002; Funk et al., 2008) and semi-supervised methods based on the similarity between unlabeled documents and a small set of manually labeled documents or clues (Turney, 2002; Goldberg and Zhu, 2006).

Sentiment analysis and opinion mining approaches have been proposed for several Slavic languages (Chetviorkin et al., 2012; Buczynski and Wawer, 2008; Smrž, 2006; Smailović et al., 2012). Methods that rely on translation, using resources developed for major languages, have also been proposed (Smrž, 2006; Steinberger et al., 2012). Thus far, there has been little work on opinion mining for Croatian. Glavaš et al. (2012) use graph-based algorithms to acquire a sentiment lexicon from a newspaper corpus. Agić et al. (2010) describe a rule-based method for detecting polarity phrases in financial domain. To the best of our knowledge, our work is the first that deals with aspect-oriented opinion mining for Croatian.

3 Aspect-Oriented Opinion Mining

Our approach consists of three steps: (1) acquisition of an opinion lexicon of domain-specific opinion clues and product aspects, (2) recognition of aspects targeted by opinion clues, and (3) prediction of overall review polarity and opinion rating.

The linguistic preprocessing includes sentence segmentation, tokenization, lemmatization, POS-tagging, and dependency parsing. We use the inflectional lexicon from Šnajder et al. (2008) for lemmatization, POS tagger from Agić et al. (2008), and dependency parser from Agić (2012). As we are dealing with noisy user-generated text, prior to any of these steps, we use GNU Aspell tool[1] for spelling correction.

Step 1: Acquisition of the opinion lexicon. We use a simple semi-automatic method to acquire opinion clues and aspects. We identify candidates for positive clues as lemmas that appear much more frequently in positive than in negative reviews (we determine review polarity based on user-assigned rating). Analogously, we consider as negative clue candidates lemmas that occur much more frequently in negative than in positive reviews. Assuming that opinion clues target product aspects, we extract as aspect candidates all lemmas that frequently co-occur with opinion clues. We then manually filter out the false positives from the lists of candidate clues and aspects.

Unlike some approaches (Popescu and Etzioni, 2007; Kobayashi et al., 2007), we do not require that clues or aspects belong to certain word categories or to a predefined taxonomy. Our approach is pragmatic – clues are words that express opinions about aspects, while aspects are words that opinion clues target. For example, we treat words like *stići* (*to arrive*) and *sve* (*everything*) as aspects, because they can be targets of opinion clues, as in *"pizza je stigla kasno"* (*"pizza arrived late"*) and *"sve super!"* (*"everything's great!"*).

Step 2: Identifying opinionated aspects. We aim to pair in each sentence the aspects with the opinion clues that target them. For example, in *"dobra pizza, ali lazanje su užasne"* (*"good pizza, but lasagna was terrible"*), the clue *dobra* (*good*) should be paired with the aspect *pizza*, and *užasne* (*terrible*) should be paired with *lazanje* (*lasagne*).

In principle, the polarity of an opinion is determined by both the opinion clue and the aspect. At an extreme, an aspect can invert the prior polarity of an opinion clue (e.g., *"cold pizza"* has a negative, whereas *"cold ice-cream"* has a positive polarity). However, given that no such cases occurred in our dataset, we chose not to consider this particular type of inversion. On the other hand, the polarity of an opinion may be inverted explicitly by the use of negations. To account for this, we use a very simple rule to recognize negations: we consider an aspect-clue pair to be negated if there is a negation word within a ± 3 token window of the opinion clue (e.g., *"pizza im nikad nije hladna"* – *"their pizza is never cold"*).

To identify the aspect-clue pairs, we train a supervised model that classifies all possible pairs within a sentence as either *paired* or *not paired*. We use four sets of features:

(1) Basic features: the distance between the aspect and the clue (in number of tokens); the number of aspects and clues in the sentence; the sentence length (in number of tokens); punctuation, other aspects, and other clues in between the aspect and the clue; the order of the aspect and the clue (i.e.,

[1] `http://aspell.net/`

which one comes before);

(2) Lexical features: the aspect and clue lemmas; bag-of-words in between the aspect and the clue; a feature indicating whether the aspect is conjoined with another aspect (e.g., *"pizza i sendvič su bili izvrsni" – "pizza and sandwich were amazing"*); a feature indicating whether the clue is conjoined with another clue (e.g., *"velika i slasna pizza" – "large and delicious pizza"*);

(3) Part-of-speech features: POS tags of the aspect and the clue word; set of POS tags in between the aspect and the clue; set of POS tags preceding the aspect/clue; set of POS tags following the aspect/clue; an agreement of gender and number between the aspect and the clue;

(4) Syntactic dependency features: dependency relation labels along the path from the aspect to the clue in the dependency tree (two features: a concatenation of these labels and a set of these labels); a feature indicating whether the given aspect is syntactically the closest to the given clue; a feature indicating whether the given clue is syntactically the closest to given aspect.

Step 3: Predicting overall review opinion. We use extracted aspects, clues, and aspect-clue pairs to predict the overall review opinion. We consider two separate tasks: (1) prediction of review polarity (positive or negative) and (2) prediction of user-assigned rating that accompanies a review. We frame the first task as a binary classification problem, and the second task as a regression problem. We use the following features for both tasks:

(1) Bag-of-word (BoW): the standard tf-idf weighted BoW representation of the review;

(2) Review length: the number of tokens in the review (longer reviews are more likely to contain more opinion clues and aspects);

(3) Emoticons: the number of positive (e.g., ":) ") and negative emoticons (e.g., ": ("");

(4) Opinion clue features: the number and the lemmas of positive and negative opinion clues;

(5) Opinionated aspect features: the number and the lemmas of positively and negatively opinionated aspects.

4 Evaluation

For experimental evaluation, we acquired a domain-specific dataset of restaurant reviews[2] from Pauza.hr,[3] Croatia's largest food ordering website. The dataset contains 3310 reviews, totaling about 100K tokens. Each review is accompanied by an opinion rating on a scale from 0.5 (worst) to 6 (best). The average user rating is 4.5, with 74% of comments rated above 4. We use these user-assigned ratings as gold-standard labels for supervised learning. Table 1 shows an example of a review (clues are bolded and aspects are underlined). We split the dataset into a development and a test set (7:3 ratio) and use the former for lexicon acquisition and model training.

(HR)	*Zaista za svaku* ***pohvalu****! Jelo su nam dostavili 15 minuta* ***ranije****. Naručili smo pizzu koja je bila* ***prepuna*** *dodataka,* ***dobro pečena****, i vrlo* ***ukusna****.*
(EN)	*Really* ***laudable****! Food was delivered 15 minutes* ***early****. We ordered pizza which was* ***filled*** *with extras,* ***well-baked****, and very* ***tasteful****.*
	Rating: 6/6

Table 1: Example of a review (text and rating)

Experiment 1: Opinionated aspects. To build a set on which we can train the aspect-clue pairing model, we sampled 200 reviews from the development set and extracted from each sentence all possible aspect-clue pairs. We obtained 1406 aspect-clue instances, which we then manually labeled as either *paired* or *not paired*. Similarly for the test set, we annotated 308 aspect-clue instances extracted from a sample of 70 reviews. Among the extracted clues, 77% are paired with at least one aspect and 23% are unpaired (the aspect is implicit).

We trained a support vector machine (SVM) with radial basis kernel and features described in Section 3. We optimized the model using 10-fold cross-validation on the training set. The baseline assigns to each aspect the closest opinion clue within the same sentence. We use stratified shuffling test (Yeh, 2000) to determine statistical significance of performance differences.

Results are shown in Table 2. All of our supervised models significantly outperform the closest clue baseline ($p < 0.01$). The *Basic+Lex+POS+Synt* model outperforms *Basic* model (F-score difference is statistically significant at $p < 0.01$), while the F-score differences between *Basic* and both *Basic+Lex* and *Basic+Lex+POS* are pairwise significant at $p < 0.05$. The F-score

[2] Available under CC BY-NC-SA license from http://takelab.fer.hr/cropinion

[3] http://pauza.hr/

Model	Precision	Recall	F1
Baseline	31.8	71.0	43.9
Basic	77.2	76.1	76.6
Basic+Lex	78.1	**82.6**	80.3
Basic+Lex+POS	80.9	79.7	80.3
Basic+Lex+POS+Synt	**84.1**	80.4	**82.2**

Table 2: Aspect-clue pairing performance

	Review polarity			Review rating	
Model	Pos	Neg	Avg	r	MAE
BoW	94.1	79.1	86.6	0.74	0.94
BoW+E	94.4	80.3	87.4	0.75	0.91
BoW+E+A	95.7	85.2	90.5	0.80	0.82
BoW+E+C	95.7	85.6	90.7	0.81	0.79
BoW+E+A+C	**96.0**	**86.2**	**91.1**	**0.83**	**0.76**

E – emoticons; *A* – opinionated aspects; *C* – opinion clues

Table 3: Review polarity and rating performance

differences between *Basic+Lex*, *Basic+Lex+POS*, and *Basic+Lex+POS+Synt* are pairwise not statistically significant ($p < 0.05$). This implies that linguistic features increase the classification performance, but there are no significant differences between models employing different linguistic feature sets. We also note that improvements over the *Basic* model are not as large as we expected; we attribute this to the noisy user-generated text and the limited size of the training set.

Experiment 2: Overall review opinion. We considered two models: a classification model for predicting review polarity and a regression model for predicting user-assigned rating. We trained the models on the full development set (2276 reviews) and evaluated on the full test set (1034 reviews). For the classification task, we consider reviews rated lower than 2.5 as negative and those rated higher than 4 as positive. Ratings between 2.5 and 4 are mostly inconsistent (assigned to both positive and negative reviews), thus we did not consider reviews with these ratings. For classification, we used SVM with radial basis kernel, while for regression we used support vector regression (SVR) model. We optimized both models using 10-fold cross-validation on the training set.

Table 3 shows performance of models with different feature sets. The model with bag-of-words features (*BoW*) is the baseline. For polarity classification, we report F1-scores for positive and negative class. For rating prediction, we report Pearson correlation (r) and mean average error (MAE).

The models that use opinion clue features (*BoW+E+C*) or opinionated aspect features (*BoW+E+A* and *BoW+E+A+C*) outperform the baseline model (difference in classification and regression performance is significant at $p < 0.05$ and $p < 0.01$, respectively; tested using stratified shuffling test). This confirms our assumption that opinion clues and opinionated aspects improve the prediction of overall review opinion. Performance on negative reviews is consistently lower than for positive reviews; this can be ascribed to the fact that the dataset is biased toward positive reviews. Models *BoW+E+A* and *BoW+E+C* perform similarly (the difference is not statistically significant at $p < 0.05$), suggesting that opinion clues improve the performance just as much as opinionated aspects. We believe this is due to (1) the existence of a considerable number (23%) of unpaired opinion clues (e.g., *užasno* (*terrible*) in *"Bilo je užasno!"* (*"It was terrible!"*)) and (2) the fact that most opinionated aspects inherit the prior polarity of the clue that targets them (also supported by the fact the *BoW+E+A+C* model does not significantly outperform the *BoW+E+C* nor the *BoW+E+A* models). Moreover, note that, in general, user-assigned ratings may deviate from the opinions expressed in text (e.g., because some users chose to comment only on some aspects). However, the issue of annotation quality is out of scope and we leave it for future work.

5 Conclusion

We presented a method for aspect-oriented opinion mining from user reviews in Croatian. We proposed a simple, semi-automated approach for acquiring product aspects and domain-specific opinion clues. We showed that a supervised model with linguistic features can effectively assign opinions to the individual product aspects. Furthermore, we demonstrated that opinion clues and opinionated aspects improve prediction of overall review polarity and user-assigned opinion rating.

For future work we intend to evaluate our method on other datasets and domains, varying in level of language complexity and correctness. Of particular interest are the domains with aspect-focused ratings and reviews (e.g., electronic product reviews). Aspect-based opinion summarization is another direction for future work.

Acknowledgments

This work has been supported by the Ministry of Science, Education and Sports, Republic of Croatia under the Grant 036-1300646-1986 and Grant 098-0982560-2566.

References

Željko Agić, Marko Tadić, and Zdravko Dovedan. 2008. Improving part-of-speech tagging accuracy for Croatian by morphological analysis. *Informatica*, 32(4):445–451.

Željko Agić, Nikola Ljubešić, and Marko Tadić. 2010. Towards sentiment analysis of financial texts in Croatian. In Nicoletta Calzolari, editor, *Proceedings of the Seventh conference on International Language Resources and Evaluation (LREC'10)*, Valletta, Malta. European Language Resources Association (ELRA).

Željko Agić. 2012. K-best spanning tree dependency parsing with verb valency lexicon reranking. In *Proceedings of 24th international Conference on Computational Linguistics (COLING 2012): Posters*, pages 1–12.

Erik Boiy and Marie-Francine Moens. 2009. A machine learning approach to sentiment analysis in multilingual web texts. *Information retrieval*, 12(5):526–558.

Aleksander Buczynski and Aleksander Wawer. 2008. Shallow parsing in sentiment analysis of product reviews. In *Proceedings of the Partial Parsing workshop at LREC*, pages 14–18.

Ilia Chetviorkin, Pavel Braslavskiy, and Natalia Loukachevich. 2012. Sentiment analysis track at romip 2011. *Dialog*.

Yoonjung Choi, Youngho Kim, and Sung-Hyon Myaeng. 2009. Domain-specific sentiment analysis using contextual feature generation. In *Proceedings of the 1st international CIKM workshop on Topic-sentiment analysis for mass opinion*, pages 37–44. ACM.

Angela Fahrni and Manfred Klenner. 2008. Old wine or warm beer: Target-specific sentiment analysis of adjectives. In *Proc. of the Symposium on Affective Language in Human and Machine, AISB*, pages 60–63.

Adam Funk, Yaoyong Li, Horacio Saggion, Kalina Bontcheva, and Christian Leibold. 2008. Opinion analysis for business intelligence applications. In *Proceedings of the first international workshop on Ontology-supported business intelligence*, page 3. ACM.

Goran Glavaš, Jan Šnajder, and Bojana Dalbelo Bašić. 2012. Semi-supervised acquisition of Croatian sentiment lexicon. In *Text, Speech and Dialogue*, pages 166–173. Springer.

Alec Go, Richa Bhayani, and Lei Huang. 2009. Twitter sentiment classification using distant supervision. *CS224N Project Report, Stanford*, pages 1–12.

Andrew B Goldberg and Xiaojin Zhu. 2006. Seeing stars when there aren't many stars: Graph-based semi-supervised learning for sentiment categorization. In *Proceedings of the First Workshop on Graph Based Methods for Natural Language Processing*, pages 45–52. Association for Computational Linguistics.

Valentin Jijkoun, Maarten de Rijke, and Wouter Weerkamp. 2010. Generating focused topic-specific sentiment lexicons. In *Proceedings of the 48th Annual Meeting of the Association for Computational Linguistics*, pages 585–594. Association for Computational Linguistics.

Hiroshi Kanayama and Tetsuya Nasukawa. 2006. Fully automatic lexicon expansion for domain-oriented sentiment analysis. In *Proceedings of the 2006 Conference on Empirical Methods in Natural Language Processing*, EMNLP '06, pages 355–363, Stroudsburg, PA, USA. Association for Computational Linguistics.

Colin Kelly, Barry Devereux, and Anna Korhonen. 2012. Semi-supervised learning for automatic conceptual property extraction. In *Proceedings of the 3rd Workshop on Cognitive Modeling and Computational Linguistics*, CMCL '12, pages 11–20, Stroudsburg, PA, USA. Association for Computational Linguistics.

Nozomi Kobayashi, Kentaro Inui, and Yuji Matsumoto. 2007. Extracting aspect-evaluation and aspect-of relations in opinion mining. In *Proceedings of the 2007 Joint Conference on Empirical Methods in Natural Language Processing and Computational Natural Language Learning (EMNLP-CoNLL)*, pages 1065–1074.

Arjun Mukherjee and Bing Liu. 2012. Aspect extraction through semi-supervised modeling. In *Proceedings of the 50th Annual Meeting of the Association for Computational Linguistics: Long Papers-Volume 1*, pages 339–348. Association for Computational Linguistics.

Bo Pang, Lillian Lee, and Shivakumar Vaithyanathan. 2002. Thumbs up? Sentiment classification using machine learning techniques. In *Proceedings of the ACL-02 conference on Empirical methods in natural language processing-Volume 10*, pages 79–86. Association for Computational Linguistics.

Ana-Maria Popescu and Oren Etzioni. 2007. Extracting product features and opinions from reviews. In *Natural language processing and text mining*, pages 9–28. Springer.

Guang Qiu, Bing Liu, Jiajun Bu, and Chun Chen. 2009. Expanding domain sentiment lexicon through double propagation. In *Proceedings of the 21st international jont conference on Artifical intelligence*, pages 1199–1204.

Jasmina Smailović, Miha Grčar, and Martin Žnidaršič. 2012. Sentiment analysis on tweets in a financial domain. In *Proceedings of the 4th Jozef Stefan International Postgraduate School Students Conference*, pages 169–175.

Pavel Smrž. 2006. Using WordNet for opinion mining. In *Proceedings of the Third International WordNet Conference*, pages 333–335. Masaryk University.

Jan Šnajder, Bojana Dalbelo Bašić, and Marko Tadić. 2008. Automatic acquisition of inflectional lexica for morphological normalisation. *Information Processing & Management*, 44(5):1720–1731.

Josef Steinberger, Mohamed Ebrahim, Maud Ehrmann, Ali Hurriyetoglu, Mijail Kabadjov, Polina Lenkova, Ralf Steinberger, Hristo Tanev, Silvia Vázquez, and Vanni Zavarella. 2012. Creating sentiment dictionaries via triangulation. *Decision Support Systems*.

Maite Taboada, Julian Brooke, Milan Tofiloski, Kimberly Voll, and Manfred Stede. 2011. Lexicon-based methods for sentiment analysis. *Computational linguistics*, 37(2):267–307.

Peter D Turney. 2002. Thumbs up or thumbs down? Semantic orientation applied to unsupervised classification of reviews. In *Proceedings of the 40th annual meeting on association for computational linguistics*, pages 417–424. Association for Computational Linguistics.

Theresa Wilson, Janyce Wiebe, and Paul Hoffmann. 2009. Recognizing contextual polarity: An exploration of features for phrase-level sentiment analysis. *Computational linguistics*, 35(3):399–433.

Alexander Yeh. 2000. More accurate tests for the statistical significance of result differences. In *Proceedings of the 18th conference on Computational linguistics-Volume 2*, pages 947–953. Association for Computational Linguistics.

Frequently Asked Questions Retrieval for Croatian Based on Semantic Textual Similarity

Mladen Karan* **Lovro Žmak†** **Jan Šnajder***
*University of Zagreb, Faculty of Electrical Engineering and Computing
Unska 3, 10000 Zagreb, Croatia
†Studio Artlan, Andrije Štangera 18, 51410 Opatija, Croatia
{mladen.karan,jan.snajder}@fer.hr lovro.zmak@studioartlan.hr

Abstract

Frequently asked questions (FAQ) are an efficient way of communicating domain-specific information to the users. Unlike general purpose retrieval engines, FAQ retrieval engines have to address the lexical gap between the query and the usually short answer. In this paper we describe the design and evaluation of a FAQ retrieval engine for Croatian. We frame the task as a binary classification problem, and train a model to classify each FAQ as either relevant or not relevant for a given query. We use a variety of semantic textual similarity features, including term overlap and vector space features. We train and evaluate on a FAQ test collection built specifically for this purpose. Our best-performing model reaches 0.47 of mean reciprocal rank, i.e., on average ranks the relevant answer among the top two returned answers.

1 Introduction

The amount of information available online is growing at an exponential rate. It is becoming increasingly difficult to navigate the vast amounts of data and isolate relevant pieces of information. Thus, providing efficient information access for clients can be essential for many businesses. Frequently asked questions (FAQ) databases are a popular way to present domain-specific information in the form of expert answers to users questions. Each FAQ consists of a question and an answer, possibly complemented with additional metadata (e.g., keywords). A FAQ retrieval engine provides an interface to a FAQ database. Given a user query in natural language as input, it retrieves a ranked list of FAQs relevant to the query.

FAQ retrieval can be considered half way between traditional document retrieval and question answering (QA). Unlike in full-blown QA, in FAQ retrieval the questions and the answers are already extracted. On the other hand, unlike in document retrieval, FAQ queries are typically questions and the answers are typically much shorter than documents. While FAQ retrieval can be approached using simple keyword matching, the performance of such systems will be severely limited due to the *lexical gap* – a lack of overlap between the words that appear in a query and words from a FAQ pair. As noted by Sneiders (1999), there are two causes for this. Firstly, the FAQ database creators in general do not know the user questions in advance. Instead, they must guess what the likely questions would be. Thus, it is very common that users' information needs are not fully covered by the provided questions. Secondly, both FAQs and user queries are generally very short texts, which diminishes the chances of a keyword match.

In this paper we describe the design and the evaluation of a FAQ retrieval engine for Croatian. To address the lexical gap problem, we take a supervised learning approach and train a model that predicts the relevance of a FAQ given a query. Motivated by the recent work on semantic textual similarity (Agirre et al., 2012), we use as model features a series of similarity measures based on word overlap and semantic vector space similarity. We train and evaluate the model on a FAQ dataset from a telecommunication domain. On this dataset, our best performing model achieves 0.47 of mean reciprocal rank, i.e., on average ranks the relevant FAQ among the top two results.

In summary, the contribution of this paper is twofold. Firstly, we propose and evaluate a FAQ retrieval model based on supervised machine learning. To the best of our knowledge, no previous work exists that addresses IR for Croatian in a supervised setting. Secondly, we build a freely available FAQ test collection with relevance judgments. To the best of our knowledge, this is the first IR test collection for Croatian.

The rest of the paper is organized as follows. In the next section we give an overview of related work. In Section 3 we describe the FAQ test collection, while in Section 4 we describe the retrieval model. Experimental evaluation is given in Section 5. Section 6 concludes the paper and outlines future work.

2 Related Work

Most prior work on FAQ retrieval has focused on the problem of lexical gap, and various approaches have been proposed for bridging it. Early work, such as Sneiders (1999), propose to manually enrich the FAQ databases with additional meta data such as the required, optional, and forbidden keywords and keyphrases. This effectively reduces FAQ retrieval to simple keyword matching, however in this case it is the manually assigned metadata that bridges the lexical gap and provides the *look and feel* of semantic search.

For anything but a small-sized FAQ database, manual creation of metadata is tedious and cost intensive, and in addition requires expert knowledge. An alternative is to rely on general linguistic resources. FAQ finder (Burke et al., 1997) uses syntax analysis to identify phrases, and then performs matching using shallow lexical semantic knowledge from WordNet (Miller, 1995). Yet another way to bridge the lexical gap is smoothing via clustering, proposed by Kim and Seo (2006). First, query logs are expanded with word definitions from a machine readable dictionary. Subsequently, query logs are clustered, and query similarity is computed against the clusters, instead of against the individual FAQs. As an alternative to clustering, query expansion is often used to perform lexical smoothing (Voorhees, 1994; Navigli and Velardi, 2003).

In some domains a FAQ engine additionally must deal with typing errors and noisy user-generated content. An example is the FAQ retrieval for SMS messages, described by Kothari et al. (2009) and Contractor et al. (2010).

Although low lexical overlap is identified as the primary problem in FAQ retrieval, sometimes it is the high lexical overlap that also presents a problem. This is particularly true for large FAQ databases in which a non-relevant document can "accidentally" have a high lexical overlap with a query. Moreo et al. (2012) address the problem of false positives using case based reasoning. Rather than considering only the words, they use phrases ("differentiator expressions") that discriminate well between FAQs.

The approaches described so far are essentially unsupervised. A number of supervised FAQ retrieval methods have been described in the literature. To bridge the lexical gap, Xue et al. (2008) use machine translation models to "translate" the user query into a FAQ. Their system is trained on very large FAQ knowledge bases, such as Yahoo answers. Soricut and Brill (2004) describe another large-scale FAQ retrieval system, which uses language and transformation models. A good general overview of supervised approaches to ranking tasks is the work by Liu (2009).

Our system falls into the category of supervised methods. In contrast to the above-described approaches, we use a supervised model with word overlap and semantic similarity features. Taking into account that FAQs are short texts, we use features that have been recently proposed for determining the semantic similarity between pairs of sentences (Šarić et al., 2012). Because we train our model to output a relevance score for each document, our approach is essentially a *pointwise* learning-to-rank approach (Qin et al., 2008).

3 Croatian FAQ test collection

The standard procedure for IR evaluation requires a test collection consisting of documents, queries, and relevance judgments. We additionally require an annotated dataset to train the model. As there currently exists no standard IR test collection for Croatian, we decided to build a FAQ test collection from scratch. We use this collection for both model training and retrieval evaluation.

To obtain a FAQ test collection, we crawled the web FAQ of Vip,[1] a Croatian mobile phone operator. For each FAQ, we retrieved both the question and the answer. In the Vip FAQ database questions are categorized into several broad categories (e.g., by type of service). For each FAQ, we also extract the category name assigned to it. We obtained a total of 1344 FAQs. After removing the

[1] `http://www.vipnet.hr/pitanja-i-odgovori/` (accessed Sep 2009)

Query	FAQ question	FAQ answer
Kako se spaja na internet? (*How to connect to the internet?*)	Što mi je potrebno da bih spojio računalo i koristio se internetom? (*What do I need to connect my computer and use the internet*)	Morate spojiti računalo sa Homebox uređajem LAN kabelom... (*You must connect your computer to the Homebox device using a LAN cable ...*)
Putujem izvan Hrvatske i želim koristiti svoj Vip mobilni uređaj. Koliko će me to koštati? (*I am traveling abroad and want to use my Vip mobile device. How much will this cost?*)	Koja je mreža najpovoljnija za razgovore, a koja za slanje SMS i MMS poruka u roamingu? (*Which network is the best for conversations, and which one for SMS and MMS messages in roaming?*)	Cijene za odlazne pozive u inozemstvu su najpovoljnije u mrežama Vodafone partnera... (*Outgoing calls cost less on networks of Vodafone partners ...*)
Kako pogledati e-mail preko mobitela? (*How to check e-mail using a mobile phone?*)	Koja je cijena korištenja BlackBerry Office usluge? (*What is the price of using the BlackBerry Office service?*)	... business e-mail usluga uračunata je u cijenu... (*... business e-mail is included in the price ...*)

Table 1: Examples of relevant answers to queries from the dataset

duplicates, 1222 unique FAQ pairs remain.

Next, we asked ten annotators to create at least twelve queries each. They were instructed to invent queries that they think would be asked by real users of Vip services. To ensure that the queries are as original as possible, the annotators were not shown the original FAQ database. Following Lytinen and Tomuro (2002), after creating the queries, the annotators were instructed to rephrase them. We asked the annotators to make between three and ten paraphrases of each query. The paraphrase strategies suggested were the following: (1) turn a query into a multi-sentence query, (2) change the structure (syntax) of the query, (3) substitute some words with synonyms, while leaving the structure intact, (4) turn the query into a declarative sentence, and (5) any combination of the above. The importance of not changing the underlying meaning of a query was particularly stressed.

The next step was to obtain the binary relevance judgments for each query. Annotating relevance for the complete FAQ database is not feasible, as the total number of query-FAQ pairs is too large. On the other hand, not considering some of the FAQs would make it impossible to estimate recall. A feasible alternative is the standard pooling method predominantly used in IR evaluation campaigns (Voorhees, 2002). In the pooling method, the top-k ranked results of each evaluated system are combined into a single list, which is then annotated for relevance judgments. For a sufficiently large k, the recall estimate will be close to real recall, as the documents that are not in the pool are likely to be non-relevant. We simulate this setting using several standard retrieval models: keyword search, phrase search, tf-idf, and language modeling. The number of combined results per query is between 50 and 150. To reduce the annotators' bias towards top-ranked examples, the retrieved results were presented in random order. For each query, the annotators gave binary judgments ("relevant" or "not relevant") to each FAQ from the pooled list; FAQs not in the pool are assumed to be not relevant. Although the appropriateness of binary relevance has been questioned (e.g., by Kekäläinen (2005)), it is still commonly used for FAQ and QA collections (Wu et al., 2006; Voorhees and Tice, 2000). Table 1 shows examples of queries and relevant FAQs.

The above procedure yields a set of pairs (Q_r, F_{rel}), where Q_r is a set of query paraphrases and F_{rel} is the set of relevant FAQs for any query paraphrase from Q_r. The total number of such pairs is 117. From this set we generate a set of pairs (q, F_{rel}), where $q \in Q_r$ is a single query. The total number of such pairs is 419, of which 327 have at least one answer ($F_{rel} \neq \emptyset$), while 92 are not answered ($F_{rel} = \emptyset$). In this work we focus on optimizing the performance on answered queries and leave the detection and handling of unanswered queries for future work. The average number of relevant FAQs for a query is 1.26, while on average each FAQ is relevant for 1.44 queries. Test collection statistics is shown in Table 2. We make the test collection freely available for research purposes.[2]

For further processing, we lemmatized the query and FAQ texts using the morphological lexicon from Šnajder et al. (2008). We removed the stopwords using a list of 179 Croatian stopwords.

[2]Available under CC BY-SA-NC license from `http://takelab.fer.hr/faqir`

	Word counts			Form	
	Min	Max	Avg	Quest.	Decl.
Queries	1	25	8	372	47
FAQ questions	4	63	7	287	4
FAQ answers	1	218	30	–	–

Table 2: FAQ test collection statistics

We retained the stopwords that constitute a part of a service name (e.g., the pronoun *"me"* (*"me"*) in *"Nazovi me"* (*"Call me"*)).

4 Retrieval model

The task of the retrieval model is to rank the FAQs by relevance to a given query. In an ideal case, the relevant FAQs will be ranked above the non-relevant ones. The retrieval model we propose is a confidence-rated classifier trained on binary relevance judgments, which uses as features the semantic textual similarity between the query and the FAQ. For a given a query-FAQ pair, the classifier outputs whether the FAQ is relevant (positive) or irrelevant (negative) for the query. More precisely, the classifier outputs a confidence score, which can be interpreted as the degree of relevance. Given a single query as input, we run the classifier on all query-FAQ pairs to obtain the confidence scores for all FAQs from the database. We then use these confidence scores to produce the final FAQ ranking.

The training set consists of pairs (q, f) from the test collection, where $q \in Q_r$ is a query from the set of paraphrase queries and $f \in F_{rel}$ is a FAQ from the set of relevant FAQs for this query (cf. Section 3). Each (q, f) pair represents a positive training instance. To create a negative training instance, we randomly select a (q, f) pair from the set of positive instances and substitute the relevant FAQ f with a randomly chosen non-relevant FAQ f'. As generating all possible negative instances would give a very imbalanced dataset, we chose to generate only $2N$ negative instances, where N is the number of positive instances. Because $|F_{rel}|$ varies depending on query q, number of instances N per query also varies; on average, N is 329.

To train the classifier, we compute a feature vector for each (q, f) instance. The features measure the semantic textual similarity between q and f. More precisely, the features measure (1) the similarity between query q and the question from f and (2) the similarity between query q and the answer from f. Considering both FAQ question and answer has proven to be beneficial (Tomuro and Lytinen, 2004). Additionally, ngram overlap features are computed between the query and FAQ category name.

As the classification model, we use the Support Vector Machine (SVM) with radial basis kernel. We use the LIBSVM implementation from Chang and Lin (2011).

4.1 Term overlap features

We expect that FAQ relevance to be positively correlated with lexical overlap between FAQ text and the user query. We use several lexical overlap features. Similar features have been proposed by Michel et al. (2011) for paraphrase classification and by Šarić et al. (2012) for semantic textual similarity.

Ngram overlap (NGO). Let T_1 and T_2 be the sets of consecutive ngrams (e.g., bigrams) in the first and the second text, respectively. NGO is defined as

$$ngo(T_1, T_2) = 2 \times \left(\frac{|T_1|}{|T_1 \cap T_2|} + \frac{|T_2|}{|T_1 \cap T_2|} \right)^{-1} \quad (1)$$

NGO measures the degree to which the first text covers the second and vice versa. The two scores are combined via a harmonic mean. We compute NGO for unigrams and bigrams.

IC weighted word overlap (ICNGO). NGO gives equal importance to all words. In practice, we expect some words to be more informative than others. The informativeness of a word can be measured by its information content (Resnik, 1995), defined as

$$ic(w) = \ln \frac{\sum_{w' \in C} freq(w')}{freq(w)} \quad (2)$$

where C is the set of words from the corpus and $freq(w)$ is the frequency of word w in the corpus. We use the HrWaC corpus from Ljubešić and Erjavec (2011) to obtain the word counts.

Let S_1 and S_2 be the sets of words occurring in the first and second text, respectively. The IC-weighted word coverage of the second text by the first text is given by

$$wwc(S_1, S_2) = \frac{\sum_{w \in S_1 \cap S_2} ic(w)}{\sum_{w' \in S_2} ic(w')} \quad (3)$$

We compute the ICNGO feature as the harmonic mean of $wwc(S_1, S_2)$ and $wwc(S_2, S_1)$.

4.2 Vector space features

Tf-idf similarity (TFIDF). The tf-idf (term frequency/inverse document frequency) similarity of two texts is computed as the cosine similarity of their tf-idf weighted bag-of-words vectors. The tf-idf weights are computed on the FAQ test collection. Here we treat each FAQ (without distinction between question, answer, and category parts) as a single document.

LSA semantic similarity (LSA). Latent semantic analysis (LSA), first introduced by Deerwester et al. (1990), has been shown to be very effective for computing word and document similarity. To build the LSA model, we proceed along the lines of Karan et al. (2012). We build the model from Croatian web corpus HrWaC from Ljubešić and Erjavec (2011). For lemmatization, we use the morphological lexicon from Šnajder et al. (2008). Prior to the SVD, we weight the matrix elements with their tf-idf values. Preliminary experiments showed that system performance remained satisfactory when reducing the vector space to only 25 dimensions, but further reduction caused deterioration. We use 25 dimensions in all experiments.

LSA represents the meaning of a w by a vector $v(w)$. Motivated by work on distributional semantic compositionality (Mitchell and Lapata, 2008), we compute the semantic representation of text T as the semantic composition (defined as vector addition) of the individual words constituting T:

$$v(T) = \sum_{w \in T} v(w) \tag{4}$$

We compute the similarity between texts T_1 and T_2 as the cosine between $v(T_1)$ and $v(T_2)$.

IC weighted LSA similarity (ICLSA). In the LSA similarity feature all words occurring in a text are considered to be equally important when constructing the compositional vector, ignoring the fact that some words are more informative than others. To acknowledge this, we use information content weights defined by (2) and compute the IC weighted compositional vector of a text T as

$$c(T) = \sum_{w_i \in T} ic(w_i) v(w_i) \tag{5}$$

Aligned lemma overlap (ALO). This feature measures the similarity of two texts by semantically aligning their words in a greedy fashion. To compare texts $T1$ and $T2$, first all pairwise similarities between words from $T1$ and words from $T2$ are computed. Then, the most similar pair is selected and removed from the list. The procedure is repeated until all words are aligned. The aligned pairs are weighted by the larger information content of the two words:

$$\begin{aligned} sim(w_1, w_2) = \\ \max(ic(w_1), ic(w_2)) \times ssim(w_1, w_2) \end{aligned} \tag{6}$$

where $ssim(w_1, w_2)$ is the semantic similarity of words w_1 and w_2 computed as the cosine similarity of their LSA vectors, and ic is the information content given by (2). The overall similarity between two texts is defined as the sum of weighted pair similarities, normalized by the length of the longer text:

$$alo(T_1, T_2) = \frac{\sum_{(w_1, w_2) \in P} sim(w_1, w_2)}{\max(length(T_1), length(T_2))} \tag{7}$$

where P is the set of aligned lemma pairs. A similar measure is proposed by Lavie and Denkowski (2009) for machine translation evaluation, and has been found out to work well for semantic textual similarity (Šarić et al., 2012).

4.3 Question type classification (QC)

Related work on QA (Lytinen and Tomuro, 2002) shows that the accuracy of QA systems can be improved by question type classification. The intuition behind this is that different types of questions demand different types of answers. Consequently, information about the type of answer required should be beneficial as a feature.

To explore this line of improvement, we train a simple question classifier on a dataset from Lombarović et al. (2011). The dataset consists of 1300 questions in Croatian, classified into six classes: *numeric*, *entity*, *human*, *description*, *location*, and *abbreviation*. Following Lombarović et al. (2011), we use document frequency to select the most frequent 300 words and 600 bigrams to use as features. An SVM trained on this dataset achieves 80.16% accuracy in a five-fold cross-validation. This is slightly worse than the best result from Lombarović et al. (2011), however we use a smaller set of lexical features. We use the question type classifier to compute two features: the question type of the query and the question type of FAQ question.

Feature	RM1	RM2	RM3	RM4	RM5
NGO	+	+	+	+	+
ICNGO	+	+	+	+	+
TFIDF	–	+	+	+	+
LSA	–	–	+	+	+
ICLSA	–	–	+	+	+
ALO	–	–	+	+	+
QED	–	–	–	+	+
QC	–	–	–	–	+

Table 4: Features used by our models

4.4 Query expansion dictionary (QED)

Our error analysis revealed that some false negatives could easily be eliminated by expanding the query with similar/related words. To this end, we constructed a small, domain-specific query expansion dictionary. We aimed to (1) mitigate minor spelling variances, (2) make the high similarity of some some cross-POS or domain-specific words explicit, and (3) introduce a rudimentary "world knowledge" useful for the domain at hand. The final dictionary contains 53 entries; Table 3 shows some examples.

5 Evaluation

5.1 Experimental setup

Because our retrieval model is supervised, we evaluate it using five-fold cross-validation on the FAQ test collection. In each fold we train our system on the training data as described in Section 4, and evaluate the retrieval performance on the queries from the test set. While each (q, F_{rel}) occurs in the test set exactly once, the same FAQ may occur in both the train and test set. Note that this does not pose a problem because the query part of the pair will differ (due to paraphrasing).

To gain a better understanding of which features contribute the most to retrieval performance, we created several models. The models use increasingly complex feature sets; an overview is given in Table 4. We leave exhaustive feature analysis and selection for future work.

As a baseline to compare against, we use a standard tf-idf weighted retrieval model. This model ranks the FAQs by the cosine similarity of tf-idf weighted vectors representing the query and the FAQ. When computing the vector of the FAQ pair, the question, answer, and category name are concatenated into a single text unit.

Model	P	R	F1
RM1	14.1	68.5	23.1
RM2	25.8	75.1	37.8
RM3	24.4	75.4	36.3
RM4	**25.7**	**77.7**	**38.2**
RM5	25.3	76.8	37.2

Table 5: Classification results

5.2 Results

Relevance classification performance. Recall that we use a binary classifier as a retrieval model. The performance of this classifier directly determines the performance of the retrieval system as a whole. It is therefore interesting to evaluate classifier performance separately. To generate the test set, in each of the five folds we sample from the test set the query-FAQ instances using the procedure described in Section 4 (N positive and $2N$ negative instance).

Precision, recall, and F1-score for each model are shown in Table 5. Model RM4 outperforms the other considered models. Model RM5, which additionally uses question type classification, performs worse than RM4, suggesting that the accuracy of question type classification is not sufficiently high. Our analysis of the test collection revealed that this can be attributed to a domain mismatch: the questions (mobile phone operator FAQ) are considerably different than those on which the question classifier was trained (factoid general questions). Moreover, some of the queries and questions in our FAQ test collection are not questions at all (cf. Table 2); e.g., *"Popravak mobitela."* (*"Mobile phone repair."*). Consequently, it is not surprising that question classification features do not improve the performance.

Retrieval performance. Retrieval results of the five considered models are given in Table 6. We report the standard IR evaluation measures: mean reciprocal rank (MRR), average precision (AP), and R-precision (RP). The best performance was obtained with RM4 model, which uses all features except the question type. The best MRR result of 0.479 (with standard deviation over five folds of ± 0.04) indicates that, on average, model RM4 ranks the relevant answer among top two results.

Performance of other models expectedly increase with the complexity of features used. However, RM5 is again an exception, performing worse than RM4 despite using additional question

Query word	Expansion words	Remark
face	facebook	A lexical mismatch that would often occur
ograničiti (*to limit*)	ograničenje (*limit*)	Cross POS similarity important in the domain explicit
cijena (*price*)	trošak (*cost*), koštati (*to cost*)	Synonyms very often used in the domain
inozemstvo (*abroad*)	roaming (*roaming*)	Introduces world knowledge
ADSL	internet	Related words often used in the domain

Table 3: Examples from query expansions dictionary

Model	MRR	MAP	RP
Baseline	0.341	21.77	15.28
RM1	0.326	20.21	17.6
RM2	0.423	28.78	24.37
RM3	0.432	29.09	24.90
RM4	**0.479**	**33.42**	**28.74**
RM5	0.475	32.37	27.30

Table 6: Retrieval results

type features, for the reasons elaborated above.

Expectedly, classification performance and retrieval performance are positively correlated (cf. Tables 5 and 6). A noteworthy case is RM4, which improves the F1-score by only 5% over RM3, yet improves IR measures by more than 10%. This suggest that, in addition to improving the classifier decisions, the QED boosts the confidence scores of already correct decisions.

A caveat to the above analysis is the fact that the query expansion dictionary was constructed base on the cross-validation result. While only a small amount of errors were corrected with the dictionary, this still makes models RM4 and RM5 slightly biased to the given dataset. An objective estimate of maximum performance on unseen data is probably somewhere between RM3 and RM4.

5.3 Error analysis

By manual inspection of false positive and false negative errors, we have identified several characteristic cases that account for the majority of highly ranked irrelevant documents.

Lexical interference. While a query does have a significant lexical similarity with relevant FAQ pairs, it also has (often accidental) lexical similarity with irrelevant FAQs. Because the classifier appears to prefer lexical overlap, such irrelevant FAQs interfere with results by taking over some of the top ranked positions from relevant pairs.

Lexical gap. Some queries ask a very similar question to an existing FAQ from the database, but paraphrase it in such a way that almost no lexical overlap remains. Even though the effect of this is partly mitigated by our semantic vector space features, in extreme cases the relevant FAQs will be ranked rather low.

Semantic gap. Taken to the extreme, a paraphrase can change a query to the extent that it not only introduces a lexical gap, but also a semantic gap, whose bridging would require logical inference and world knowledge. An example of such query is *"Postoji li mogućnost korištenja Vip kartice u Australiji?"* (*"Is it possible to use Vip sim card in Australia?"*). The associated FAQ question is *"Kako mogu saznati postoji li GPRS/EDGE ili UMTS/HSDPA roaming u zemlji u koju putujem?"* (*"How can I find out if there is GPRS/EDGE or UMTS/SPA roaming in the country to which I am going?"*).

Word matching errors. In some cases words which should match do not. This is most often the case when one of the words is missing from the morphological lexicon, and thus not lemmatized. A case in point is the word *"Facebook"*, or its colloquial Croatian variants *"fejs"* and *"face"*, along with their inflected forms. Handling this is especially important because a significant number of FAQs from our dataset contain such words. An obvious solution would be to complement lemmatization with stemming.

5.4 Cutoff strategies

Our model outputs a list of all FAQs from the database, ranked by relevance to the input query. As low-ranked FAQs are mostly not relevant, presenting the whole ranked list puts an unnecessary burden on the user. We therefore explored some strategies for limiting the number of results.

First N (FN). This simply returns the N best ranked documents.

Measure threshold criterion (MTC). We define a threshold on FAQ relevance score, and re-

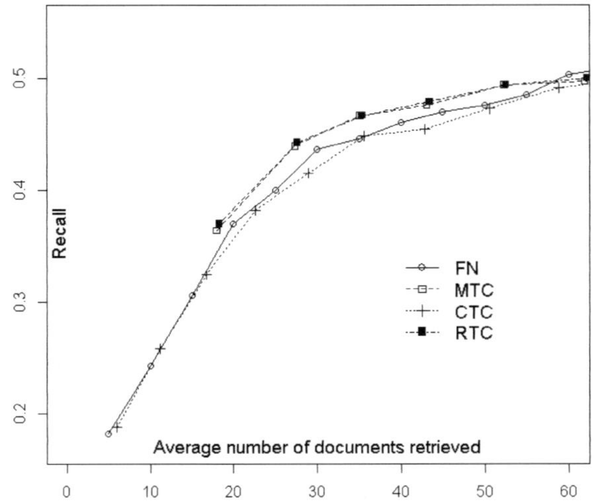

Figure 1: Recall vs. average number of documents retrieved (for various cutoff strategies)

turn only the FAQs for which the classifier confidence is above a specified threshold.

Cumulative threshold criterion (CTC). We define a threshold for cumulative relevance score. The top-ranked FAQs for which the sum of classifier confidences is below the threshold are returned.

Relative threshold criterion (RTC). Returns all FAQs whose relevance is within the given percentage of the top-ranked FAQ relevance.

A good cutoff strategy should on average return a smaller number of documents, while still retaining high recall. To reflect this requirement we measure the recall vs. average number of retrieved documents (Fig. 1). While there is no substantial difference between the four strategies, MTC and RTC perform similarly and slightly better than FN and CTC. As the number of documents increases, the differences between the different cutoff strategies diminish.

5.5 Performance and scalability

We have implemented the FAQ engine using in-house code in Java. The only external library used is the Java version of LIBSVM. Regarding system performance, the main bottleneck is in generating the features. Since all features depend on the user query, they cannot be precomputed. Computationally most intensive feature is ALO (cf. Section 4.2), which requires computing a large number of vector cosines.

The response time of our FAQ engine is acceptable – on our 1222 FAQs test collection, the results are retrieved within one second. However, to retrieve the results, the engine must generate features and apply a classifier to every FAQ from the database. This makes the response time linearly dependent on the number of FAQs. For larger databases, a preprocessing step to narrow down the scope of the search would be required. To this end, we could use a standard keyword-based retrieval engine, optimized for high recall. Unfortunately, improving efficiency by precomputing the features is impossible because it would require the query to be known in advance.

6 Conclusion and Perspectives

We have described a FAQ retrieval engine for Croatian. The engine uses a supervised retrieval model trained on a FAQ test collection with binary relevance judgments. To bridge the notorious lexical gap problem, we have employed a series of features based on semantic textual similarity between the query and the FAQ. We have built a FAQ test collection on which we have trained and evaluated the model. On this test collection, our model achieves a very good performance with an MRR score of 0.47.

We discussed a number of open problems. Error analysis suggests that our models prefer the lexical overlap features. Consequently, most errors are caused by deceivingly high or low word overlap. One way to address the former is to consider not only words themselves, but also syntactic structures. A simple way to do this is to use POS patterns to detect similar syntactic structures. A more sophisticated version could make use of dependency relations obtained by syntactic parsing.

We have demonstrated that even a small, domain-specific query expansion dictionary can provide a considerable performance boost. Another venue of research could consider the automatic methods for constructing a domain-specific query expansion dictionary. As noted by a reviewer, one possibility would be to mine query logs collected over a longer period of time, as employed in web search (Cui et al., 2002) and also FAQ retrieval (Kim and Seo, 2006).

From a practical perspective, future work shall focus on scaling up the system to large FAQ databases and multi-user environments.

Acknowledgments

This work has been supported by the Ministry of Science, Education and Sports, Republic of Croatia under the Grant 036-1300646-1986. We thank the reviewers for their constructive comments.

References

Eneko Agirre, Mona Diab, Daniel Cer, and Aitor Gonzalez-Agirre. 2012. SemEval-2012 task 6: A pilot on semantic textual similarity. In *Proceedings of the First Joint Conference on Lexical and Computational Semantics*, pages 385–393. Association for Computational Linguistics.

Robin D. Burke, Kristian J. Hammond, Vladimir Kulyukin, Steven L. Lytinen, Noriko Tomuro, and Scott Schoenberg. 1997. Question answering from frequently asked question files: experiences with the FAQ Finder system. *AI magazine*, 18(2):57.

Chih-Chung Chang and Chih-Jen Lin. 2011. LIBSVM: A library for support vector machines. *ACM Transactions on Intelligent Systems and Technology*, 2:27:1–27:27. Software available at `http://www.csie.ntu.edu.tw/~cjlin/libsvm`.

Danish Contractor, Govind Kothari, Tanveer A. Faruquie, L. Venkata Subramaniam, and Sumit Negi. 2010. Handling noisy queries in cross language FAQ retrieval. In *Proceedings of the EMNLP 2010*, pages 87–96. Association for Computational Linguistics.

Hang Cui, Ji-Rong Wen, Jian-Yun Nie, and Wei-Ying Ma. 2002. Probabilistic query expansion using query logs. In *Proceedings of the 11th international conference on World Wide Web*, pages 325–332. ACM.

Scott Deerwester, Susan T. Dumais, George W. Furnas, Thomas K. Landauer, and Richard Harshman. 1990. Indexing by latent semantic analysis. *Journal of the American society for information science*, 41(6).

Mladen Karan, Jan Šnajder, and Bojana Dalbelo Bašić. 2012. Distributional semantics approach to detecting synonyms in Croatian language. In *Information Society 2012 - Eighth Language Technologies Conference*, pages 111–116.

Jaana Kekäläinen. 2005. Binary and graded relevance in IR evaluations—comparison of the effects on ranking of IR systems. *Information processing & management*, 41(5):1019–1033.

Harksoo Kim and Jungyun Seo. 2006. High-performance FAQ retrieval using an automatic clustering method of query logs. *Information processing & management*, 42(3):650–661.

Govind Kothari, Sumit Negi, Tanveer A. Faruquie, Venkatesan T. Chakaravarthy, and L. Venkata Subramaniam. 2009. SMS based interface for FAQ retrieval. In *Proceedings of the Joint Conference of the 47th Annual Meeting of the ACL and the 4th International Joint Conference on Natural Language Processing of the AFNLP*, volume 2, pages 852–860.

Alon Lavie and Michael J. Denkowski. 2009. The METEOR metric for automatic evaluation of machine translation. *Machine translation*, 23(2-3):105–115.

Tie-Yan Liu. 2009. Learning to rank for information retrieval. *Foundations and Trends in Information Retrieval*, 3(3):225–331.

Nikola Ljubešić and Tomaž Erjavec. 2011. HrWaC and SlWaC: compiling web corpora for Croatian and Slovene. In *Text, Speech and Dialogue*, pages 395–402. Springer.

Tomislav Lombarović, Jan Šnajder, and Bojana Dalbelo Bašić. 2011. Question classification for a Croatian QA system. In *Text, Speech and Dialogue*, pages 403–410. Springer.

Steven Lytinen and Noriko Tomuro. 2002. The use of question types to match questions in FAQ Finder. In *AAAI Spring Symposium on Mining Answers from Texts and Knowledge Bases*, pages 46–53.

Jean-Baptiste Michel, Yuan Kui Shen, Aviva P. Aiden, Adrian Veres, Matthew K. Gray, et al. 2011. Quantitative analysis of culture using millions of digitized books. *Science*, 331(6014):176.

George A. Miller. 1995. WordNet: a lexical database for English. *Communications of the ACM*, 38(11):39–41.

Jeff Mitchell and Mirella Lapata. 2008. Vector-based models of semantic composition. *Proceedings of ACL-08: HLT*, pages 236–244.

Alejandro Moreo, Maria Navarro, Juan L. Castro, and Jose M. Zurita. 2012. A high-performance FAQ retrieval method using minimal differentiator expressions. *Knowledge-Based Systems*.

Roberto Navigli and Paola Velardi. 2003. An analysis of ontology-based query expansion strategies. In *Proceedings of the 14th European Conference on Machine Learning, Workshop on Adaptive Text Extraction and Mining, Cavtat-Dubrovnik, Croatia*, pages 42–49.

Tao Qin, Tie-Yan Liu, Jun Xu, and Hang Li. 2008. How to make letor more useful and reliable. In *Proceedings of the ACM Special Interest Group on Information Retrieval 2008 Workshop on Learning to Rank for Information Retrieval*, pages 52–58.

Philip Resnik. 1995. Using information content to evaluate semantic similarity in a taxonomy. In *eprint arXiv: cmp-lg/9511007*, volume 1, page 11007.

Frane Šarić, Goran Glavaš, Mladen Karan, Jan Šnajder, and Bojana Dalbelo Bašić. 2012. TakeLab: systems for measuring semantic text similarity. In *Proceedings of the First Joint Conference on Lexical and Computational Semantics*, pages 441–448. Association for Computational Linguistics.

Jan Šnajder, Bojana Dalbelo Bašić, and Marko Tadić. 2008. Automatic acquisition of inflectional lexica for morphological normalisation. *Information Processing & Management*, 44(5).

Eriks Sneiders. 1999. Automated FAQ answering: continued experience with shallow language understanding. In *Question Answering Systems. Papers from the 1999 AAAI Fall Symposium*, pages 97–107.

Radu Soricut and Eric Brill. 2004. Automatic question answering: beyond the factoid. In *Proceedings of HLT-NAACL*, volume 5764.

Noriko Tomuro and Steven Lytinen. 2004. Retrieval models and Q and A learning with FAQ files. *New Directions in Question Answering*, pages 183–194.

Ellen M. Voorhees and Dawn M. Tice. 2000. Building a question answering test collection. In *Proceedings of the 23rd annual international ACM SIGIR conference on Research and development in information retrieval*, pages 200–207. ACM.

Ellen M. Voorhees. 1994. Query expansion using lexical-semantic relations. In *SIGIR'94*, pages 61–69. Springer.

Ellen M. Voorhees. 2002. The philosophy of information retrieval evaluation. In *Evaluation of cross-language information retrieval systems*, pages 355–370. Springer.

Chung-Hsien Wu, Jui-Feng Yeh, and Yu-Sheng Lai. 2006. Semantic segment extraction and matching for internet FAQ retrieval. *Knowledge and Data Engineering, IEEE Transactions on*, 18(7):930–940.

Xiaobing Xue, Jiwoon Jeon, and W Bruce Croft. 2008. Retrieval models for question and answer archives. In *Proceedings of the 31st annual international ACM SIGIR conference on Research and development in information retrieval*, pages 475–482. ACM.

Parsing Russian: a Hybrid Approach

Dan Skatov, Sergey Liverko,
Vladimir Okatiev, Dmitry Strebkov
Russian Federation, Nizhny Novgorod
Dictum Ltd
{ds,liverko,oka,strebkov}@dictum.ru

Abstract

We present an approach for natural language parsing in which dependency and constituency parses are acquired simultaneously. This leads to accurate parses represented in a specific way, richer than constituency or dependency tree. It also allows reducing parsing time complexity. Within the proposed approach, we show how to treat some significant phenomena of the Russian language and also perform a brief evaluation of the parser implementation, known as *DictaScope Syntax*.

1 Introduction

A syntactic parser inputs a sentence and produces information on syntactic relationships between parts of the sentence. It is an open question which method is the most convenient one to represent these relationships. In this paper, we are focusing on two of those methods. The first one, a *constituency tree (CT)*, is a representation of a sentence by a set of nested fragments — groups, each group corresponding to a syntactically coherent phrase. The second one, a *dependency tree (DT)*, expresses relationships by a set of syntactic links between pairs of tokens.

Figure 1 demonstrates correspondence between CT and DT: one is clearly derivable from another. In applications, one usually needs to transform CT into DT due to the following fact: if a tree is correct, then subjects, objects and adverbials of some predicate X are always direct children of the node X in DT. With a traditional CT framework these children can be obtained in much less intuitive way by browsing up and down through constituents, as shown in Figure 1 by dotted lines. According to this comparison, DT transparently maps onto the level of semantic representation, thereby DT-s are considered most appropriate in applications (Jurafsky and Martin, 2009) like sentiment analysis and fact extraction.

Figure 1: A constituency tree (upper) and a dependency tree (lower) for a sentence *"A blue ball lies on the sand"*.

Constituency parsing. Despite the usefulness of DT-s, CT-s have a longer history of application as a computational model. For now, probabilistic constituency parser by (Charniak, 1997) and its derivatives are considered the state of the art for English. Unfortunately, the framework of constituency parsing, taken alone, is not productive for languages such as Russian. It turns out that the number of rules in a grammar start to grow fast if one tries to describe an inflecting language with a free word order explicitly. As a result, pure constituency parsers are not well known for Russian. It has recently been confirmed by a Russian syntactic parsers task at the Dialogue conference (see http://www.dialog-21.ru), at which several parsers were presented and all of them used DT formalism as a basis.

Dependency parsing. Modern algorithmic approaches to dependency parsing are based on machine learning techniques and are supported by open-source implementations. Unfortunately, large DT-s corpora are not widely available for Russian to train these parsers. The need for the corpora also brings complications when one wants to achieve high precision parsing a given subject domain, and then to switch to parse another domain: eventually one will need a separate corpus for each domain. There is a consent among researches that a "long tail" of special error cases is definitely hard to fix in pure machine learning frameworks (Sharov and Nivre, 2011), while it is necessary for high precision. In contrast to English, dependency parsing is traditional for Russian computational linguistics. As a result, modern Russian parsers produce DT-s. These parsers are mainly rule-based with an optional statistical component (Toldova et al., 2012) and standard expert-verified data sets such as verb subcategorization frames, which are called "control models" or "set of valences" in Russian. None of the rule-based parsers that were presented at the Dialogue task are freely available.

Unfortunately, the practice of using DT-s has revealed some of their significant deficiencies. The most frequently discussed one is the representation of homogenous parts of the sentence (Testelets, 2001). Figure 2 shows some known methods. One can observe that there must be a syntactic agreement between the group of homogenous parts `1-3` and their parent `4-6`[1] by `Number`, which is `Plural`, but it is impossible to capture this relation in a DT where only words can hold grammar values. No representation among A-E in Figure 2 keeps this information for the group. Things get worse if one tries to represent an agreement for two groups of homogenous parts, like in 2.F. In addition, it is common to modify the parsing algorithm, but not the set of decision rules, directly in order to get nonprojective[2] DT-s (McDonald et al., 2005). The list of open problems can be extended further: paired conjunctions, nested sentences, introductory phrases etc.

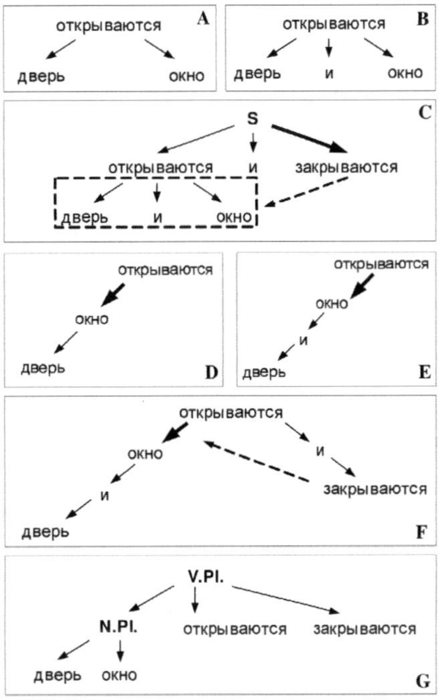

Figure 2: Uncertainty with the representation of homogenous parts in dependency trees for *"дверь$_1$ и$_2$ окно$_3$ открываются$_4$ и$_5$ закрываются$_6$" "door$_1$ and$_2$ window$_3$ open$_4$ and$_5$ close$_6$"*

Toward the hybrid approach. It would be possible to resolve problems with homogenous parts if additional vertices could be added to the DT, like in Figure 2.G, representing supplementary constituents with synthesized grammar values. Unfortunately, known approaches for dependency parsing assume that all vertices are predefined before the algorithm starts, so it is impossible to include new vertices on the fly without inventing new parsing methods.

The idea of combining dependencies and constituencies directly is not a new one. For Russian, (Gladkij, 1985) suggested designating a standard relation between predicate and subject by a syntactic link, along with adding a separate constituent for compound predicative groups like *"должен уступить"* from *"Дорогу$_1$ должен$_2$ уступить$_3$ водитель$_4$" "The driver$_4$ must$_2$ give$_3$ way$_1$ (to smb.)..."*, which has a nonprojective DT. This solution immediately reduces the number of overlapping dependency links for compound predicates, because links that tend to over-

[1]In examples, we put indices for words in correspondence with English translation (often with omitted articles *"a"*, *"the"*), refer to any word by its index, and to a phrase by indices of its starting and finishing word.

[2]Dependency tree is called *projective* if each subtree corresponds to a continuous fragment of the source sentence. There is evidence that more than 80% of the sentences are usually projective in European natural languages. A famous example of nonprojectivity for Russian is *"Я$_1$ памятник$_2$ себе$_3$ воздвиг$_4$ нерукотворный$_5$" "I$_1$'ve raised$_4$ a monument$_2$ for myself$_3$ not made by hands$_5$"* from Pushkin, where link `4→1` overlaps `2→5`.

lap are packed inside the constituent. In (Kurohashi and Nagao, 1994) constituents for groups of homogenous parts are prebuilt to be treated as single units during the next step by a dependency parser for Japanese. In (Okatiev et al., 2010) preprocessing of certain tokens connected to constituents is performed before the dependency parsing. In (Wang and Zong, 2010) a third-party black-box dependency parser is used to improve the results of author's constituency parser, achieving 10% boost in F_1. Additionally, there is evidence that ABBYY Compreno (Anisimovich et al., 2012) tracks the order in sequences of consecutive tokens so it actually exploits some kind of constituents throughout the process of dependency parsing.

In this paper, we propose a method of representing a parse tree, which is a combination of CT and DT and eliminates some disadvantages of both. Then we describe syntactic rules that guide the process of simultaneous bottom-up acquisition of multiple syntactically ambiguous DT-s and CT-s for a given sentence, ranked by syntactic relevance. In addition, we discuss some properties of the rule base that is built in the framework of proposed rules description language. After that, we show that it is possible to extend the classical Cocke-Younger-Kasami algorithm (Kasami, 1965) to use grammar rules of arbitrary arity without grammar binarization and to exploit intermediate DT-s to increase efficiency. Moreover, we demonstrate how to achieve a reasonable ranking of solutions without using any additional statistical information. In conclusion, we discuss possible extensions of the approach.

2 Representing the Parse Tree

Our goal is to achieve the most complete representation of syntactic relations between words and/or chunks of a given sentence. The subject of semantic representation, e.g. semantic labeling of predicate participants or questions on the edges, are not discussed further. We assume that such information can be surfaced either during the process of analysis or directly afterwards by semantic interpretation of resulting parse trees.

As it was mentioned, it is possible to avoid disadvantages of DT-s if one finds a way to bring additional vertices to these trees. Though it is not natural for DT-s to have such vertices, it is common for constituents in CT-s to acquire derived grammar values. Thereafter, instead of building a parse tree of a completely new type, we obtain the representation that consists of three components: 1) constituency tree — CT, 2) dependency tree — DT, 3) hybrid tree — HT. CT strictly corresponds to a system of syntactic rules given preliminarily, and DT is built by instructions from rules at each step of the bottom-up analysis driven by this system. A hybrid representation, HT, that is based on DT but depicts homogenous parts, dependent clauses and nested sentences in a particular way. As a next step, we declare a balanced system of agreements between these different representations.

Assumptions for a constituency tree. We only require that CT correctly corresponds to the given sentence, and phrases of CT do not need to correspond to the expected expressions of VP, NP, AP etc. E.g., one can declare a specific rule that generates a constituent that simultaneously corresponds to a subject and a verb, e.g. *"должен уступить водитель"*. Such a phrase corresponds both to VP and NP and is atypical, but the corresponding rule can produce a proper fragment of a nonprojective DT and HT, which is the main goal in this context. To summarize, in the proposed model constituencies play an utilitarian role, they are treated like carriers for parts of DT and are borrowed at certain decision points to form a resulting HT.

Assumptions for a dependency tree. During the parsing, a *hypothesis of syntactic locality* is considered, that states: tokens that are close linearly in a sentence are more likely to have a syntactic relationship. If there are several methods to represent a syntactic phenomenon, we choose a method that fits it best. Recalling Figure 2, one can observe that in 2.A and 2.B two links correspond to different linear distances between corresponding vertices, while in C–F each link corresponds to a unity distance. Let us call the latter kind of homogeneity representation "a chain scheme" and require syntactic rules to follow it.

The following assumptions are made: 1) prepositions become roots of the corresponding prepositional phrases; 2) subordinate conjunctions become roots of the corresponding dependent clauses; 3) punctuation marks, quotes and coordination conjunctions are removed from DT and will be properly presented in HT.

The following link types are expected: agreement (`Adj+Noun`, `Noun+Noun`, etc), control

(Verb+Noun, prepositional phrases etc), contiguity (for adverbs, particles etc.), isolation for dependent clauses and coordination for chains of homogenous parts. For cases when a synthesized grammar value is needed like in Figure 2.G, we do not expect a special new vertex to be introduced in DT. Instead, each vertex of DT contains a reference to the corresponding constituency in CT, which holds its own grammar value. By default, this value is inherited from the head element of the constituent, but can be overridden, which is the case for homogeneity.

Assumptions for a hybrid tree are revealed by the example in Figure 3, where an XML-file is represented for a HT of a sentence with two dependent clauses 8-11 and 12-19, a nested sentence 1-19 and homogenous nouns 17 and 19. Only significant details are shown in the figure — shortened grammar values (N for Noun etc) as GV and wordforms as W. Full representation also includes normal forms, detailed grammar values, tokens' positions and link types.

Subordinate clauses are presented under Subord tag as a nested group, while nested sentences are located under S tag. The group of two homogenous nouns is placed under Coord, but, unlike corresponding DT, homogenous members do not form a chain and are located on a single level inside a special Group tag. Such Group can have any number of dependent elements which are placed between </Group> and </Coord> (shown in Figure 4 below). There, the agreement by number between the group of two nouns 2-4 and the adjective 1 is taken into account, and the adverb 10 adjoins to the group of verbs 6 and 9 but not to a single verb.

An intensive research has been performed by (Okatiev et al., 2010) on the role of punctuation for Russian. According to it, one has to distinguish roles of punctuation marks and conjunctions (which together are called junctions) to deduce correct parses. For this reason roles are marked in a hybrid XML tree. One punctuation mark or a conjunction can possess several roles: it can be an isolator (Isol, bounds dependent phrases), a separator (Sepr, is used to separate homogenous parts inside coordinated groups) and a connector (Conn, indicates nested sentences, e.g. quotation marks). Isolators and connectors always play an opening or a closing role for one or several clauses. In the sentence from Figure 3, the

```
<S T="«Я не могу … он">
<V W="объясняет" GV="V">
  <S T="Я не могу требовать…">
    <Conn W='«'/>
    <V W="могу" GV="V">
      <V W="Я" GV="Pron">
      <V W="не" GV="Part">
      <V W="требовать" GV="V">
        <V W="бережливости" GV="N">
          <V W="от">
            <V W="людей">
              <Subord GrV="V">
                <Isol W=","/>
                <V W="работают GV="V">
                  <V W="которые" GV="Pron">
                  <V W="на" GV="Pr">
                    <V W="меня" GV="Pron">
                  </V>
                </V>
                <Isol W=","/>
              </Subord>
            </V>
          </V>
        </V>
      </V>
      <Subord GrV="V">
        <Isol W=","/>
        <Isol W="если"/>
        <V W="буду" GV="V">
          <V W="проводить" GV="V">
            <V W="время" GV="N">
              <V W="в" GV="Prep">
                <Coord>
                  <Group GrV="N">
                    <V W="роскоши" GV="N">
                    <Sepr W="и"/>
                    <V W="комфорте" GV="N">
                  </Group>
                </Coord>
              </V>
            </V>
          </V>
        </V>
      </Subord>
    </V>
    <Conn W='»'/>
  </S>
  <Conn W="—"/>
  <V W="он">
</V>
</S>
```

Figure 3: A HT for "*«Я*$_1$ *не*$_2$ *могу*$_3$ *требовать*$_4$ *бережливости*$_5$ *от*$_6$ *людей*$_7$, *которые*$_8$ *на*$_9$ *меня*$_{10}$ *работают*$_{11}$, *если*$_{12}$ *буду*$_{13}$ *проводить*$_{14}$ *время*$_{15}$ *в*$_{16}$ *роскоши*$_{17}$ *и*$_{18}$ *комфорте*$_{19}$*»*, — *объясняет*$_{20}$ *он*$_{21}$"
"*«I*$_1$ *can*$_3$ *not*$_2$ *require*$_4$ *thrift*$_5$ *of*$_6$ *people*$_7$ *who*$_8$ *work*$_{11}$ *for*$_9$ *me*$_{10}$ *if*$_{12}$ *I* *spend*$_{14}$ *time*$_{15}$ *in*$_{16}$ *luxury*$_{17}$ *and*$_{18}$ *comfort*$_{19}$*»*, — *he*$_{21}$ *explains*$_{20}$".

comma between 11 and 12 is a closing isolator for clause 8-11 and also and opening isolator for 12-18. Therefore this comma is mentioned twice in shown XML file in the beginning and the ending of the corresponding <Subord>-s. In general, HT contains at least as many vertices as there are tokens in a sentence, and possible duplicates correspond to punctuation marks and conjunctions.

Another case of multiple roles for the punctuation is shown by the example "*Круг*$_1$, *закрашенный*$_2$ *синим*$_3$, *равнобедренный*$_4$

треугольник$_5$ *и*$_6$ *жёлтый*$_7$ *квадрат*$_8$*"* *"Circle*$_1$*, shaded*$_2$ *in*$_2$ *blue*$_3$*, isosceles*$_4$ *triangle*$_5$ *and*$_6$ *yellow*$_7$ *square*$_8$*"* where the comma between `3` and `4` is an ending isolator for `2-3` and also a separator for parts `1` and `5` of a group of homogenous nouns. In addition, the case of an isolating group of a comma and a following conjunction, like *", если" ", if"*, is always being discussed: is it a single token, should one remove a comma or leave it, etc. In this case, this group is just a pair of consecutive isolators in HT XML, see Figures 3 and 4.

```
<S>
<Coord>
   <Group GV="Verb">
      <Sepr W="как"/>
      <V W="открываются" GV="Verb"/>
      <Sepr W=","/>
      <Sepr W="так и"/>
      <V W="закрываются" GV="Verb"/>
   </Group>
   <Coord>
      <Group GV="Noun">
         <V W="дверь" GV="Noun"/>
         <Sepr W="и"/>
         <V W="окно" GV="Noun"/>
      </Group>
      <V W="Большие" GV="Adj"/>
   </Coord>
   <V W="тихо" GV="Adv"/>
</Coord>
</S>
```

Figure 4: A HT for *"Большие*$_1$ *дверь*$_2$ *и*$_3$ *окно*$_4$ *как*$_5$ *открываются*$_6$*, так*$_7$ *и*$_8$ *закрываются*$_9$ *тихо*$_{10}$*" "The large*$_1$ *door*$_2$ *and*$_3$ *window*$_4$ *both*$_5$ *open*$_6$ *and*$_{7,8}$ *close*$_9$ *silently*$_{10}$*"*.

The way in which paired conjunctions are treated in HT is synchronized with the representation of single coordinative conjunctions. E.g., *"как ..., так и ..." "both ... and ..."* is followed by a rule *"S → как S, так и S"*, where *"S"*-s denote clauses, yielding the parse in Figure 4, which is difficult to obtain in a pure DT.

3 The Rule Base

Linguistic data. We use a set of subcategorization frames for about 25 000 verbs, deverbatives and other predicative words, which is collected at our side through standard techniques of collocations and lexics aquisition from (Manning and Schütze, 1999). A morphological dictionary consists of about 5 mln wordforms.

Morphological hierarchy. In many cases, it is useful to unite different parts of speech into one metapart which possesses some common properties. E.g., participles share properties of verbs and adjectives. For verbs, the class `ComVerb` is introduced, which includes `Verb` in both finite and infinite forms, `Participle` and `Transgressive`, for adjectives — the class `ComAdj` with `FullAdj`, `ShortAdj` and `Participle`. This concept leads to the reduction in the number of syntactic rules.

The language of syntactic rules is shown by an example that describes a coordination relation between an adjective and a noun:

```
// Высокая спинка "high back"
AgreeNounAdj {
  T: [ComAdj] [ComNoun];
  C: NumberGenderCaseAgree (PH1, PH2);
  Main: 2; L: 2=>Agreement=>1;
}
```

Section `T` declares that a template should check grammar values of consecutive phrases `PH1` and `PH2`, while section `C` checks required properties of them. If phrases fit `T` and `C`, then a DT is built according to `L` section by a link from the main word of the second constituent to the main word of the first, plus trees of `PH1` and `PH2`. The second phrase is declared the head one (`Main: 2`) for the new phrase built by `AgreeNounAdj` rule.

Coordination. It is possible to override grammar value of a new phrase `PH`, which is shown by an example of homogenous nouns:

```
// Яблоко, груша "apple, pear"
CoordNounComma {
  T: [ComNoun] <,> [ComNoun];
  C: (PH1.Case == PH2.Case) && !PH1.IsCoord
     && PH2.NormalForm != "который";
  Main: 1; L: 1=>Coord=>2; J: 1<=Sepr;
  A: PH.Number = NUMBER_PL;
     PH.IsCoord = true;
}
```

`Number` of the entire phrase is set to `Plural`. In addition, the role of the comma is set to `Sepr`. `IsCoord` property is introduced to phrases to prune the propagation of different bracketings. E.g., for a chain of nouns *"A и B, C и D"* a large number of bracketings are possible: *"[[A и B], [C и D]]", "[A и [B, [C и D]]]"* etc. To prune this to exactly one correct bracketing, we deny chaining phrases that both contain chains of nonunity length and allow only left-to-right chains by a check `!PH1.IsCoord`.

Ambiguous compounds. Some compounds in Russian have their own grammar values in certain contexts. E.g., *"по причине" "by reason of"* is sometimes a preposition equivalent to *"из-за" "because of"* (as preposition): *"[судили [по [причине и следствию]]]" "judged on reason and consequence"* vs. *"[опоздал [по причине]* *пробок]" "was late by reason of traffic jams"*. In contrast to context rules for such constructions, we use pure syntactic rules for testing both versions, introducing a compound version by the rule:

```
CompoundPrep {
  T: [Any] [Any];
  C: IsCompoundPrep (PH1, PH2);
  Main: 1; L: 1=>Compound=>2;
  A: PH.Type = PHRASE_PREP;
}
```

Nonprojective parses for compound predicates are processed by the following rule which produces a nonprojective DT. Despite nonprojectivity, it brings no problem for CT parsing process:

```
// Дорогу должен уступить…
ControlNonProjectLeft {
  T: [Any] [Any] [Any];
  C: PredicModel (PH2, PH3) &&
     IsFreeValence (PH2, PH3) &&
     PredicModel (PH3, PH1) &&
     IsFreeValence (PH3, PH1);
  Main: 2;
  L: 2=>Control=>3; 3=>Control=>1;
  A: FillValence (PH, PH3);
}
```

Punctuation. Roles of junctions guide the parsing process. E.g., we consider that a junction that has exactly one role, which is ending isolator, is equivalent to a whitespace. Let us see how the rule `AgreeNounAdj` will parse the example under this assumption: *"синий$_1$, как$_2$ море$_3$, оттенок$_4$" "shade$_4$, as blue$_1$ as$_2$ a sea$_3$"*. One can verify that, due to consideration, the second comma no longer prevents this phrase from being covered by `AgreeNounAdj`. Another way to track these roles is to reject false control in genitive, e.g. *"много$_1$ [кругов$_2$, заполненных$_3$ белым$_4$, квадратов$_5$], эллипсов$_6$" "lots$_1$ of$_1$ circles$_2$, shaded$_3$ in$_3$ white$_4$, squares$_5$, ellipses$_6$"*.

Overall base. For Russian, we have built a rule base with 90 rules, divided into 7 groups, one for each type of syntactic relations to be included into DT. These rules exploit 20 predicates in criterion sections and 10 additional phrase properties.

4 The Algorithm

We provide a modification of the Cocke-Yanger-Kasami algorithm (CYK) to find DT-s by corresponding CT-s that can be derived by rules described above and that are best in a specified way.

In our interpretation, CYK has the following structure. It inputs a sentence of n tokens. Empty $n \times n$ matrix M is set up and its main diagonal is filled with one-token phrases, each phrase at a cell $M[i][i]$ takes some grammar value from the i-th token of the sentence, $i = 1, \dots, n$ as its head. CYK iterates all diagonals from the main diagonal of M to its upper-right cell $M[1][n]$. Each cell on the diagonal of length $k \in \{n-1, \dots, 1\}$ will contain only phrases of exactly k consecutive tokens, so $M[1][n]$ will contain exactly those phrases that correspond to consecutive tokens, i.e. the entire sentence.

For CYK, it is traditionally assumed that each rule has exactly two nonterminals, and grammars formed by such rules are called *binarized grammars* (also known as *"in Chomsky normal form"*). Now consider the binarized rule $R : Ph_1 Ph_2 \rightarrow Ph$. If one wants to derive a phrase Ph of consecutive tokens by this rule, then one should look at consecutive phrases Ph_1 and Ph_2 with properties defined by R and of j and $k - j$ tokens correspondently. So, standing at $M[i][i + n - k]$, $i \in \{1, \dots, k\}$, CYK searches for Ph_1 in j cells in the current row to the left and then for Ph_2 in $k - j$ lower diagonals in the current column to the bottom, checking them by R if both Ph_1 and Ph_2 are found for some j and storing corresponding Ph in $M[i][i + n - k]$. Figure 5 shows M at the moment when CYK has finished for a particular input.

Adj высокая	N_3= Adj+N_1	N_5= Adj+N_4 N_6= N_3+N_2
	N_1 спинка	N_4= N_1+N_2
		N_2 стула

Figure 5: The CYK matrix after *"высокая$_1$ спинка$_2$ стула$_3$" "high$_1$ chair$_3$ back$_2$"*.

Rules of arbitrary arity. Surprisingly, the extension of CYK for grammars that are not binarized is not widely discussed in literature. Instead, issues of binarization and special classes of grammars that do not lead to exponential growth of the binarized version are proposed (Lange and Leiß, 2009). Indeed, due to the author's experience, researchers argue to reject using CYK, because the increase in the size of the grammar through binarization degrades the performance significantly. Although it is true, we further show that it is not necessary at all to binarize grammar to use CYK.

To use the rule system proposed earlier, we modify CYK in the following way. Consider the rule $R : Ph_1\ Ph_2\ \ldots\ Ph_r \rightarrow Ph$. One can treat it as a rule $R' : Ph_1\ PhL \rightarrow Ph$, where $PhL = Ph_2\ Ph_3\ \ldots\ Ph_r$. In this way, the problem reduces to the former case of binarized grammar. When a reduction is applied to PhL recursively and finally some Ph_r is fixed, a set of $Ph_1, \ldots, Ph_r$ can be checked against R. This check is performed as described in Section 3. One can verify that modification increases the worst run time of CYK by a polynomial multiplier $\mathcal{O}(n^r)$, and it is always an overestimation for natural languages, for which the case $r \geq 4$ is rare. Moreover, a big room for optimization is left. E.g., it is possible to extract checks from R that correspond to $Ph_1, \ldots, Ph_m$, $m < r$, and apply them before all r phrases are collected to be checked.

Equivalency of phrases. In Figure 5 two final parses are derived by two different ways but these parses correspond exactly to the same phrase with no syntactic ambiguity. When $n > 5$, matrix cells' content becomes too large due to this effect, which leads to a significant decrease in CYK performance. Let us recall that the main goal of the process is to obtain correct DT-s. Let us notice then that two parse results in $M[1][3]$ from Figure 5 carry the same DT. Therefore it is necessary to merge phrases in a cell if they carry identical DT-s. Let us assume that CYK had already put S phrases in a cell, and a new phrase P is pending. CYK then checks P against all elements of S and declines to add P in S at the first time when it finds some $p \in P$ that carry the same DT as P.

Notice that it is insufficient to merge two phrases only by properties of the head. E.g., for "*Я*$_1$ *не*$_2$ *посещал*$_3$ *палаты*$_4$ *мер*$_5$ *и*$_6$ *весов*$_7$" "*I*$_1$ *did*$_3$ *not*$_2$ *attend*$_3$ *the Chamber*$_4$ *of Weights*$_5$ *and*$_6$ *Measures*$_7$" the first possible phrasal coverage is `[1 2 3 [4 [5 6 7]]]`, the second is `[1 2 3 [[4 5] 6 [7]]]`, and it is not known which is correct at a syntactic level. For both coverages, the head of the group is the same verb with subject and object slots filled, while the underlying DT-s differ.

Shallow weighting. Due to a high level of ambiguity in natural languages, a huge amount of phrases can be obtained in subcells even when the merging of phrases takes place as described above. Therefore it is necessary to delete some portion of irrelevant phrases from subcells.

For every phrase that arises in any step of CYK, let us add a weight to this phrase by the following scheme. For each edge $e = (i, j)$ of the corresponding DT that forms a link from i-th to j-th word of a sentence, we attach a weight $|j - i|^q$. The weight W of the phrase is a sum of weights of all of the edges of its DT.

For every cell of M, after the set of phrases S is complete by CYK, S is sorted by the weights of phrases. After S is sorted, it turns out to be separated into layers by the weights. Finally, only α top layers are left in a cell. Our evaluation has showed that $q = 2$ and $\alpha = 2$ are sufficient.

Processing mistypings as if the correction variants were additional grammar values of tokens, being incorporated into the algorithm by a scheme given by (Erekhinskaya et al., 2011), improves F_1 up to 20% on real-world texts from the Internet without significant loss in the performance.

Partial parses in case there is an error in an input that are good enough and look much like ones from pure dependency parsers can be obtained by the proposed algorithm, in contrast to shift-reduce approaches, in which only some left part of the sentence with an error is parsed.

5 Evaluation

There is a lack of corpora for Russian to evaluate parsers. In 2012, a task for Russian syntactic parsers was held during the Dialogue conference. The evaluation was conducted as follows: every parser processed a set of thousands of separate sentences from news and fiction, and then a "golden standard" of 800 sentences was selected and verified by several assessors. During evaluation, some mistakes, such as prepositional phrase attachment, were not taken into account as syntactic parsers are originally not intended to deal with semantics. Ignoring this, the method of evaluation was exactly UAS (*unlabeled attach score*, i.e. a number of nodes in a DT that have correct parents, see (McDonald et al., 2005)).

Our previous version of *DictaScope Syntax* parser, which was based on a modification of Eisner's algorithm (Erekhinskaya et al., 2011), took part in that task in 2012, resulting with 5-th place out of 7 (systems have been ranged by F_1), with 86,3% precision, 98% recall and 0,917 F_1. Our current evaluation of the new version of *DictaScope Syntax* parser, based on methods proposed in this paper, follows the technique from the

Dialogue-2012 task (Toldova et al., 2012). We took 800 entries from the same set of sentences and marked them up in HT XML format. In evaluation we followed the same principles as described in (Toldova et al., 2012), reaching 93.1% precision, 97% recall and 95% F_1, which correspond to the 3rd place out of 7, with a lag of half percent from the second place. We have also marked up a corpus from Internet-forums and Wikipedia of 300 sentences, reaching 87% F_1.

Note on complexity. It is known that for a sentence of n tokens CYK is $\mathcal{O}(n^3)$ algorithm by worst case complexity, and this complexity can be reduced to $\mathcal{O}(n^{2.38})$ by algebraic tricks (Valiant, 1975). We have performed a time complexity evaluation of our parser on a corpus of 1 mln Russian sentences from Internet-news, averaging the time for every fixed length of the sentence. We evaluated sentences with lengths from 3 to 40 tokens, 12 tokens average length. Evaluation has showed the performance of 25 sentences per second average for one kernel of 3GHz Intel Quad. The evaluation has also led to a plot given in Figure 6.

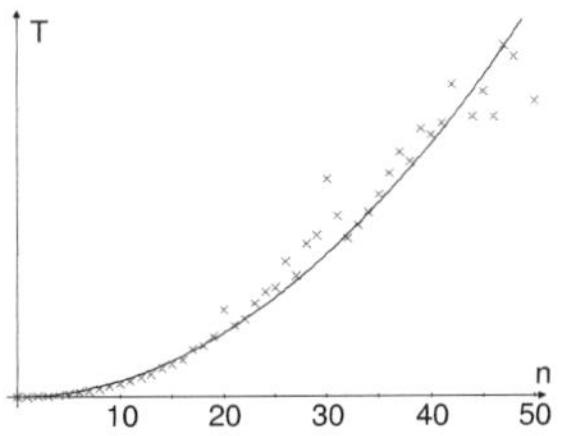

Figure 6: Average complexity of parsing as a function of the number of tokens

It can be verified that the plot corresponds only to An^2 for some A, but not to An^3. We can explain it in the following way. With our grammar and Russian language, we have noticed that for a completed upper-triangular matrix of CYK, nonempty cells on each row are denser near the main diagonal. Following this, for the part of the row that forms m cells to the right of the main diagonal, the density of nonempty cells in it is $p_m \leq \frac{c}{m}$ for some c. Now assume that 1) the maximum cost of the rule checking operation and 2) the maximum number of phrases' combinations that need to be verified against the rule base are some constants which depend on rules, 3) τ is the number of rules which are stored in a vocabulary with a key formed by grammar values from templates. Then, the total number of rule checks is

$$T_{total} \leq c \cdot \sum_{k=n-1}^{1} \sum_{i=1}^{k} \sum_{j=1}^{n-k} p_{n-k} \cdot \log \tau \leq$$
$$\leq c \cdot \log \tau \cdot \sum_{k=1}^{n-1} \sum_{i=1}^{k} \sum_{j=1}^{n-k} \frac{C}{n-k} =$$
$$= c \cdot C \cdot \log \tau \cdot \sum_{k=1}^{n-1} k = \mathcal{O}\left(n^2 \log \tau\right) .$$

6 Discussion

In this paper we proposed a method of parsing Russian, based on a hybrid representation of the result, which is derived from a dependency tree with elements of the corresponding constituency tree to model phenomena like homogenous members, nested sentences and junction roles. This approach led to the elimination of some disadvantages of both representations. We also presented a rule system and an algorithm to acquire a ranked set of syntactically ambiguous representations of that kind for a given sentence. Properties of the Cocke–Younger–Kasami algorithm and its modifications, remarkable for natural language parsing, are particularly discussed. The *DictaScope Syntax* parser, based on the proposed results, is embedded in a commercial NLP system, that is adopted in *Kribrum.ru* — a service for Internet-based reputation management.

The natural question is whether this approach can be extended to parse other languages. We perform the development of rule systems for English and Arabic, and preliminary evaluation demonstrates results comparable to those for Russian.

We also intend to propose the described HT XML format as a standard markup language for syntax parse trees by building the freely available corpus for languages that lack such linguistic resources, e.g. for Russian.

References

Konstantin Anisimovich, Konstantin Druzhkin, Filipp Minlos, M. Petrova, Vladimir Selegey, and K. Zuev. 2012. Syntactic and Semantic parser based on ABBYY Compreno linguistic technologies. *In Proceedings of the International Conference "Dialogue-2012"*, 2:91–103.

Eugene Charniak. 1997. Statistical parsing with a context-free grammar and word statistics. *In Proceedings of the Fourteenth National Conference on Artificial Intelligence.*

Tatiana Erekhinskaya, Anna Titova, and Vladimir Okatiev. 2011. Syntax parsing for texts with misspellings in DictaScope Syntax. *In Proceedings of the International Conference "Dialogue-2011"*, pages 186–195.

Alexey Gladkij. 1985. *Syntactic structures of natural language in automated systems for human-machine interaction*. Science, Moscow, USSR.

Daniel Jurafsky and James H. Martin. 2009. *Speech and Language Processing: An Introduction to Natural Language Processing, Speech Recognition, and Computational Linguistics. 2-nd edition*. Prentice-Hall.

Tadao Kasami. 1965. *An efficient recognition and syntax-analysis algorithm for context-free languages. Scientific report AFCRL-65-758*. Air Force Cambridge Research Lab, Bedford, MA.

Sadao Kurohashi and Makoto Nagao. 1994. Japanese dependency/case structure analyzer.

Martin Lange and Hans Leiß. 2009. To CNF or not to CNF? An Efficient Yet Presentable Version of the CYK Algorithm. *Informatica Didactica*.

Christopher D. Manning and Hinrich Schütze. 1999. *Foundations of Statistical Natural Language Processing*. The MIT Press, Cambridge, Massachusetts.

Ryan McDonald, Fernando Pereira, Kiril Ribarov, and Jan Hajic. 2005. Non-projective dependency parsing using spanning tree algorithms. *In Proc. of the Joint Conf. on Human Language Technology and Empirical Methods in Natural Language Processing (HLT/EMNLP)*.

Vladimir Okatiev, Tatiana Erekhinskaya, and Tatiana Ratanova. 2010. Secret punctuation marks. *In Proceedings of the International Conference "Dialogue-2010"*, pages 356–362.

Sergey Sharov and Joakim Nivre. 2011. The proper place of men and machines in language technology. processing Russian without any linguistic knowledge. *In Proceedings of the International Conference "Dialogue-2011"*, pages 591–604.

Jacov Testelets. 2001. *Introduction to general syntax*. RSUH, Moscow, Russia.

Svetlana Toldova, Elena Sokolova, Irina Astaf'eva, Anastasia Gareyshina, A. Koroleva, Dmitry Privoznov, E. Sidorova, L. Tupikina, and Olga Lyashevskaya. 2012. NLP evaluation 2011–2012: Russian syntactic parsers. *In Proceedings of the International Conference "Dialogue-2012"*, 2:77–90.

Leslie Valiant. 1975. General context-free recognition in less than cubic time. *Journal of Computer and System Sciences*, 2(10):308–314.

Zhiguo Wang and Chengqing Zong. 2010. Phrase structure parsing with dependency structure. *International Conference on Computational Linguistics*.

GPKEX: Genetically Programmed Keyphrase Extraction from Croatian Texts

Marko Bekavac and **Jan Šnajder**
University of Zagreb, Faculty of Electrical Engineering and Computing
Text Analysis and Knowledge Engineering Lab
Unska 3, 10000 Zagreb, Croatia
{marko.bekavac2, jan.snajder}@fer.hr

Abstract

We describe GPKEX, a keyphrase extraction method based on genetic programming. We represent keyphrase scoring measures as syntax trees and evolve them to produce rankings for keyphrase candidates extracted from text. We apply and evaluate GPKEX on Croatian newspaper articles. We show that GPKEX can evolve simple and interpretable keyphrase scoring measures that perform comparably to more complex machine learning methods previously developed for Croatian.

1 Introduction

Keyphrases are an effective way of summarizing document contents, useful for text categorization, document management, and search. Unlike *keyphrase assignment*, in which documents are assigned keyphrases from a predefined taxonomy, *keyphrase extraction* selects phrases from the text of the document. Extraction is preferred in cases when a taxonomy is not available or when its construction is not feasible, e.g., if the set of possible keyphrases is too large or changes often. Manual keyphrase extraction is extremely tedious and inconsistent, thus methods for automatic keyphrase extraction have attracted a lot of research interest.

In this paper we describe GPKEX, a keyphrase extraction method based on genetic programming (GP), an evolutionary optimization technique inspired by biological evolution (Koza and Poli, 1992). GP is similar to genetic algorithms except that the individual solutions are expressions, rather than values. We use GP to evolve keyphrase scoring measures, represented as abstract syntax trees. The advantage of using GP over black-box machine learning methods is in the interpretability of the results: GP yields interpretable expressions, revealing the relevant features and their relationships, thus offering some insight into keyphrase usage. Furthermore, GP can evolve simple scoring measures, providing an efficient alternative to more complex machine learning methods.

We apply GPKEX to Croatian language and evaluate it on a dataset of newspaper articles with manually extracted keyphrases. Our results show that GPKEX performs comparable to previous supervised and unsupervised approaches for Croatian, but has the advantage of generating simple and interpretable keyphrase scoring measures.

2 Related Work

Keyphrase extraction typically consist of two steps: candidate extraction and candidate scoring. Supervised approaches include decision tree models (Turney, 1999; Ercan and Cicekli, 2007), naïve Bayes classifier (Witten et al., 1999; McCallum and Nigam, 1998; Frank et al., 1999), and SVM (Zhang et al., 2006). Unsupervised approaches include clustering (Liu et al., 2009), graph-based methods (Mihalcea and Tarau, 2004), and language modeling (Tomokiyo and Hurst, 2003). Many more methods were proposed and evaluated within the SemEval shared task (Kim et al., 2010). Recent approaches (Jiang et al., 2009; Wang and Li, 2011; Eichler and Neumann, 2010) acknowledge keyphrase extraction as a highly subjective task and frame it as a learning-to-rank problem.

Keyphrase extraction for Croatian has been addressed in both supervised and unsupervised setting. Ahel et al. (2009) use a naïve Bayes classifier with phrase position and tf-idf (term frequency/inverse document frequency) as features. Saratlija et al. (2011) use distributional semantics to build topically related word clusters, from which they extract keywords and expand them to keyphrases. Mijić et al. (2010) use filtering based on morphosyntactic tags followed by tf-idf scoring.

To the best of our knowledge, GPKEX is the first application of GP to keyphrase extraction. Although we essentially approach the problem as a classification task (we train on binary relevance judgments), GPKEX produces continuous-valued scoring measures, thus keyphrases can eventually be ranked and evaluated in a rank-based manner.

3 GPKEX

GPKEX (Genetically Programmed Keyphrase Extraction) consists of two steps: keyphrase candidate extraction and the genetic programming of keyphrase scoring measures (KSMs).[1]

3.1 Step 1: Keyphrase candidate extraction

Keyphrase candidate extraction starts with text preprocessing followed by keyphrase feature extraction. A keyphrase candidate is any sequence of words from the text that (1) does not span over (sub)sentence boundaries and (2) matches any of the predefined POS patterns (sequences of POS tags). The POS patterns are chosen based on the analysis of the training set (cf. Section 4).

After the candidates have been extracted, each candidate is assigned 11 features. We distinguish between three groups of features. The first group are the frequency-based features: the relative term frequency (the ratio between the number of phrase occurrences in a document and the total number of phrases in the document), inverse document frequency (the ratio between the total number of documents in the training set and the number of documents in which the phrase occurs), and the tf-idf value. These features serve to eliminate the irrelevant and non-discriminative phrases. The second group are the position-based features: the position of the first occurrence of a phrase in the text (i.e., the number of phrases in the text preceding the first occurrence of the candidate phrase), the position of the last occurrence, the occurrence in document title, and the number of occurrences in the first, second, and the last third of the document. These features serve to capture the relation between phrase relevance and the distribution of the phase within the document. The last group of features concerns the keyphrase surface form: its length and the number of discriminative words it contains (these being defined as the 10 words from the document with the highest tf-idf score).

[1]GPKEX is freely available for download from `http://takelab.fer.hr/gpkex`

3.2 Step 2: Genetic programming

Genetic expressions. Each keyphrase scoring measure (KSM) corresponds to one genetic expression, represented as a syntax tree (see Fig. 1). We use the above-described keyphrase features as outer nodes of an expression. For inner nodes we use binary ($+$, $-$, $\times$, and $/$) and unary operators ($\log \cdot$, $\cdot \times 10$, $\cdot/10$, $1/\cdot$). We randomly generate the initial population of KSMs and use fitness-proportionate selection to guide the evolution process.

Fitness function. The fitness function scores KSMs according to their ability to extract correct keyphrases. We measure this by comparing the extracted keyphrases against the gold-standard keyphrases (cf. Section 4). We experimented with a number of fitness functions; simple functions, such as Precision at n (P@n) or Mean Reciprocal Rank (MRR), did not give satisfactory results. Instead, we define the fitness of a KSM s as

$$f(s) = \frac{1}{|D|} \sum_{d \in D} \begin{cases} \frac{|C_d^k|}{minRank(C_d^k)} & C_d^k \neq \emptyset, \\ \frac{1}{minRank(C_d^\infty)} & \text{otherwise} \end{cases} \quad (1)$$

where D is the set of training documents, C_d^k is the set of correct keyphrases within top k-ranked keyphrases extracted from document $d \in D$, and $minRank(C_d^k)$ is the highest rank (the smallest number) of keyphrase from set C_d^k. Parameter k defines a cutoff threshold, i.e., keyphrase ranked below rank k are discarded. If two KSMs extract the same number of correct keyphrases in top k results, the one with the highest-ranked correct keyphrase will be scored higher. To ensure that the gradient of the fitness function is non-zero, a KSM that extracts no correct keyphrases within the first k results is assigned a score based on the complete set of correctly extracted keyphrases (denoted C_d^∞). The fitness scores are averaged over the whole document collection. Based on preliminary experiments, we set the cutoff value to $k = 15$.

Parsimony pressure. Supervised models often face the problem of overfitting. In GP, overfitting is typically controlled by parsimony pressure, a regularization term that penalizes complex expressions. We define the regularized fitness function as

$$f_{reg} = \frac{f}{1 + N/\alpha} \quad (2)$$

where f is the non-regularized fitness function given by (1), N is the number of nodes in the expression, and parameter α defines the strength of parsimony pressure. Note that in both regularized and non-regularized case we limit the size of an expression to a maximum depth of 17, which is often used as the limit (Riolo and Soule, 2009).

Crossover and mutation. Two expressions chosen for crossover exchange subtrees rooted at random nodes, resulting in a child expression with parts from both parent expressions. We use a population of 500 expressions and limit the number of generations to 50, as we observe that results stagnate after that point. To retain the quality of solution throughout the generations, we employ the elitist strategy and copy the best-fitted individual into the next generation. Moreover, we use mutation to prevent early local optimum trapping. We implement mutation as a randomly grown subtree rooted at a randomly chosen node. Each expression has a 5% probability of being mutated, with 10% probability of mutation at inner nodes.

4 Evaluation

Data set and preprocessing. We use the dataset developed by Mijić et al. (2010), comprising 1020 Croatian newspaper articles provided by the Croatian News Agency. The articles have been manually annotated by expert annotators, i.e., each document has an associated list of keyphrases. The number of extracted keyphrases per document varies between 1 and 7 (3.4 on average). The dataset is divided in two parts: 960 documents each annotated by a single annotator and 60 documents independently annotated by eight annotators. We use the first part for training and the second part for testing.

Based on dataset analysis, we chose the following POS patterns for keyphrase candidate filtering: N, AN, NN, NSN, V, U (N – noun, A – adjective, S – preposition, V – verb, U – unknown). Although a total of over 200 patterns would be needed to cover all keyphrases from the training set, we use only the six most frequent ones in order to reduce the number of candidates. These patterns account for cca. 70% of keyphrases, while reducing the number of candidates by cca. 80%. Note that we chose to only extract keyphrases of three words or less, thereby covering 93% of keyphrases. For lemmatization and (ambiguous) POS tagging, we use the inflectional lexicon from Šnajder et al. (2008), with additional suffix removal after lemmatization.

Evaluation methodology. Keyphrase extraction is a highly subjective task and there is no agreed-upon evaluation methodology. Annotators are often inconsistent: they extract different keyphrases and also keyphrases of varying length. What is more, an omission of a keyphrase by one of the annotators does not necessarily mean that the keyphrase is incorrect; it may merely indicate that it is less relevant. To account for this, we use rank-based evaluation measures. As our method produces a ranked list of keyphrases for each document, we can compare this list against a gold-standard keyphrase ranking for each document. We obtain the latter by aggregating the judgments of all annotators; the more annotators have extracted a keyphrase, the higher its ranking will be.[2] Following Zesch and Gurevych (2009), we consider the morphological variants when matching the keyphrases; however, we do not consider partial matches.

To evaluate a ranked list of extracted keyphrases, we use the generalized average precision (GAP) measure proposed by Kishida (2005). GAP generalizes average precision to multi-grade relevance judgments: it takes into account both precision (all correct items are ranked before all incorrect ones) and the quality of ranking (more relevant items are ranked before less relevant ones).

Another way of evaluating against keyphrases extracted by multiple annotators is to consider the different levels of agreement. We consider as *strong agreement* the cases in which a keyphrase is extracted by at least five annotators, and as *weak agreement* the cases in which at least two annotators have extracted a keyphrase. For both agreement levels separately, we compare the extracted keyphrases against the manually extracted keyphrases using rank-based IR measures of Precision at Rank 10 (P@10) and Recall at Rank 10 (R@10). Because GP is a stochastic algorithm, to account for randomness we made 30 runs of each experiment and report the average scores. On these samples, we use the unpaired t-test to determine the significance in performance differences. As baseline to compare against GPKEX, we use keyphrase extraction based on tf-idf scores (with the same preprocessing and filtering setup as for GPKEX).

Tested configurations. We tested four evolution configurations. Configuration A uses the parameter setting described in Section 3.2, but without parsimony pressure. Configurations B and C use parsimony pressure defined by (2), with $\alpha = 1000$

[2]The annotated dataset is available under CC BY-NC-SA license from `http://takelab.fer.hr/gpkex`

		Strong agreement		Weak agreement	
Config.	GAP	P@10	R@10	P@10	R@10
A	**13.0**	**8.3**	28.7	**28.7**	8.4
B	12.8	8.2	**30.2**	28.4	**8.5**
C	12.5	7.7	27.3	27.3	7.7
D	9.9	5.1	25.9	20.4	7.3
tf-idf	7.4	5.8	22.3	21.5	12.4
UKE	6.0	5.8	32.6	15.3	15.8

Table 1: Keyphrase ranking results.

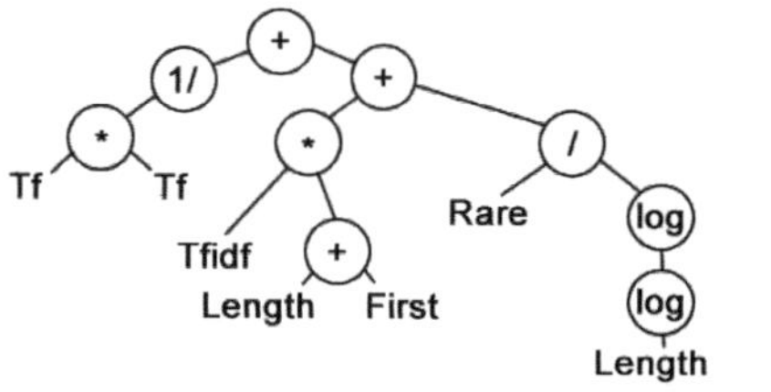

$$\frac{1}{\mathsf{Tf}*\mathsf{Tf}} + \mathsf{Tfidf} * (\mathsf{Length} + \mathsf{First}) + \frac{\mathsf{Rare}}{\log(\log \mathsf{Length})}$$

Figure 1: The best-performing KSM expression.

and $\alpha = 100$, respectively. Configuration D is similar to A, but uses all POS patterns attested for keyphrases in the dataset.

Results. Results are shown in Table 1. Configurations A and B perform similarly across all evaluation measures (pairwise differences are not significant at p<0.05, except for R@10) and outperform the baseline (differences are significant at p<0.01). Configuration C is outperformed by configuration A (differences are significant at p<0.05). Configuration D outperforms the baseline, but is outperformed by other configurations (pairwise differences in GAP are significant at p<0.05), indicating that conservative POS filtering is beneficial. Since A and B perform similar, we conclude that applying parsimony pressure in our case only marginally improved GAP (although it has reduced KSM size from an average 30 nodes for configuration A to an average of 20 and 9 nodes for configurations B and C, respectively). We believe there are two reasons for this: first, the increase in KSM complexity also increases the probability that the KSM will be discarded as not computable (e.g., the right subtree of a '/' node evaluates to zero). Secondly, our fitness function is perhaps not fine-grained enough to allow more complex KSMs to emerge gradually, as small changes in keyphrase scores do not immediately affect the value of the fitness function.

In absolute terms, GAP values are rather low. This is mostly due to wrong ranking, rather than the omission of correct phrases. Furthermore, the precision for strong agreement is considerably lower than for weak agreement. This indicates that GPKEX often assigns high scores to less relevant keyphrases. Both deficiencies may be attributed to the fact that we do not learn to rank, but train on dataset with binary relevance judgments.

The best-performing KSM from configuration A is shown in Fig. 1 (simplified form). Length is the length of the phrase, First is the position of the first occurrence, and Rare is the number of discriminative words in a phrase (cf. Section 3.1). Tfidf, First, and Rare features seem to be positively correlated with keyphraseness. This particular KSM extracts on average three correct keyphrases (weak agreement) within the first 10 results.

Our results are not directly comparable to previous work for Croatian (Ahel et al., 2009; Mijić et al., 2010; Saratlija et al., 2011) because we use a different dataset and/or evaluation methodology. However, to allow for an indirect comparison, we re-evaluated the results of unsupervised keyphrase extraction (UKE) from Saratlija et al. (2011); we show the result in the last row of Table 1. GPKEX (configuration A) outperforms UKE in terms of precision (GAP and P@10), but performs worse in terms of recall. In terms of F1@10 (harmonic mean of P@10 and R@10), GPKEX performs better than UKE at the strong agreement level (12.9 vs. 9.9), but worse at the weak agreement level (13.0 vs. 15.6). For comparison, Saratlija et al. (2011) report UKE to be comparable to supervised method from Ahel et al. (2009), but better than the tf-idf extraction method from Mijić et al. (2010).

5 Conclusion

GPKEX uses genetically programmed scoring measures to assign rankings to keyphrase candidates. We evaluated GPKEX on Croatian texts and showed that it yields keyphrase scoring measures that perform comparable to other machine learning methods developed for Croatian. Thus, scoring measures evolved by GPKEX provide an efficient alternative to these more complex models. The focus of this work was on Croatian, but our method could easily be applied to other languages as well.

We have described a preliminary study. The next step is to apply GPKEX to directly learn keyphrase ranking. Using additional (e.g., syntactic) features might further improve the results.

Acknowledgments

This work has been supported by the Ministry of Science, Education and Sports, Republic of Croatia under the Grant 036-1300646-1986. We thank the reviewers for their constructive comments.

References

Renee Ahel, B Dalbelo Bašic, and Jan Šnajder. 2009. Automatic keyphrase extraction from Croatian newspaper articles. *The Future of Information Sciences, Digital Resources and Knowledge Sharing*, pages 207–218.

Kathrin Eichler and Günter Neumann. 2010. DFKI KeyWE: Ranking keyphrases extracted from scientific articles. In *Proceedings of the 5th international workshop on semantic evaluation*, pages 150–153. Association for Computational Linguistics.

Gonenc Ercan and Ilyas Cicekli. 2007. Using lexical chains for keyword extraction. *Information Processing & Management*, 43(6):1705–1714.

Eibe Frank, Gordon W. Paynter, Ian H. Witten, Carl Gutwin, and Craig G. Nevill-Manning. 1999. Domain-specific keyphrase extraction. In *Proceedings of IJCAI '99*, pages 668–673. Morgan Kaufmann Publishers Inc.

Xin Jiang, Yunhua Hu, and Hang Li. 2009. A ranking approach to keyphrase extraction. In *Proceedings of the 32nd international ACM SIGIR conference on Research and development in information retrieval*, pages 756–757. ACM.

Su Nam Kim, Olena Medelyan, Min-Yen Kan, and Timothy Baldwin. 2010. SemEval-2010 task 5: Automatic keyphrase extraction from scientific articles. In *Proceedings of the 5th International Workshop on Semantic Evaluation*, pages 21–26. Association for Computational Linguistics.

Kazuaki Kishida. 2005. *Property of average precision and its generalization: An examination of evaluation indicator for information retrieval experiments*. National Institute of Informatics.

John R. Koza and Riccardo Poli. 1992. *Genetic Programming: On the programming of computers by Means of Natural Selection*. MIT Press.

Zhiyuan Liu, Peng Li, Yabin Zheng, and Maosong Sun. 2009. Clustering to find exemplar terms for keyphrase extraction. In *Proceedings of EMNLP 2009*, pages 257–266, Singapore. ACL.

Andrew McCallum and Kamal Nigam. 1998. A comparison of event models for Naïve Bayes text classification. In *AAAI-98 workshop on learning for text categorization*, pages 41–48. AAAI Press.

Rada Mihalcea and Paul Tarau. 2004. TextRank: Bringing order into texts. In *Proceedings of EMNLP*, volume 4. Barcelona, Spain.

Jure Mijić, B Dalbelo Bašic, and Jan Šnajder. 2010. Robust keyphrase extraction for a large-scale Croatian news production system. In *Proceedings of FASSBL*, pages 59–66.

Rick Riolo and Terence Soule. 2009. *Genetic Programming Theory and Practice VI*. Springer.

Josip Saratlija, Jan Šnajder, and Bojana Dalbelo Bašić. 2011. Unsupervised topic-oriented keyphrase extraction and its application to Croatian. In *Text, Speech and Dialogue*, pages 340–347. Springer.

Jan Šnajder, Bojana Dalbelo Bašić, and Marko Tadić. 2008. Automatic acquisition of inflectional lexica for morphological normalisation. *Information Processing & Management*, 44(5):1720–1731.

Takashi Tomokiyo and Matthew Hurst. 2003. A language model approach to keyphrase extraction. In *Proceedings of the ACL 2003 workshop on Multiword expressions: analysis, acquisition and treatment-Volume 18*, pages 33–40. Association for Computational Linguistics.

Peter Turney. 1999. Learning to extract keyphrases from text. Technical report, National Research Council, Institute for In- formation Technology.

C. Wang and S. Li. 2011. CoRankBayes: Bayesian learning to rank under the co-training framework and its application in keyphrase extraction. In *Proceedings of the 20th ACM international conference on Information and knowledge management*, pages 2241–2244. ACM.

Ian H Witten, Gordon W Paynter, Eibe Frank, Carl Gutwin, and Craig G Nevill-Manning. 1999. Kea: Practical automatic keyphrase extraction. In *Proceedings of the fourth ACM conference on Digital libraries*, pages 254–255. ACM.

Torsten Zesch and Iryna Gurevych. 2009. Approximate matching for evaluating keyphrase extraction. In *Proceedings of the 7th International Conference on Recent Advances in Natural Language Processing*, pages 484–489.

Kuo Zhang, Hui Xu, Jie Tang, and Juanzi Li. 2006. Keyword extraction using support vector machine. In *Advances in Web-Age Information Management*, volume 4016 of *LNCS*, pages 85–96. Springer Berlin / Heidelberg.

Lemmatization and Morphosyntactic Tagging of Croatian and Serbian

Željko Agić* **Nikola Ljubešić*** **Danijela Merkler**†
*Department of Information and Communication Sciences
†Department of Linguistics
Faculty of Humanities and Social Sciences, University of Zagreb
Ivana Lučića 3, 10000 Zagreb, Croatia
zagic@ffzg.hr nljubesi@ffzg.hr dmerkler@ffzg.hr

Abstract

We investigate state-of-the-art statistical models for lemmatization and morphosyntactic tagging of Croatian and Serbian. The models stem from a new manually annotated SETIMES.HR corpus of Croatian, based on the SETimes parallel corpus. We train models on Croatian text and evaluate them on samples of Croatian and Serbian from the SETimes corpus and the two Wikipedias. Lemmatization accuracy for the two languages reaches 97.87% and 96.30%, while full morphosyntactic tagging accuracy using a 600-tag tagset peaks at 87.72% and 85.56%, respectively. Part of speech tagging accuracies reach 97.13% and 96.46%. Results indicate that more complex methods of Croatian-to-Serbian annotation projection are not required on such dataset sizes for these particular tasks. The SETIMES.HR corpus, its resulting models and test sets are all made freely available.

1 Introduction

Part of speech tagging (POS tagging) is an natural language processing task in which words are annotated with the corresponding grammatical categories – parts of speech: verb, noun, adjective, pronoun, etc. – in a given context. It is also frequently called morphosyntactic tagging (MSD tagging, i.e., tagging with morphosyntactic descriptions), especially when addressing highly inflected languages, for which the tagging process often includes assigning additional subcategories to words, such as gender and case for nouns or tense and person for verbs. POS/MSD tagging is a well-known task and an important preprocessing step in natural language processing. It is often preceded or followed by lemmatization – the process of mapping inflected word forms to corresponding base forms or lemmas. State of the art in POS/MSD tagging and lemmatization across languages is generally achieved – both in terms of per token accuracy and speed and robustness – by statistical methods, which involve training annotation models on manually annotated corpora.

In this paper, we investigate the possibility of utilizing statistical models trained on corpora of Croatian in lemmatization and MSD tagging of Croatian and Serbian. We present a new manually annotated corpus of Croatian – the SETIMES.HR corpus. We test a number of lemmatizers and MSD taggers on Croatian and Serbian test sets from two different domains and consider options of annotation transfer between the two languages. We also outline a first version of the Multext East v5 tagset and three usable reductions of this tagset. Special emphasis is given to rapid resource development and public availability of our research. Thus, the SETIMES.HR corpus, the test sets and the best lemmatization and MSD tagging models are made publicly available.[1] In the following section, we discuss related work on lemmatization and tagging of Croatian and Serbian. We then present the SETIMES.HR corpus and the test sets, selected lemmatizers and morphosyntactic taggers and the experimental method. Finally we provide a discussion of the evaluation results and indicate future work directions.

2 Related work

The task of tagging English sentences with parts of speech is generally considered a closed issue. This is due to the fact that, over the course of the past 11 years, from (Brants, 2000) to (Søgaard, 2011), the current state of the art in tagging English has improved by 1.04 – to 97.50% in terms of per token accuracy. This is, however, not the case for languages with richer morphology and free sentence

[1] http://nlp.ffzg.hr/resources/models/

word order, such as Croatian and Serbian.

Current state of the art for statistical MSD tagging of Croatian is reported at 86.05% (Agić et al., 2008). It involves a hidden Markov model trigram tagger CroTag, trained on the Croatia Weekly 100 thousand wordform (100 kw) subcorpus of Croatian newspaper text from Croatian National Corpus (Tadić, 2009), manually MSD-tagged and lemmatized using the Multext East v3 tagset (MTE v3) (Erjavec, 2004) and Croatian Lemmatization Server (Tadić, 2005) for guided annotation. The tagger is not publicly available. Just recently, the Croatia Weekly corpus has been made publicly available through META-SHARE.[2] Another line of research reports on a prototype constraint grammar tagger for Croatian (Peradin and Šnajder, 2012), which scores at 86.36% using a MTE-based tagset. This tagger is also not publicly available as it is in prototype stage and it currently does not analyze out-of-vocabulary word forms. The top score for lemmatizing Croatian text is reported at 96.96% by combining CroTag and Croatian Morphological Lexicon (Agić et al., 2009). The lemmatizer is not publicly available.

Lemmatization and tagging of Serbian text was recently addressed in (Gesmundo and Samardžić, 2012a; Gesmundo and Samardžić, 2012b). It involves BTagger, a combined bidirectional tagger-lemmatizer tool which implements a lemmatization-as-tagging paradigm. Models are trained on the Serbian Multext East 1984 corpus, they are publicly available[3] under a permissive license, reaching overall accuracies of 97.72% for lemmatization and 86.65% for MSD tagging. It should be noted, however, that BTagger evaluation in terms of spatial and temporal complexity was not documented and that the results provided for Serbian are obtained on specific in-domain data, i.e., a corpus of fiction and are thus not directly comparable to, e.g., results for Croatian on the Croatia Weekly newspaper corpus.

Other lines of research in Serbian lemmatization and tagging exists. Delić et al. (2009) deals with transformation-based tagging of Serbian text, but it does not provide state-of-the-art results or freely available resources. Rule-based approaches to processing Serbian using NooJ [4] and similar linguistic development environments have been thoroughly explored (Vitas et al., 2003). Several resources relevant for Serbian lemmatization and tagging are provided to the public. The Serbian version of Jules Verne 60 kw manually lemmatized and MTE-tagged corpus implements a small deviation from MTE v4 and deals with specific fictional closed-vocabulary data. SrpLemKor is a 3.7 Mw corpus of Serbian newspaper text, automatically lemmatized and POS-tagged using TreeTagger (Schmid, 1995) with a tagset of 16 POS tags. A morphological dictionary of 85 thousand Serbian lemmas with sligtly deviated MTE v4 tagset is available through NooJ. Public availability of these resources is enabled through META-SHARE, with somewhat more restrictive licensing that involves non-commercial use in all cases and for some of them it also imposes no redistribution.

Related work on lemmatizer and tagger comparison exists for many languages. Restraining the search to closely related Slavic languages, extensive work in this domain has been done for Bulgarian (Georgiev et al., 2012), Czech (Spoustová et al., 2007) and Slovene (Erjavec and Džeroski, 2004; Rupnik et al., 2008). For Croatian, preliminary work on tagger evaluation for tagger voting has been conducted (Agić et al., 2010).

3 SETIMES.HR corpus

SETIMES.HR is a new manually lemmatized and MSD-tagged corpus of Croatian. It is built on top of the SETimes parallel newspaper corpus involving 10 languages from the SEE region,[5] Croatian and Serbian included. This initial dataset selection was deliberate in terms of enabling us with possibility of cross-lingual annotation projection and other cross-lingual experiments. SETIMES.HR was annotated by experts using the Croatian Lemmatization Server (HML)[6] (Tadić, 2005) to facilitate the process. We made a number of changes to the initial annotation provided by human annotators. Namely, HML provides MSD tags using an undocumented alteration of the initial MTE tagset, which we corrected to conform entirely to the MTE v4 standard (Erjavec, 2012). Also, for certain lemmas HML provides lemmatization with morphosemantic cues encoded by lemma numbering – e.g. *biti1* (en. *to be*) and *biti2* (en. *to beat*) – which we omitted as they are used only in the process of generating the morphological lexicon (Tadić and Fulgosi, 2003)

[2]http://metashare.elda.org/

[3]https://github.com/agesmundo/BTagger

[4]http://www.nooj4nlp.net/

[5]http://www.nljubesic.net/resources/corpora/setimes/

[6]http://hml.ffzg.hr

Corpus	Sent's	Tokens	Types	Lemmas
SETIMES.HR	4 016	89 785	18 089	8 930
set.test.hr	100	2 297	1 270	991
set.test.sr	100	2 320	1 251	981
wiki.test.hr	100	1 887	1 027	802
wiki.test.sr	100	1 953	1 055	795

Table 1: Stats for SETIMES.HR and test sets

		set.test		wiki.test	
Tagset	SETIMES.HR	hr	sr	hr	sr
MTE v4	660	235	236	188	192
MTE v5	663	233	234	192	195
MTE v5r1	618	213	216	176	180
MTE v5r2	634	216	217	178	181
MTE v5r3	589	196	199	162	166

Table 2: Tagset variation in tag counts

and are thus not required for purposes of lemmatization and MSD tagging. We make the resulting 90 kw SETIMES.HR corpus, along with the four test sets, publicly available under the CC-BY-SA-3.0 license.[7] Corpus stats are given in Table 1.

For purposes of this experiment, we propose an alteration of the baseline MTE v4 tagset in form of a first version for the MTE v5 standard.[8] The biggest changes in the new version are participal adjectives and adverbs moving from the verbal subset – which was very complex in v4 – to the adjectival and adverbial subsets. Additionally, acronyms are moved from the abbreviation subset to the noun subset. A general shrinking of the length of many tags was performed as well because from v4 onwards the MTE standard does not require one tagset for all languages in the standard. We also suggest three reductions of the suggested MTE v5 tagset:

1. without adjective definiteness (v5r1),
2. without common (Nc) vs. proper (Np) distinction for nouns (v5r2) and
3. without both (v5r3).

Adjectival definiteness is a category which is easy to implement in a morphological lexicon, but is very hard to distinguish in context as many of its variants are homographs. We question the distinction between common and proper nouns as well since they are contextually very hard to discriminate. On the other hand, some foreign proper nouns are inflected by specific paradigms and suffix tries used on unknown words could profit from this distinction. Stats for the MTE v5 and the reduced tagset versions in comparison with the baseline MTE v4 tagset version of SETIMES.HR are given in Table 2. They reflect the design choices we made: MTE v5 has a comparable amount of tags as MTE v4, gaining additional tags in the adjective subset, but losing tags in the verb and abbreviation subsets, while the reductions subsequently lower the overall MSD tag count.

[7]http://creativecommons.org/licenses/by-sa/3.0/

[8]http://nl.ijs.si/ME/V5/msd/html/

4 Experiment setup

In this section, we define specific experiment goals and the experiment design. We also present the datasets and tools used in the experiment.

4.1 Objectives

The principal goal of this experiment is to provide prospective users with freely available – downloadable, retrainable and usable, both for research purposes and for commercial use – state-of-the-art lemmatization and tagging modules for Croatian and Serbian. An additional goal of our experiment is to inspect lemmatization and tagging tools available under permissive licenses and give an overview regarding their accuracy and time complexity when used on languages of morphological complexity such as Croatian and Serbian.

Regarding the previously discussed constraints on existing corpora and tools for Croatian and Serbian tagging and lemmatization, our objective implies exclusive usage of the SETIMES.HR corpus in the experiment.[9] Since SETIMES.HR is part of the SETimes parallel corpus which, among other languages, includes both Croatian and Serbian, manually annotated SETIMES.HR text has a freely available Serbian equivalent. Our first course of action was thus to train a number of taggers and lemmatizers on SETIMES.HR and test it on Croatian and Serbian held out text to verify state-of-the-art accuracy on Croatian text and to observe whether the expected decline in accuracy on Serbian text is substantial or not.

In case of substantial decrease in accuracy for lemmatizing and tagging Serbian using Croatian models, we designed multiple schemes for projecting annotation from SETIMES.HR to its Serbian

[9]Considering corpora of Croatian and Serbian stated in related work, we chose not to use non-MTE resources and corpora of fiction as an experiment basis. Importance of encoding the full set of morphological features from the MTE tagset is illustrated by its benefits for dependency parsing of Croatian (Agić and Merkler, 2013).

equivalent from the SETimes parallel corpus. The general directions for identifying the bitext subset for annotation projection were using parallel sentences which have the highest longest common subsequence or using statistical machine translation to produce Serbian sentences with minimum difference to the Croatian counterpart. Projecting tags on a bitext of high similarity would include heuristics of annotating the variation with the same morphosyntactic category if the variation was one token long or annotating it with the existing model for tagging if the variation was longer than that. Lemmatization of the single-token variation would be reapplied if the token ending in both languages was identical while other cases would be annotated with the existing lemmatization model.

4.2 Experiment workflow

We do four batches of experiments:

1. to identify the best available tool and underlying paradigm for lemmatization and tagging of both languages by observing overall accuracy and execution time,
2. to establish the need for annotation projection from Croatian SETIMES.HR corpus to its Serbian counterpart,
3. to select the best of the proposed MTE-based tagsets for both tasks and
4. to provide in-depth evaluation of the selected top-performing lemmatizer and tagger on both languages by using the top-performing tagset.

In the first experiment batch, we test the tools only on Croatian data from SETimes. The second batch establishes the need for – or needlessness of – annotation projection for improved processing of Serbian text by testing the tools selected in the first batch on both languages. The in-depth evaluation of the third and fourth experiment batch includes, for both languages and all test sets, observing the influence of tagset selection to overall accuracy and investigating tool performance in more detail. We measure precision, recall and F_1 scores for selected parts of speech and inspect lemmatization and tagging confusion matrices for detailed analysis and possible prediction of tool operation in real-world language processing environments.

We aim for the experiment to serve as underlying documentation for enabling prospective users in implementing more complex natural language processing systems for Croatian and Serbian by using these resources. Additionally, the overview of the usability of tools available is informative for researchers developing basic language technologies for other languages. We test statistical significance of observed differences in our results by using the approximate randomization test.

4.3 Datasets

All models are trained on SETIMES.HR. To at least partially avoid the possible pitfall of exclusive in-domain testing, we define two test sets for each language. The first test set consists of 100 Croatian-Serbian parallel sentence pairs taken by random sampling from the relative complement of the SETimes parallel corpus and SETIMES.HR. The second test set is taken from the Croatian and Serbian Wikipedia by manually selecting 20 matching Wikipedia articles and manually extracting 100 approximate sentence pairs. We chose manual over random sampling from Wikipedia to account for the fact that a certain number of articles is virtually identical between the two Wikipedias due to language similarity and mutual copying between Wikipedia users. All four test sets were manually annotated using the same procedure that was used for SETIMES.HR. The stats are given in Table 1. In addition, we have verified the difference between language test sets by measuring lexical coverage using HML as a high-coverage morphological lexicon of Croatian. For the Croatian SETimes and Wikipedia samples, we detected 5.2% and 3.9% out-of-vocabulary word forms and 11.40% and 8.86% were observed for the corresponding Serbian samples, supporting well-foundedness of the test sets in terms of maintaining the differences between the two languages.

4.4 Lemmatizers and taggers

As lemmatizers and taggers with permissive licensing schemes and documented cross-lingual state-of-the-art performance have become largely available, we chose not to implement our own but to obtain a set of tools and test them using our data, i.e., train them on the SETIMES.HR corpus and test them on Croatian and Serbian SETimes and Wikipedia test samples. We selected the tools on the basis of availability and underlying stochastic paradigms as to identify the best tools and best paradigms.

We tested hidden Markov model trigram taggers HunPos[10] (Halácsy et al., 2007) and lemmatization-capable PurePos[11] (Orosz and Novák, 2012),

[10] https://code.google.com/p/hunpos/

[11] https://github.com/ppke-nlpg/purepos

Tool	Lem.	MSD	Train (sec)	Test (sec)
BTagger	96.22	86.63	24 864.47	87.01
CST	**97.78**	–	**1.80**	**0.03**
+ lex	97.04	–	1.87	0.12
HunPos	–	**87.11**	**1.10**	**0.11**
+ lex	–	84.81	10.79	0.45
PurePos	74.40	86.63	5.49	4.42
SVMTool	–	84.99	1 897.08	3.28
TreeTagger	90.51	85.07	7.49	0.19
+ lex	94.12	87.01	17.48	0.31

Table 3: Preliminary evaluation

lemmatization-capable decision-tree-based TreeTagger[12] (Schmid, 1995), support vector machine tagger SVMTool[13] (Giménez and Màrquez, 2004) and CST's[14] data-driven rule-based lemmatizer (Ingason et al., 2008). Keeping in mind the previously mentioned state-of-the-art scores on Serbian 1984 corpus and statistical lemmatization capability, we also tested BTagger (Gesmundo and Samardžić, 2012a; Gesmundo and Samardžić, 2012b). Since some lemmatizers and taggers are capable of using an external morphological lexicon, we used a MTE v5r1 version of Apertium's lexicon of Croatian[15] (Peradin and Tyers, 2012) where applicable.[16] All tools are well-documented and successfully applied across languages, as indicated in related work.

5 Results and discussion

A discussion of the experiment results follows in the next four subsections. Each subsection represents one batch of experiments. First we select the best lemmatizer and tagger, next we check for a need of annotation projection to the Serbian corpus, then the best MTE-based tagset using the best tool combination. Finally we provide a more detailed insight into the results of the top-performing pair of selected tools and tagset.

5.1 Tool selection

Results of the first experimental batch, consisting of testing the selected set of lemmatizers and taggers on the MTE v5r1 version of Croatian SETimes test set, are given in Table 3. In terms of lemmatization and tagging accuracy as well as processing speed in both training and testing, the top performing tools are CST lemmatizer and HunPos tagger. Thus, we chose these two for further investigation in the following batches of experiments. It should be noted that, even though its performance is comparable to the one of CST and HunPos, BTagger was not chosen for the other batches primarily because of its temporal complexity, as it is orders of magnitude higher than for the selected tools. Given that lemmatization and tagging are considered prerequisites for further processing of text tata, the data itself often being fed to these modules in large quantities (e.g., web corpora), we insist on the significance of temporal complexity in tool selection. The other results are comparable with previous research in tagging Croatian. Where applicable, we tried assisting the tools by providing Apertium's lexicon as an optional input for improved lemmatization and tagging. Only TreeTagger lemmatization and tagging benefited from lexicon inclusion. However, it should be noted that TreeTagger implements a very simple approach to lemmatization, as it only performs dictionary matching and does not lemmatize unknown words. Inclusion of a larger lexicon such as HML might be more beneficial for all the tools.

	set.test		wiki.test	
POS	hr	sr	hr	sr
HunPos	**97.04**	**95.47**	94.25	**96.46**
+ lex	96.60	95.09	**94.62**	95.58
MSD				
HunPos	**87.11**	**85.00**	**80.83**	**82.74**
+ lex	84.81	81.59	78.49	79.20

Table 4: Overall tagging accuracy with and without the inflectional lexicon

	set.test		wiki.test	
Model	hr	sr	hr	sr
CST	**97.78**	**95.95**	**96.59**	96.30
+ lex	97.04	95.52	96.38	**96.61**

Table 5: Overall lemmatization accuracy with and without the inflectional lexicon

5.2 Annotation projection

HunPos tagging accuracy on all Croatian and Serbian test sets for both POS only and full MSD is given in Table 4 for the default variant and for the

[12] http://www.cis.uni-muenchen.de/ schmid/tools/TreeTagger/
[13] http://www.lsi.upc.edu/ nlp/SVMTool/
[14] http://cst.dk/online/lemmatiser/uk/
[15] http://www.apertium.org/
[16] As with already existing Croatian annotated corpora, HML is not fully MTE compliant. For future work, we might utilize a compliant version in our experiment and resulting models, being that its coverage is generally greater than the one of Apertium's lexicon due to size difference.

Tagset	set.test		wiki.test	
POS	hr	sr	hr	sr
MTE v4	96.08	94.61	93.96	95.85
MTE v5	97.04	95.52	**94.30**	96.40
MTE v5r1	97.04	95.47	94.25	**96.46**
MTE v5r2	97.00	**95.60**	94.20	96.30
MTE v5r3	**97.13**	95.56	94.09	96.15
MSD				
MTE v4	86.24	83.45	80.45	81.98
MTE v5	86.77	84.48	80.46	82.43
MTE v5r1	87.11	85.00	80.83	82.74
MTE v5r2	87.11	84.96	81.20	82.38
MRE v5r3	**87.72**	**85.56**	**81.52**	**82.79**

Table 6: HunPos POS and MSD tagging accuracy for all tagsets

	set.test		wiki.test	
Tagset	hr	sr	hr	sr
MTE v4	97.78	95.82	96.66	96.11
MTE v5	97.82	95.86	**96.81**	**96.30**
MTE v5r1	97.78	95.95	96.59	**96.30**
MTE v5r2	**97.87**	**95.99**	96.75	96.20
MTE v5r3	97.74	**95.99**	96.54	96.20

Table 7: CST lemmatization accuracy for all tagsets

one using Apertium's lexicon. These results serve as the first decision point regarding the need for Croatian-to-Serbian annotation projection, the second one being the lemmatization scores in Table 5. Here we observed an unsubstantial decrease in POS and MSD tagging between Croatian and Serbian test sets – the observed difference is, in fact, more substantial across domains than across languages. Overall, Croatian and Serbian scores differ less than 3%. Results for Serbian Wikipedia sample are even consistently better than for Croatian Wikipedia, emphasizing domain significance over language difference. The tagger does not benefit from the inclusion of the inflectional lexicon in POS tagging and it even incurs a substantial 2% to 4% penalty in MSD tagging. Since such observations were not made while including the lexicon with the TreeTagger tool – which implements the simplest form of dictionary lemmatization – we performed a small results analysis and noticed an unnaturally high percentage of categories that are as expected present in the lexicon, but very rare in the training corpus (like the vocative case) pointing to a naïve implementation of the procedure. Thus we chose not to use the lexicon in further observations. Lack of more substantial differences

Tagsets	v5	v5r1	v5r2	v5r3
v4	0.268	$<$0.05	$<$0.05	$<$0.01
v5	/	$<$0.01	$<$0.05	$<$0.01
v5r1	/	/	0.877	$<$0.05
v5r2	/	/	/	$<$0.01

Table 8: Statistical significance of differences in full MSD tagging between tagsets (p-values using approximate randomization)

in tagging scores between Croatian and Serbian for this specific test scenario implied no need for annotation projection.

This is further supported by overall lemmatization scores in Table 5. Even with the observed lexical differences between the languages, as we indicated in the description of the test sets by measuring lexical coverage using HML, the learned CST lemmatizer rules are more robust considering language alteration than the trigram tagging model of HunPos. Lemmatization accuracy stays in the margins of approximately 97%±1% for both languages. Average accuracy on Croatian is less than 2% higher than for Serbian and the domain patterns observed for tagging are also observed for lemmatization. Benefits of an inflectional lexicon for lemmatization are minor, if any, which can be followed back to the small size of the lexicon and high quality of the CST lemmatizer. On the contrary, TreeTagger's simple lemmatization does gain four points by using the lexicon, but it initially performs seven points worse than CST.

5.3 Tagset selection

Tables 6 and 7 show the influence of tagset design on tagging and lemmatization accuracy. They are accompanied by Table 8, i.e., results of testing statistical significance of differences between the tagsets in the task of full MSD tagging from Table 6. Statistical significance is calculated with all test sets merged into one. Differences in lemmatization accuracy are virtually non-existent regarding the tagset choice. Full MSD tagging follows the usual pattern of inverse proportionality between tagset size and overall accuracy. It should be noted that MTE v5 accuracy is not significantly higher than MTE v4 accuracy ($p = 0.268$), but we consider the new tagset to be easier to use for humans since its tags are shortened by removing placehodlers for features used in other MTE languages. Considering that only tagging accuracy using the MTE v5r3 tagset is significantly better than tagging using all

	Croatian			Serbian		
POS	P	R	F_1	P	R	F_1
Adj	94.33	90.14	92.19	94.34	93.98	94.16
	66.80	63.83	65.28	66.79	66.54	66.66
Adv	84.56	82.73	83.63	82.57	73.77	77.92
	84.56	82.73	83.63	82.57	73.77	77.92
Conj	95.29	93.82	94.55	97.92	95.29	96.59
	94.12	92.66	93.38	96.89	94.28	95.57
Noun	95.70	96.34	96.02	95.42	96.59	96.00
	76.78	77.30	77.04	75.38	76.30	75.84
Num	94.57	97.75	96.13	96.51	93.26	94.86
	91.30	94.38	92.81	94.19	91.01	92.57
Prep	98.10	99.72	98.90	98.45	98.70	98.57
	95.93	97.52	96.72	94.30	94.55	94.42
Pron	95.97	97.54	96.75	95.78	97.42	96.59
	81.85	83.20	82.52	81.43	82.83	82.12
Verb	95.88	98.07	96.96	95.23	95.72	95.47
	93.81	95.96	94.87	93.36	93.84	93.60

Table 9: Precision (P), recall (R) and F_1 score for POS only (1st column) and full MSD (2nd column) on Croatian and Serbian

other suggested tagsets, we chose this tagset and tagging model for further observation of lemmatization and tagging properties in the remainder of the paper. Still, in this section, we present the results on all tagsets to serve as underlying documentation of the observed differences, mainly because of the fact that only MTE v4 is officially supported at this moment and MTE v5 is a newly-introduced prototype that displays better performance in this specific experiment.

5.4 In-depth analysis

In Table 9 we merge SETimes and Wikipedia test sets by language and provide POS and MSD tagging precision, recall and F_1 score for selected Croatian and Serbian parts of speech. In terms of POS only, the most difficult-to-tag part of speech is the adverb, followed by the adjective in both Croatian and Serbian. The other categories are consistently POS-tagged with an F_1 score of approximately 95% or higher. The decrease for adverbs and adjectives is somewhat more evident in precision than in recall and the POS confusion matrix for both languages, given in Table 10, shows that these two parts of speech are often mistaken for each other by the tagger. Regarding full MSD tagging using the MTE v5r3 tagset, for both languages, the lowest F_1 scores are observed for adjectives (approximately 66%), nouns (76%) and pronouns (82%). This is most likely due to the fact that these parts of speech have the largest tagset subsets, making it easier for the tagger to get confused.[17] Performance for other parts of speech is satisfactory, especially for verbs, keeping in mind, e.g., possible subsequent dependency parsing of the two languages. The absolute difference between POS and MSD tagging score is most substantial for adjectives (approximately 27%), indicating that certain MSD features might be triggering the decrease. This is partially supported by our tagset design investigation as dropping adjective definiteness atribute yielded substantial overall tagging accuracy increase when compared with the tagsets in which this attribute is still encoded.

In Table 10 we provide a part of speech confusion matrix for Croatian and Serbian on test sets merged by language. In Croatian test sets, the most frequent confusions are those between adjectives and nouns (28.9%), nouns and verbs (14.5%), adjectives and adverbs (11.6%) and nouns and adverbs (6.9%). In Serbian text, the tagger most frequently confuses nouns – for adjectives (21.1%), verbs (20%) and adverbs (16%). Merging the test sets by language mostly evens out the tagging differences as there is a total of 173 MSD confusions in Croatian test sets and only 3 more, i.e., 175 in the Serbian test sets.

POS scores for both languages neared the level of human error in our experiment. Keeping that in mind, upon observing the confusion instances themselves, we spotted a confusion between adjectives and nouns (e.g. names of countries (*Hrvatska* (en. *Croatia*, *Croatian*)), homographic forms (*strana* (en. *foreign*, *side*), *svet* (en. *world*, *holy*)) and confusion between adjectives and adverbs. Adverbs and prepositions are sometimes confused with nouns, especially for nouns in instrumental case (e.g. *godinama* (en. *year*, *yearly*), *tijekom* (en. *duration*, *during*)). Conjuctions are at times incorrently tagged because various words can have a conjuctional function, most frequently pronouns and adverbs: *što* (en. *what*), *kako* (en. *how*), *kada* (en. *when*). Interestingly, there is some confusion between nouns and verbs in Wikipedia test sets, while in SETimes test sets there are almost none. This confusion arises from the homographic forms – e.g. *mora* (en. *must*, *seas*) – or from nouns with

[17] There are 589 MTE v5r3 tags in SETIMES.HR. Out of these, 164 are used for tagging adjectives, 42 for nouns and 268 for pronouns, thus accounting for 80.47% of the tagset. There are also 50 verb tags.

POS	Abbr	Adj	Adv	Conj	Noun	Num	Part	Prep	Pron	Res	Verb
Abbr		0	0	0	1	3	0	0	0	0	0
Adj	0		20	0	50	0	1	0	3	1	4
Adv	0	10		9	12	0	0	2	0	0	2
Conj	0	0	5		2	0	5	5	7	0	0
Noun	0	37	28	0		4	0	1	5	7	25
Num	2	4	0	0	2		0	0	0	0	0
Part	0	0	0	3	0	0		0	0	0	3
Prep	0	0	2	3	2	0	1		0	0	0
Pron	0	2	1	9	3	0	1	0		0	1
Res	0	0	1	0	4	0	0	2	0		0
Verb	0	9	4	0	35	1	2	1	0	1	

Table 10: POS confusion matrix for Croatian (top right) and Serbian (bottom left)

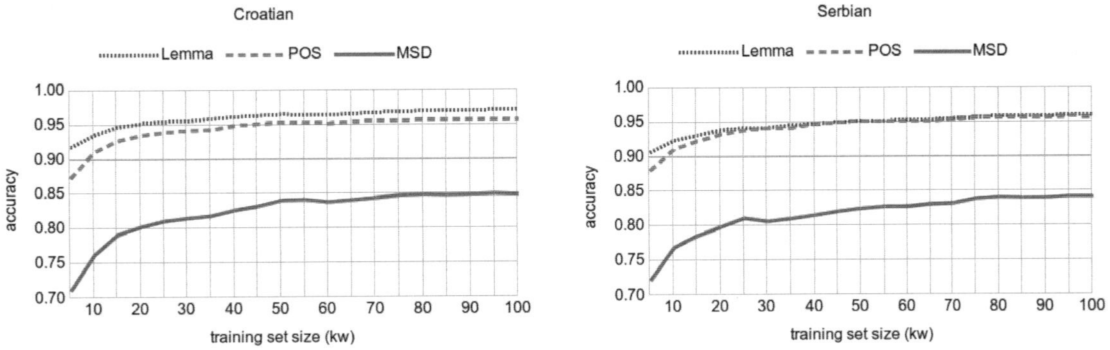

Figure 1: Learning curves for Croatian and Serbian lemmatization and tagging

suffixes *-la* and *-lo*, which are used for denoting participles in feminine and neuter gender, or with suffix *-ti*, which is also a suffix for infinitive.

Most MSD tag confusions arise from the fact that the same suffix can denote different cases in different declensions. We observed confused number and gender category (mostly in adjectives in masculine and neuter gender), but the most frequent confusion occurs for accusative forms in masculine gender, which have different suffixes when they denote animacy (suffix is the same as in the genitive case: *pobjednika* (en. *winner*), *kandidata* (en. *candidate*)) and when they denote inanimacy (suffix is the same as in the nominative case: *metak* (en. *bullet*), *bubnjar* (en. *drummer*)).

In lemmatization, as in POS tagging, errors are generally very infrequent. Some occur with adjectives, when an assigned lemma represents a definite form of an adjective, instead of an indefinitive form (and less frequently vice versa). Besides, adjectives are sometimes confused with adverbs (e.g., target lemma is *značajno* (en. *significantly*), but the lemma *značajan* (en. *significant*) is assigned, and vice versa). Other less frequent examples include cases in which the assigned lemma is not in its canonical form, but a case other than the nominative case, or when the assigned lemma is a word stem. A small number of errors also occurs due to slight differences in Croatian and Serbian wordforms, e.g., when a Serbian nominative form is not a nominative form in Croatian (*planeta* as Serbian nominative and Croatian genitive, *planet* being the Croatian nominative).

Figure 1 provides lemmatization, POS and MSD tagging learning curves for both languages on merged test sets. Apart from the slight difference in lemmatization scores in favor of Croatian, the learning curves and overall scores on merged test sets are virtually identical. The easiest task to learn is lemmatization while the most complex one is applying MSD.

6 Conclusions and future work

In this paper, we have addressed the issue of lemmatization and morphosyntactic tagging of two generally under-resourced languages, Croatian and Serbian. Our goal was to provide the general public with freely available language resources and state-of-the-art models for lemmatization and tagging of these two languages in terms of accuracy, robustness and speed. We also aimed at using lemmatization and tagging as a platform for implicit comparison of the two languages in natural language processing terms, as to provide partial insight to how difficult and lossy – or, more desireably, how easy and straightforward – would it be to port linguistic resources and language processing tools from one language to another.

While developing the models, we completed a series of experiments. We used the Croatian text from the freely available SETimes parallel corpus to create a new manually lemmatized and morphosyntactically tagged corpus of Croatian – the SETIMES.HR corpus. Beside the Multext East v4 morphosyntactic tagset specification for Croatian which was used for initial corpus annotation, we designed and implemented a first version of the Multext East v5 tagset and its three reductions and applied these to SETIMES.HR. Using SETimes and Wikipedia as starting point resources, we created two gold standard test sets for each language in order to test existing state-of-the-art lemmatizers and taggers. We ran preliminary tests on a number of tools to select CST lemmatizer and HunPos tagger as tools of choice considering observed accuracy, training time and text processing time. In an in-depth evaluation of these tools, we obtained peak overall lemmatization accuracy of 97.87% and 96.30% for Croatian and Serbian and full morphosyntactic tagging accuracy of 87.72% and 85.56%, with basic part of speech tagging accuracy at 97.13% and 96.46%. In this specific test scenario and with this specific training set, we have shown the differences in results between Croatian and Serbian not to be significant enough to justify an effort in more elaborate strategy of adapting Croatian models to Serbian data – simply training the models on Croatian text from SETIMES.HR corpus and using them on Serbian text provided state-of-the-art results in lemmatization and tagging, while maintaining and even topping previously documented state of the art for Croatian.

The SETIMES.HR corpus, Croatian and Serbian test sets and top-performing lemmatization and tagging models are publicly available and freely downloadable[18] under the CC-BY-SA-3.0 license.

Our future work plans include both enlarging and enhancing SETIMES.HR. The presented learning curves show significant room for improvement by annotating additional data. The dataset already serves as a basis for the SETIMES.HR treebank of Croatian (Agić and Merkler, 2013), implementing a novel dependency syntactic formalism and enabling experiments with joint dependency parsing of Croatian and Serbian. Should dependency parsing experiments show the need for more elaborate language adaptation strategies, we will most likely implement them also on the level of lemmas and morphosyntactic tags before addressing syntactic issues. This will possibly be helped by statistical machine translation between Croatian and Serbian to enhance bitext similarity and empower projection strategies. An effort could be made to adapt existing Croatian and Serbian resources and subsequently to attempt achieving better lemmatization and tagging performance by combining these with SETIMES.HR. We will use the models presented in this paper to annotate the web corpora of Croatian and Serbian (Ljubešić and Erjavec, 2011) – hrWaC and srWaC.

[18]http://nlp.ffzg.hr/resources/models/

Acknowledgement

The research leading to these results has received funding from the European Union Seventh Framework Programme FP7/2007-2013 under grant agreement n° PIAP-GA-2012-324414 (project Abu-MaTran).

References

Željko Agić and Danijela Merkler. 2013. Three Syntactic Formalisms for Data-Driven Dependency Parsing of Croatian. In *Text, Speech and Dialogue. Lecture Notes in Computer Science*. Springer.

Željko Agić, Marko Tadić, and Zdravko Dovedan. 2008. Improving Part-of-Speech Tagging Accuracy for Croatian by Morphological Analysis. *Informatica*, 32(4):445–451.

Željko Agić, Marko Tadić, and Zdravko Dovedan. 2009. Evaluating Full Lemmatization of Croatian Texts. In *Recent Advances in Intelligent Information Systems*, pages 175–184. Exit Warsaw.

Željko Agić, Marko Tadić, and Zdravko Dovedan. 2010. Tagger Voting Improves Morphosyntactic Tagging Accuracy on Croatian Texts. In *Proceedings of ITI*, pages 61–66.

Thorsten Brants. 2000. TnT: A Statistical Part-of-Speech Tagger. In *Proceedings of ANLP*, pages 224–231.

Vlado Delić, Milan Sečujski, and Aleksandar Kupusinac. 2009. Transformation-Based Part-of-Speech Tagging for Serbian Language. In *Proceedings of CIMMACS*.

Tomaž Erjavec and Sašo Džeroski. 2004. Machine Learning of Morphosyntactic Structure: Lemmatizing Unknown Slovene Words. *Applied Artificial Intelligence*, 18:17–41.

Tomaž Erjavec. 2004. MULTEXT-East Version 3: Multilingual Morphosyntactic Specifications, Lexicons and Corpora. In *Proceedings of LREC*.

Tomaž Erjavec. 2012. MULTEXT-East: Morphosyntactic Resources for Central and Eastern European Languages. *Language Resources and Evaluation*, 46(1):131–142.

Georgi Georgiev, Valentin Zhikov, Kiril Simov, Petya Osenova, and Preslav Nakov. 2012. Feature-Rich Part-of-speech Tagging for Morphologically Complex Languages: Application to Bulgarian. In *Proceedings of EACL*, pages 492–502.

Andrea Gesmundo and Tanja Samardžić. 2012a. Lemmatisation as a Tagging Task. In *Proceedings of ACL*.

Andrea Gesmundo and Tanja Samardžić. 2012b. Lemmatising Serbian as Category Tagging with Bidirectional Sequence Classification. In *Proceedings of LREC*.

Jesús Giménez and Lluís Màrquez. 2004. SVMTool: A general POS Tagger Generator Based on Support Vector Machines. In *Proceedings of LREC*.

Péter Halácsy, András Kornai, and Csaba Oravecz. 2007. HunPos: An Open Source Trigram Tagger. In *Proceedings of ACL*, pages 209–212.

Anton Karl Ingason, Sigrún Helgadóttir, Hrafn Loftsson, and Eiríkur Rögnvaldsson. 2008. A Mixed Method Lemmatization Algorithm Using a Hierarchy of Linguistic Identities (HOLI). In *Proceedings of GoTAL*, pages 205–216.

Nikola Ljubešić and Tomaž Erjavec. 2011. hrWaC and slWaC: Compiling Web Corpora for Croatian and Slovene. In *Text, Speech and Dialogue*, pages 395–402. Springer.

György Orosz and Attila Novák. 2012. PurePos – An Open Source Disambiguator. In *Proceedings of NLPCS*.

Hrvoje Peradin and Jan Šnajder. 2012. Towards a Constraint Grammar Based Morphological Tagger for Croatian. In *Text, Speech and Dialogue*, pages 174–182. Springer.

Hrvoje Peradin and Francis M. Tyers. 2012. A Rule-Based Machine Translation System from Serbo-Croatian to Macedonian. In *Proceedings of FREERBMT12*, pages 55–65.

Jan Rupnik, Miha Grčar, and Tomaž Erjavec. 2008. Improving Morphosyntactic Tagging of Slovene Language Through Meta-Tagging. *Informatica*, 32(4):437–444.

Helmut Schmid. 1995. Improvements in Part-of-Speech Tagging With an Application to German. In *Proceedings of ACL SIGDAT Workshop*.

Anders Søgaard. 2011. Semi-Supervised Condensed Nearest Neighbor for Part-of-Speech Tagging. In *Proceedings of ACL-HLT*, pages 48–52.

Drahomíra "johanka" Spoustová, Jan Hajič, Jan Votrubec, Pavel Krbec, and Pavel Květoň. 2007. The Best of Two Worlds: Cooperation of Statistical and Rule-Based Taggers for Czech. In *Proceedings of BSNLP*, pages 67–74.

Marko Tadić and Sanja Fulgosi. 2003. Building the Croatian Morphological Lexicon. In *Proceedings of EACL 2003 Workshop on Morphological Processing of Slavic Languages*, pages 41–46.

Marko Tadić. 2005. Croatian Lemmatization Server. *Southern Journal of Linguistics*, 29(1):206–217.

Marko Tadić. 2009. New Version of the Croatian National Corpus. *After Half a Century of Slavonic Natural Language Processing*, pages 199–205.

Duško Vitas, Cvetana Krstev, Ivan Obradović, Ljubomir Popović, and Gordana Pavlović-Lažetić. 2003. An Overview of Resources and Basic Tools for Processing of Serbian Written Texts. In *Proceedings of the Workshop on Balkan Language Resources, 1st Balkan Conference in Informatics*.

Modernizing Historical Slovene Words with Character-Based SMT

Yves Scherrer
ALPAGE
Université Paris 7 Diderot & INRIA
5 Rue Thomas Mann, Paris, France
yves.scherrer@inria.fr

Tomaž Erjavec
Dept. of Knowledge Technologies
Jožef Stefan Institute
Jamova cesta 39, Ljubljana, Slovenia
tomaz.erjavec@ijs.si

Abstract

We propose a language-independent word normalization method exemplified on modernizing historical Slovene words. Our method relies on character-based statistical machine translation and uses only shallow knowledge. We present the relevant lexicons and two experiments. In one, we use a lexicon of historical word–contemporary word pairs and a list of contemporary words; in the other, we only use a list of historical words and one of contemporary ones. We show that both methods produce significantly better results than the baseline.

1 Introduction

A lot of recent work deals with detecting and matching cognate words in corpora of closely related language varieties. This approach is also useful for processing historical language (Piotrowski, 2012), where historical word forms are matched against contemporary forms, thus normalizing the varied and changing spelling of words over time. Such normalization has a number of applications: it enables better full-text search in cultural heritage digital libraries, makes old texts more understandable to today's readers and significantly improves further text processing by allowing PoS tagging, lemmatization and parsing models trained on contemporary language to be used on historical texts.

In this paper, we try to match word pairs of different historical stages of the Slovene language. In one experiment we use character-based machine translation to learn the character correspondences from pairs of words. In the second experiment, we start by extracting noisy word pairs from monolingual[1] lexicons; this experiment simulates a situation where bilingual data is not available.

The rest of this paper is structured as follows: Section 2 presents related work, Section 3 details the dataset used, Section 4 shows the experiments and results, and Section 5 concludes.

2 Related Work

The most common approach to modernizing historical words uses (semi-) hand-constructed transcription rules, which are then applied to historical words, and the results filtered against a contemporary lexicon (Baron and Rayson, 2008; Scheible et al., 2010; Scheible et al., 2011); such rules are often encoded and used as (extended) finite state automata (Reffle, 2011). An alternative to such deductive approaches is the automatic induction of mappings. For example, Kestemont et al. (2010) use machine learning to convert 12th century Middle Dutch word forms to contemporary lemmas.

Word modernization can be viewed as a special case of transforming cognate words from one language to a closely related one. This task has traditionally been performed with stochastic transducers or HMMs trained on a set of cognate word pairs (Mann and Yarowsky, 2001). More recently, character-based statistical machine translation (C-SMT) (Vilar et al., 2007; Tiedemann, 2009) has been proposed as an alternative approach to translating words between closely related languages and has been shown to outperform stochastic transducers on the task of name transliteration (Tiedemann and Nabende, 2009).

For the related task of matching cognate pairs in bilingual non-parallel corpora, various language-independent similarity measures have been proposed on the basis of string edit distance (Kondrak and Dorr, 2004). Cognate word matching has been shown to facilitate the extraction of translation lexicons from comparable corpora (Koehn and Knight, 2002; Kondrak et al., 2003; Fišer and Ljubešić, 2011).

[1] For lack of a better term, we use "monolingual" to refer to a single diachronic state of the language, and "bilingual" to refer to two diachronic states of the language.

For using SMT for modernizing historical words, the only work so far is, to the best of our knowledge, Sánchez-Martínez et al. (2013).

3 The Dataset

In this section we detail the dataset that was used in the subsequent experiments, which consists of a frequency lexicon of contemporary Slovene and training and testing lexicons of historical Slovene.[2]

3.1 The Lexicon of Contemporary Slovene

Sloleks is a large inflectional lexicon of contemporary Slovene.[3] The lexicon contains lemmas with their full inflectional paradigms and with the word forms annotated with frequency of occurrence in a large reference corpus of Slovene. For the purposes of this experiment, we extracted from Sloleks the list of its lower-cased word forms (930,000) together with their frequency.

3.2 Corpora of Historical Slovene

The lexicons used in the experiments are constructed from two corpora of historical Slovene.[4] The texts in the corpora are, *inter alia* marked up with the year of publication and their IANA language subtag (`sl` for contemporary Slovene alphabet and `sl-bohoric` for the old, pre-1850 Bohorič alphabet). The word tokens are annotated with the attributes *nform*, *mform*, *lemma*, *tag*, *gloss*, where only the first two are used in the presented experiments.

The *nform* attribute contains the result of a simple normalization step, consisting of lower-casing, removal of vowel diacritics (which are not used in contemporary Slovene), and conversion of the Bohorič alphabet to the contemporary one. Thus, we do not rely on the C-SMT model presented below to perform these pervasive, yet deterministic and fairly trivial transformations.

The modernized form of the word, *mform* is the word as it is (or would be, for extinct words) written today: the task of the experiments is to predict the correct *mform* given an *nform*.

[2]The dataset used in this paper is available under the CC-BY-NC-SA license from `http://nl.ijs.si/imp/experiments/bsnlp-2013/`.

[3]Sloleks is encoded in LMF and available under the CC-BY-NC-SA license from `http://www.slovenscina.eu/`.

[4]The data for historical Slovene comes from the IMP resources, see `http://nl.ijs.si/imp/`.

Period	Texts	Words	Verified
18B	8	21,129	21,129
19A	9	83,270	83,270
19B	59	146,100	146,100
Σ	75	250,499	250,499

Table 1: Size of goo300k corpus.

Period	Texts	Words	Verified
18B	11	139,649	15,466
19A	13	457,291	17,616
19B	270	2,273,959	65,769
Σ	293	2,870,899	98,851

Table 2: Size of foo3M corpus.

The two corpora were constructed by sampling individual pages from a collection of books and editions of one newspaper, where the pages (but not necessarily the publications) of the two corpora are disjoint:[5]

- **goo300k** is the smaller, but fully manually annotated corpus, in which the annotations of each word have been verified;[6]
- **foo3M** is the larger, and only partially manually annotated corpus, in which only the more frequent word forms that do not already appear in goo300k have verified annotations.

The texts have been marked up with the time period in which they were published, e.g., 18B meaning the second half of the 18th century. This allows us to observe the changes to the vocabulary in 50-year time slices. The sizes of the corpora are given in Table 1 and Table 2.

3.3 Lexicons of Historical Slovene

From the two corpora we have extracted the training and testing lexicons, keeping only words (e.g., discarding digits) that have been manually verified. The training lexicon, L_{goo} is derived from the goo300k corpus, while the test lexicon, L_{foo} is derived from the foo3M corpus and, as

[5]The corpora used in our experiments are slightly smaller than the originals: the text from two books and one newspaper issue has been removed, as the former contain highly idiosyncratic ways of spelling words, not seen elsewhere, and the latter contains a mixture of the Bohorič and contemporary alphabet, causing problems for word form normalization. The texts older than 1750 have also been removed from goo300k, as such texts do not occur in foo3M, which is used for testing our approach.

[6]A previous version of this corpus is described in (Erjavec, 2012).

Period	Pairs	Ident	Diff	OOV
18B	6,305	2,635	3,670	703
19A	18,733	12,223	6,510	2,117
19B	30,874	24,597	6,277	4,759
Σ	45,810	31,160	14,650	7,369

Table 3: Size of L_{goo} lexicon.

Period	OOV	Pairs	Ident	Diff
18B	660	3,199	493	2,706
19A	886	3,638	1,708	1,930
19B	1,983	10,033	8,281	1,752
Σ	3,480	16,029	9,834	6,195

Table 4: Size of L_{foo} lexicon.

mentioned, contains no ⟨*nform*, *mform*⟩ pairs already appearing in L_{goo}. This setting simulates the task of an existing system receiving a new text to modernize.

The lexicons used in the experiment contain entries with *nform*, *mform*, and the per-slice frequencies of the pair in the corpus from which the lexicon was derived, as illustrated in the example below:

```
benetkah      benetkah   19A:1 19B:1
aposteljnov apostolov  19A:1 19B:1
aržati        aržetu*    18B:2
```

The first example is a word that has not changed its spelling (and was observed twice in the 19th century texts), while the second and third have changed their spelling. The asterisk on the third example indicates that the *mform* is not present in Sloleks. We exclude such pairs from the test lexicon (but not from the training lexicon) since they will most likely not be correctly modernized by our model, which relies on Sloleks. The sizes of the two lexicons are given in Table 3 and Table 4. For L_{goo} we give the number of pairs including the OOV words, while for L_{foo} we exclude them; the tables also show the numbers of pairs with identical and different words. Note that the summary row has smaller numbers than the sum of the individual rows, as different slices can contain the same pairs.

4 Experiments and Results

We conducted two experiments with the data described above. In both cases, the goal is to create C-SMT models for automatically modernizing historical Slovene words. In each experiment, we create three different models for the three time periods of old Slovene (18B, 19A, 19B).

The first experiment follows a supervised setup: we train a C-SMT model on ⟨*historical word, contemporary word*⟩ pairs from L_{goo} and test the model on the word pairs of L_{foo}. The second experiment is unsupervised and relies on monolingual data only: we match the old Slovene words from L_{goo} with modern Slovene word candidates from Sloleks; this noisy list of word pairs then serves to train the C-SMT model. We test again on L_{foo}.

4.1 Supervised Learning

SMT models consist of two main components: the translation model, which is trained on bilingual data, and the language model, which is trained on monolingual data of the target language. We use the word pairs from L_{goo} to train the translation model, and the modern Slovene words from L_{goo} to train the language model.[7] As said above, we test the model on the word pairs of L_{foo}. The experiments have been carried out with the tools of the standard SMT pipeline: GIZA++ (Och and Ney, 2003) for alignment, Moses (Koehn et al., 2007) for phrase extraction and decoding, and IRSTLM (Federico et al., 2008) for language modelling. After preliminary experimentation, we settled on the following parameter settings:

- We have obtained the best results with a 5-gram language model. The beginning and the end of each word were marked by special symbols.
- The alignments produced by GIZA++ are combined with the *grow-diag-final* method.
- We chose to disable distortion, which accounts for the possibility of swapping elements; there is not much evidence of this phenomenon in the evolution of Slovene.
- We use *Good Turing discounting* to adjust the weights of rare alignments.
- We set 20% of L_{goo} aside for *Minimum Error Rate Training*.

The candidates proposed by the C-SMT system are not necessarily existing modern Slovene words. Following Vilar et al. (2007), we added a

[7] It is customary to use a larger dataset for the language model than for the translation model. However, adding the Sloleks data to the language model did not improve performances.

Period	Total	Baseline	Supervised		Unsupervised	
			No lex filter	With lex filter	No lex filter	With lex filter
18B	3199	493 (15.4%)	2024 (63.3%)	2316 (72.4%)	1289 (40.3%)	1563 (48.9%)
19A	3638	1708 (46.9%)	2611 (71.8%)	2941 (80.0%)	2327 (64.0%)	2644 (72.7%)
19B	10033	8281 (82.5%)	8707 (86.8%)	9298 (92.7%)	8384 (83.6%)	8766 (87.4%)

Table 5: Results of the supervised and the unsupervised experiments on L_{foo}.

lexicon filter, which selects the first candidate proposed by the C-SMT that also occurs in Sloleks.[8]

The results of these experiments, with and without lexicon filter, are shown in Table 5. As a baseline, we consider the words that are identical in both language varieties. Without lexicon filter, we obtain significant improvements over the baseline for the first two time spans, but as the language varieties become closer and the proportion of identical words increases, the SMT model becomes less efficient. In contrast to Vilar et al. (2007), we have found the lexicon filter to be very useful: it improves the results by nearly 10% absolute in 18B and 19A, and by 5% in 19B.

4.2 Unsupervised Learning

The supervised approach requires a bilingual training lexicon which associates old words with modern words. Such lexicons may not be available for a given language variety. In the second experiment we investigate what can be achieved with purely monolingual data. Concretely, we propose a bootstrapping step to collect potential cognate pairs from two monolingual word lists (the historical words of L_{goo}, and Sloleks). We then train the C-SMT system on these hypothesized pairs.

The bootstrapping step consists of searching, for each historical word of L_{goo}, its most similar modern words in Sloleks.[9] The similarity between two words is computed with the BI-SIM measure (Kondrak and Dorr, 2004). BI-SIM is a measure of graphemic similarity which uses character bigrams as basic units. It does not allow crossing alignments, and it is normalized by the length of the longer string. As a result, this measure captures a certain degree of context sensitivity, avoids counterintuitive alignments and favours associations between words of similar lengths. BI-SIM is a language-independent measure and therefore well-suited for this bootstrapping step.

For each old Slovene word, we keep the correspondences that maximize the BI-SIM value, but only if this value is greater than 0.8.[10] For the 18B slice, this means that 812 out of 1333 historical words (60.9%) have been matched with at least one modern word; 565 of the matches (69.6%, or 42.4% of the total) were correct.

These word correspondences are then used to train a C-SMT model, analogously to the supervised approach. As for the language model, it is trained on Sloleks, since the modernized forms of L_{goo} are not supposed to be known. Due to the smaller training set size, MERT yielded unsatisfactory results; we used the default weights of Moses instead. The other settings are the same as reported in Section 4.1. Again, we conducted experiments for the three time slices. We tested the system on the word pairs of the L_{foo} lexicon, as above. Results are shown in Table 5.

While the unsupervised approach performs significantly less well on the 18B period, the differences gradually diminish for the subsequent time slices; the model always performs better than the baseline. Again, the lexicon filter proves useful in all cases.

5 Conclusion

We have successfully applied the C-SMT approach to modernize historical words, obtaining up to 57.0% (absolute) accuracy improvements with the supervised approach and up to 33.5% (absolute) with the unsupervised approach. In the future, we plan to extend our model to modernize entire texts in order to take into account possible tokenization changes.

[8]In practice, we generated 50-best candidate lists with Moses, and applied the lexicon filter on that lists. In case none of the 50 candidates occurs in Sloleks, the filter returns the candidate with the best Moses score.

[9]In order to speed up the process and remove some noise, we excluded hapaxes from L_{goo} and all but the 20,000 most frequent words from Sloleks. We also excluded words that contain less than four characters from both corpora, since the similarity measures proved unreliable on them.

[10]This threshold has been chosen empirically on the basis of earlier experiments, and allows us to eliminate correspondences that are likely to be wrong. If several modern words correspond to the same old word, we keep all of them.

Acknowledgements

The authors thank the anonymous reviewers for their comments — all errors, of course, remain our own. This work has been partially funded by the LabEx EFL (ANR/CGI), operation LR2.2, by the EU IMPACT project "Improving Access to Text" and the Google Digital Humanities Research Award "Language models for historical Slovenian".

References

Alistair Baron and Paul Rayson. 2008. VARD 2: A tool for dealing with spelling variation in historical corpora. In *Proceedings of the Postgraduate Conference in Corpus Linguistics*, Birmingham, UK. Aston University.

Tomaž Erjavec. 2012. The goo300k corpus of historical Slovene. In *Proceedings of the Eighth International Conference on Language Resources and Evaluation, LREC'12*, Paris. ELRA.

Marcello Federico, Nicola Bertoldi, and Mauro Cettolo. 2008. IRSTLM: an open source toolkit for handling large scale language models. In *Proceedings of Interspeech 2008*, Brisbane.

Darja Fišer and Nikola Ljubešić. 2011. Bilingual lexicon extraction from comparable corpora for closely related languages. In *Proceedings of the International Conference on Recent Advances in Natural Language Processing (RANLP'11)*, pages 125–131.

Mike Kestemont, Walter Daelemans, and Guy De Pauw. 2010. Weigh your words – memory-based lemmatization for Middle Dutch. *Literary and Linguistic Computing*, 25:287–301.

Philipp Koehn and Kevin Knight. 2002. Learning a translation lexicon from monolingual corpora. In *Proceedings of the ACL 2002 Workshop on Unsupervised Lexical Acquisition (SIGLEX 2002)*, pages 9–16, Philadelphia.

Philipp Koehn, Hieu Hoang, Alexandra Birch, Chris Callison-Burch, Marcello Federico, Nicola Bertoldi, Brooke Cowan, Wade Shen, Christine Moran, Richard Zens, Chris Dyer, Ondrej Bojar, Alexandra Constantin, and Evan Herbst. 2007. Moses: Open source toolkit for statistical machine translation. In *Proceedings of the 45th Annual Meeting of the Association for Computational Linguistics (ACL'07), demonstration session*, Prague.

Grzegorz Kondrak and Bonnie Dorr. 2004. Identification of confusable drug names: A new approach and evaluation methodology. In *In Proceedings of COLING 2004*, pages 952–958.

Grzegorz Kondrak, Daniel Marcu, and Kevin Knight. 2003. Cognates can improve statistical translation models. In *Proceedings of NAACL-HLT 2003*.

Gideon S. Mann and David Yarowsky. 2001. Multipath translation lexicon induction via bridge languages. In *Proceedings of the Second Meeting of the North American Chapter of the Association for Computational Linguistics (NAACL 2001)*, pages 151–158, Pittsburgh.

Franz Josef Och and Hermann Ney. 2003. A systematic comparison of various statistical alignment models. *Computational Linguistics*, 29(1):19–51.

Michael Piotrowski. 2012. *Natural Language Processing for Historical Texts*. Synthesis Lectures on Human Language Technologies. Morgan & Claypool.

Ulrich Reffle. 2011. Efficiently generating correction suggestions for garbled tokens of historical language. *Natural Language Engineering*, 17:265–282.

Silke Scheible, Richard J. Whitt, Martin Durrell, and Paul Bennett. 2010. Annotating a Historical Corpus of German: A Case Study. In *Proceedings of the LREC 2010 Workshop on Language Resources and Language Technology Standards*, Paris. ELRA.

Silke Scheible, Richard J. Whitt, Martin Durrell, and Paul Bennett. 2011. A Gold Standard Corpus of Early Modern German. In *Proceedings of the 5th Linguistic Annotation Workshop*, pages 124–128, Portland, Oregon, USA, June. Association for Computational Linguistics.

Felipe Sánchez-Martínez, Isabel Martínez-Sempere, Xavier Ivars-Ribes, and Rafael C. Carrasco. 2013. An open diachronic corpus of historical Spanish: annotation criteria and automatic modernisation of spelling. Research report, Departament de Llenguatges i Sistemes Informàtics, Universitat d'Alacant, Alicante. `http://arxiv.org/abs/1306.3692`.

Jörg Tiedemann and Peter Nabende. 2009. Translating transliterations. *International Journal of Computing and ICT Research*, 3(1):33–41. Special Issue of Selected Papers from the fifth international conference on computing and ICT Research (ICCIR 09), Kampala, Uganda.

Jörg Tiedemann. 2009. Character-based PSMT for closely related languages. In *Proceedings of the 13th Conference of the European Association for Machine Translation (EAMT 2009)*, pages 12 – 19, Barcelona.

David Vilar, Jan-Thorsten Peter, and Hermann Ney. 2007. Can we translate letters? In *Proceedings of the Second Workshop on Statistical Machine Translation*, pages 33–39, Prague.

Improving English-Russian sentence alignment through POS tagging and Damerau-Levenshtein distance

Andrey Kutuzov
National Research University Higher School of Economics
Moscow, Russia
Myasnitskaya str. 20
akutuzov72@gmail.com

Abstract

The present paper introduces approach to improve English-Russian sentence alignment, based on POS-tagging of automatically aligned (by HunAlign) source and target texts. The initial hypothesis is tested on a corpus of bitexts. Sequences of POS tags for each sentence (exactly, nouns, adjectives, verbs and pronouns) are processed as "words" and Damerau-Levenshtein distance between them is computed. This distance is then normalized by the length of the target sentence and is used as a threshold between supposedly mis-aligned and "good" sentence pairs. The experimental results show precision 0.81 and recall 0.8, which allows the method to be used as additional data source in parallel corpora alignment. At the same time, this leaves space for further improvement.

1 Introduction

Parallel multilingual corpora have long ago become a valuable resource both for academic and for industrial computational linguistics. They are employed for solving problems of machine translation, for research in comparative language studies and many more.

One of difficult tasks in parallel multilingual corpora building is alignment of its elements with each other, that is establishing a set of links between words and phrases of source and target language segments (Tiedemann, 2003). Alignment can be done on the level of words, sentences, paragraphs or whole documents in text collection. Most widely used are word and sentence alignment, and the present paper deals with the latter one.

Word alignment is an essential part of statistical machine translation workflow. However, usually it can only be done after sentence alignment is already present. Accordingly, there have been extensive research on the ways to improve it.

Basic algorithm of sentence alignment simply links sentences from source and target text in order of their appearance in the texts. E.g., sentence number 1 in the source corresponds to sentence number 1 in the target etc. But this scheme by design can't handle one-to-many, many-to-one and many-to-many links (a sentence translated by two sentences, two sentences translated by one, etc) and is sensitive to omissions in source or translated text.

Mainstream ways of coping with these problems and increasing alignment quality include considering sentence length (Gale and Church, 1991) and using bilingual dictionaries (Och and Ney, 2000) or cognates (Simard et al., 1992) to estimate the possibility of sentences being linked. Kedrova and Potemkin (2008) showed that these ways provide generally good results for Russian as well.

But often this is not enough. Sentence length can vary in translation, especially when translation language is typologically different from the source one. As for bilingual dictionaries, it is sometimes problematic to gather and compile a useful set of them.

Thus, various additional methods were proposed, among them using part-of speech data from both source and target texts. It is rather commonplace in word alignment (Tiedemann, 2003; Toutanova et al., 2002). Using part-of speech tagging to improve sentence alignment for Chinese-English parallel corpus is presented in (Chen and Chen, 1994). In the current paper we propose to use similar approach in aligning English-Russian translations.

2 Setting up the Experiment

We test the part-of-speech based approach to improve quality of sentence alignment in our parallel corpus of learner translations available at http://rus-ltc.org. Only English to Russian translations were selected, as of now. The workflow was as follows.

All source and target texts were automatically aligned with the help of HunAlign software (Varga et al., 2005) together with its wrapper LF Aligner by András Farkas (http://sourceforge.net/projects/aligner). The choice of aligner was based on high estimation by researchers (cf. (Kaalep and Veskis, 2007)) and its open-source code. Sentence splitting was done with a tool from Europarl v3 Preprocessing Tools (http://www.statmt.org/europarl) written by Philipp Koehn and Josh Schroeder. Proper lists of non-breaking prefixes were used for both Russian and English.

HunAlign uses both bilingual dictionaries and Gale-Church sentence-length information. Its results are quite good, considering the noisiness of our material. However, about 30 percent of sentences are still mis-aligned. The reasons behind this are different, but mostly it is sentence splitter errors (notwithstanding its preparation for Russian), omissions or number of sentences changing during translation. Here is a typical example:

"And these two fuels are superior to ethanol, Liao says, because they have a higher energy density, do not attract water, and are noncorrosive". ||| "Эти два вида топлива явно превосходят этанол по своим свойствам."

0 ||| "По словам Ляо, они обладают более высокой энергетической плотностью, не содержат воду, а значит некоррозийные."

The translator transformed one English sentence into two Russian sentences. Consequently, aligner linked the first Russian sentence to the source one, and the second sentence is left without its source counterpart (null link). It should be said that in many cases HunAlign manages to cope with such problems, but not always, as we can see in the example above.

The cases of mis-alignment must be human corrected, which is very time-expensive, especially because there is no way to automatically assess the quality of alignment. HunAlign's internal measure of quality is often not very helpful. For example, for the first row of the table above it assigned rather high quality mark of 0.551299. Trying to predict alignment correctness with the help of Hun quality mark only for the whole our data set resulted in precision 0.727 and recall 0.548, which is much lower than our results presented below.

We hypothesize that source and target sentence should in most cases correspond in the number and order of content parts of speech (POS). This data can be used to trace mis-aligned sentences and perhaps to find correct equivalents for them. In order to test this hypothesis, our source and target texts were POS-tagged using Freeling 3.0 suite of language analyzers (Padró and Stanilovsky, 2012). Freeling gives comparatively good results in English and Russian POS-tagging, using Markov trigram scheme trained on large disambiguated corpus.

Freeling tag set for English follows that of Penn TreeBank, while Russian tag set, according to Freeling manual, corresponds to EAGLES recommendations for morphosyntactic annotation of corpora described on http://www.ilc.cnr.it/EAGLES96/home.html (Monachini and Calzolari, 1996). It is not trivial to project one scheme onto another completely, except for the main content words – nouns, verbs and adjectives. Moreover, these three parts of speech are the ones used in the paper by Chen and Chen (1994), mentioned above. So, the decision was made to take into consideration only the aforementioned lexical classes, with optional inclusion of pronouns (in real translations they often replace nouns and vice versa).

Thus, each sentence was assigned a "POS watermark", indicating number and order of content words in it. Cf. the following sentence:

"Imagine three happy people each win $1 million in the lottery."

and its "POS watermark":

VANVNN,

where N is noun, A is adjective and V is verb.

Here is the same analysis for its Russian translation counterpart:

"Представим себе трех счастливых людей, которые выиграли в лотерею по миллиону долларов."

Corresponding "POS watermark":

VPANVNNN,

where N is noun, V is verb, A is adjective and P is pronoun.

Nouns and verbs are marked identically in Penn

and EAGLES schemes. Adjectives in Penn are marked as JJ, so this mark was corrected to A, which is also the mark for adjectives in EAGLES. We considered to be 'pronouns' (P) those words which are marked as "E" in EAGLES and "PRP" in Penn.

Thus, each content word is represented as one letter strictly corresponding to one lexical class. Therefore our "POS watermark" can be thought of as a kind of "word". The difference between these "words" is computed using Damerau-Levenshtein distance (Damerau, 1964). Basically, it is the number of corrections, deletions, additions and transpositions needed to transform one character sequence into another. We employ Python implementation of this algorithm by Michael Homer (published at http://mwh.geek.nz/2009/04/26/python-damerau-levenshtein-distance).

According to it, the distance between POS watermarks of two sentence above is 2. It means we need only two operations – adding one pronoun and one noun – to get target POS structure from source POS structure. At the same time, the distance between VPVNANNNNNNNNNNVN and NVNNANANANN is as high as 10, which means that POS structures of these sentences are quite different. Indeed, the sentences which generated these structures are obviously mis-aligned:

"If a solar panel ran its extra energy into a vat of these bacteria, which could use the energy to create biofuel, then the biofuel effectively becomes a way to store solar energy that otherwise would have gone to waste." ||| "Однако они вырабатывают энергии больше, чем требуется."

One can suppose that there is correlation between Damerau-Levenshtein distance and the quality of alignment: the more is the distance the more is the possibility that the alignment of these two sentences has failed in one or the other way. In the following chapter we present the results of the preliminary experiment on our parallel texts.

3 The Results

We performed testing of the hypothesis over 170 aligned English-Russian bi-texts containing 3263 sentence pairs. As of genres of original texts, they included essays, advertisements and informational passages from mass media. The dataset was hand-annotated and mis-aligned sentence pairs marked (663 pairs, 20 percent of total dataset).

Damerau-Levenshtein distances for all sentences were computed and we tried to find optimal distance threshold to cut "bad" sentence pairs from "good" ones.

For this we used Weka software (Hall et al., 2009) and its Threshold Selector – a meta-classifier that selects a mid-point threshold on the probability output by a classifier (logistic regression in our case). Optimization was performed for "bad" class, and we used both precision and F-measure for determining the threshold, with different results presented below. The results were evaluated with 3-fold cross-validation over the entire dataset.

Initially, on the threshold 7 we achieved precision 0.78, recall 0.77 and F-measure 0.775 for the whole classifier. F-measure for detecting only mis-aligned sentences was as low as 0.464.

In order to increase the quality of detection we tried to change the settings: first, to change the number of "features", i.e., parts of speech considered. "Minimalist" approach with only nouns and adjectives lowered F-measure to 0.742. However, considering nouns, adjectives and verbs without pronouns seemed more promising: using the same distance threshold 7 we got precision 0.787 and recall 0.78 with F-measure 0.783. F-measure for detecting mis-aligned sentences also got slightly higher, up to 0.479. So, general estimate is even higher than when using pronouns.

Moving further in an effort to improve the algorithm, we found that Damerau-Levenshtein distance shows some kind of dis-balance when comparing short and long "words". Short "words" receive low distance estimates simply because the number of characters is small and it's "easier" to transform one into another, even if the "words" are rather different. At the same time, long "words" tend to receive higher distance estimates because of higher probability of some variance in them, even if the "words" represent legitimate sentence pairs. Cf. the following pairs:

- distance between PVPVAA and ANAN is estimated as 5,
- distance between NNNNVAANNVVN-NVNNNVV and NNNNVANANPAN-NANVN is estimated as 7.

Meanwhile, the first sentence pair is in fact mis-aligned, and the second one is quite legitimate. It is obvious that "word" length influences results of distance estimation and it should be somehow compensated.

Thus, the penalty was assigned to all distances, depending on the length of original sentences. Then this "normalized" distance was used as a threshold. We tried employing the length of the source sentence, of target sentence and the average of both. The length of the target (translated) sentence gave the best results.

So, the equation is as follows:

$DLnorm = \frac{DL(sP,tP)}{LEN(tP)}$,

where DLnorm is "normalized" distance, DL is original Damerau-Levenshtein distance, sP is "POS watermark" for source sentence, tP is "POS watermark" for target sentence and LEN is length in characters.

With nouns, verbs, adjectives and pronouns this normalization gives considerably better results:

Precision 0.813

Recall 0.802

F-Measure 0.807

After removing pronouns from consideration, at the optimal threshold of 0.21236, recall gets slightly higher:

Precision 0.813

Recall 0.803

F-Measure 0.808

Even "minimalist" nouns-and-adjectives approach improves after normalization:

Precision: 0.792

Recall: 0.798

F-Measure: 0.795

Overall results are presented in the Table 1.

Methods without target length penalty provide considerably lower overall performance, thus, methods with the penalty should be used.

Depending on particular aim, one can vary the threshold used in classification. In most cases, mis-aligned pairs are of more interest than "good pairs". If one's aim is to improve precision of "bad pairs" detection, the threshold of 0.8768 will give 0.851 precision for this, at the expense of recall as low as 0.1. If one wants more balanced output, the already mentioned threshold of 0.21236 is optimal, providing mis-aligned pairs detection precision of 0.513 and recall of 0.584.

Figure 1 presents distribution of "good" and "bad" pairs in our data set in relation to Damerau-Levenshtein distance (X axis). Correctly aligned pairs are colored gray and incorrectly aligned ones black. Correlation between alignment correctness and Levenshtein value can be clearly seen. At the same time, internal HunAlign quality measure (Y axis) does not show any stable influence on alignment correctness, as we already mentioned above.

Method	**Precision**	**Recall**	**F-Measure**
Nouns, adjectives, verbs and pronouns without length penalty.	0.78	0.77	0.775
Nouns, adjectives and verbs without length penalty.	0.787	0.78	0.783
Nouns and adjectives without length penalty.	0.764	0.728	0.742
Nouns and adjectives with target length penalty.	0.792	0.798	0.795
Nouns, adjectives, verbs and pronouns with target length penalty.	0.813	0.802	0.807
Nouns, adjectives and verbs with target length penalty.	**0.813**	**0.803**	**0.808**

Table 1. Overall performance of pairs classifier depending on the method.

4 Discussion and Further Research

The experimental results presented above show that number and order of POS in source and target sentences in English-Russian translations are similar to the degree that makes possible to use this similarity in order to check alignment correctness. The method of calculating Damerau-Levenshtein distance between POS "watermarks" of source and target sentences can be applied for detecting mis-aligned sentence pairs as an additional factor, influencing the decision to mark the pair as "bad".

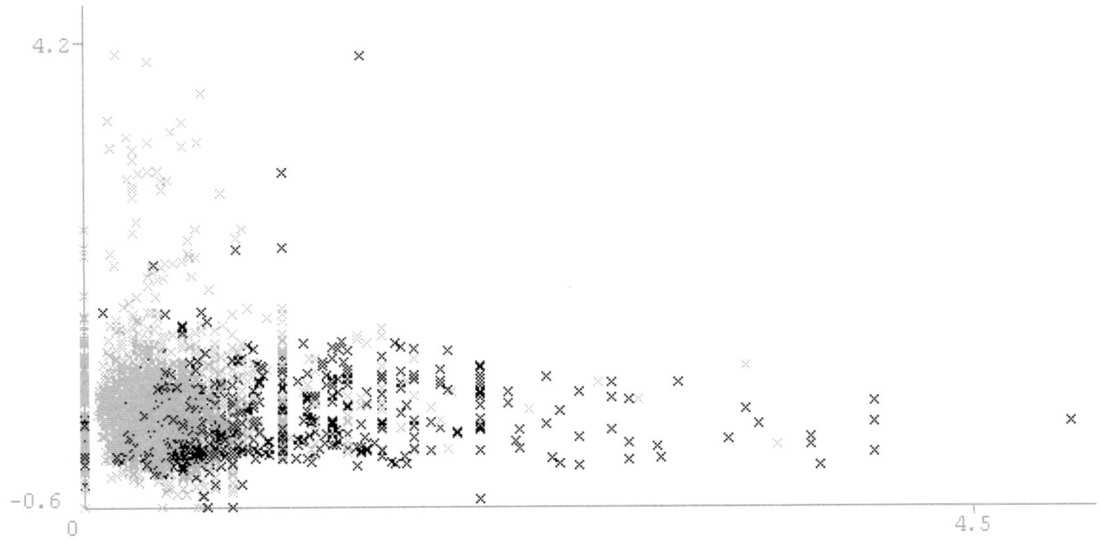

Figure 1. Levenshtein distance (X axis) and alignment correctness (color)

However, some pairs show anomalies in this aspect. For example, the pair below is characterized by normalized POS Damerau-Levenshtein distance of enormous 2.6, however, human assessor marked it as "good":

"An opinion poll released by the independent Levada research group found that only 6 per cent of Russians polled sympathised with the women and 51 per cent felt either indifference, irritation or hostility." ||| "А вот 51 процент опрошенных испытывают к ним равнодушие и даже враждебность."

Translator omitted some information she considered irrelevant, but the pair itself is aligned correctly.

On the other hand, cf. two consecutive pairs below:

"The British Museum? The Louvre?" ||| "Британский музей?"

"The Metropolitan?" ||| "Лувра?"

Normalized distance for the first pair is 0.3333, and this correctly classifies it as "bad". The second target sentence must have belonged to the first pair and the second pair is obviously bad, but its distance equals to zero (because both part contain exactly one noun), so it will be incorrectly classified as "good" with any threshold.

Such cases are not detected with the method described in this paper.

Our plans include enriching this method with heuristic rules covering typical translational transformations for particular language pair. For example, English construction "verb + pronominal direct object" is regularly translated to "pronominal direct object + verb" in Russian:

"She loves him" ||| "Она его любит".

Also we plan to move from passively marking mis-aligned pairs and leaving the actual correction to human to actively searching for possible equivalent candidates among other sentence pairs, especially among those with null links. The difficult part here is designing the method to deal with "partially correct" alignment, for example, like in the pair below:

"The magic number that defines this "comfortable standard" varies across individuals and countries, but in the United States, it seems to fall somewhere around $75,000." ||| "Волшебная цифра, которой определяется уровень комфорта, зависит от самого человека, а также от страны, в которой он проживает."

In the experiment above we considered such pairs to be mis-aligned. But ideally, the second part of the source sentence should be detached and start "looking for" appropriate equivalent. Whether this can be done with the help of POS-tagging (or, perhaps, syntactic parsing), further research will show.

The same is true about the possibility to apply this method to Russian-English translations or translations between typologically distant languages.

5 Conclusion

In this paper, approach to improve English-Russian sentence alignment was introduced, based on part-of-speech tagging of automatically aligned source and target texts. Sequences of POS-marks for each sentence (exactly, nouns, adjectives, verbs and pronouns) are processed as "words" and Damerau-Levenshtein distance between them is computed. This distance is then normalized by the length of the target sentence and is used as a threshold between supposedly mis-aligned and "good" sentence pairs.

The experimental results show precision 0.81 and recall 0.8 for this method. This performance alone allows the method to be used in parallel corpora alignment, but at the same time leaves space for further improvement.

Acknowledgments

The study was implemented in the framework of the Basic Research Program at the National Research University Higher School of Economics (HSE) in 2013.

References

Kuang-hua Chen and Hsin-Hsi Chen. 1994. A part-of-speech-based alignment algorithm. In *Proceedings of the 15th conference on Computational linguistics - Volume 1*, COLING '94, pages 166–171, Stroudsburg, PA, USA. Association for Computational Linguistics.

William A. Gale and Kenneth W. Church. 1991. A program for aligning sentences in bilingual corpora. In *Proceedings of the 29th annual meeting on Association for Computational Linguistics*, ACL '91, pages 177–184, Stroudsburg, PA, USA. Association for Computational Linguistics.

Mark Hall, Eibe Frank, Geoffrey Holmes, Bernhard Pfahringer, Peter Reutemann, and Ian H. Witten. 2009. The weka data mining software: an update. *SIGKDD Explor. Newsl.*, 11(1):10–18, November.

Heiki-Jaan Kaalep and Kaarel Veskis. 2007. Comparing parallel corpora and evaluating their quality. In *Proceedings of MT Summit XI*, pages 275–279.

G.E. Kedrova and S.B. Potemkin. 2008. Alignment of un-annotated parallel corpora. In *Papers from the annual international conference 'Dialogue'*, volume 7, pages 431–436, Moscow, Russia.

Monica Monachini and Nicoletta Calzolari. 1996. Eagles synopsis and comparison of morphosyntactic phenomena encoded in lexicons and corpora. a common proposal and applications to european languages. Technical report, Paris, France.

Franz Josef Och and Hermann Ney. 2000. A comparison of alignment models for statistical machine translation. In *Proceedings of the 18th conference on Computational linguistics - Volume 2*, COLING '00, pages 1086–1090, Stroudsburg, PA, USA. Association for Computational Linguistics.

Lluís Padró and Evgeny Stanilovsky. 2012. Freeling 3.0: Towards wider multilinguality. In Nicoletta Calzolari (Conference Chair), Khalid Choukri, Thierry Declerck, Mehmet Uğur Doğan, Bente Maegaard, Joseph Mariani, Jan Odijk, and Stelios Piperidis, editors, *Proceedings of the Eight International Conference on Language Resources and Evaluation (LREC'12)*, Istanbul, Turkey, may. European Language Resources Association (ELRA).

Michel Simard, George F. Foster, and Pierre Isabelle. 1992. Using cognates to align sentences in bilingual corpora. In *Proceedings of the Fourth International Conference on Theoretical and Methodological Issues in Machine Translation*, pages 67–81.

Jörg Tiedemann. 2003. Combining clues for word alignment. In *Proceedings of the tenth conference on European chapter of the Association for Computational Linguistics - Volume 1*, EACL '03, pages 339–346, Stroudsburg, PA, USA. Association for Computational Linguistics.

Kristina Toutanova, H. Tolga Ilhan, and Christopher D. Manning. 2002. Extensions to hmm-based statistical word alignment models. In *Proceedings of the ACL-02 conference on Empirical methods in natural language processing - Volume 10*, EMNLP '02, pages 87–94, Stroudsburg, PA, USA. Association for Computational Linguistics.

D. Varga, L. Németh, P. Halácsy, A. Kornai, V. Trón, and V. Nagy. 2005. Parallel corpora for medium density languages. In *Recent Advances in Natural Language Processing (RANLP 2005)*, pages 590–596.

Identifying False Friends between Closely Related Languages

Nikola Ljubešić
Faculty of Humanities and Social Sciences
University of Zagreb
Ivana Lučića 3
10000 Zagreb, Croatia
nikola.ljubesic@ffzg.hr

Darja Fišer
Faculty of Arts
University of Ljubljana
Aškerčeva 2
1000 Ljubljana, Slovenija
darja.fiser@ff.uni-lj.si

Abstract

In this paper we present a corpus-based approach to automatic identification of false friends for Slovene and Croatian, a pair of closely related languages. By taking advantage of the lexical overlap between the two languages, we focus on measuring the difference in meaning between identically spelled words by using frequency and distributional information. We analyze the impact of corpora of different origin and size together with different association and similarity measures and compare them to a simple frequency-based baseline. With the best performing setting we obtain very good average precision of 0.973 and 0.883 on different gold standards. The presented approach works on non-parallel datasets, is knowledge-lean and language-independent, which makes it attractive for natural language processing tasks that often lack the lexical resources and cannot afford to build them by hand.

1 Introduction

False friends are words in two or more languages that are orthographically or semantically similar but do not have the same meaning, such as the noun *burro*, which means *butter* in Italian but *donkey* in Spanish (Allan, 2009). For that reason, they represent a dangerous pitfall for translators, language students as well as bilingual computer tools, such as machine translation systems, which would all benefit greatly from a comprehensive collection of false friends for a given language pair.

False friends between related languages, such as English and French, have been discussed by lexicographers, translators and language teachers for decades (Chacón Beltrán, 2006; Granger and Swallow, 1988; Holmes and Ramos, 1993). However, they have so far played a minor role in NLP and have been almost exclusively limited to parallel data (Inkpen et al., 2005; Nakov and Nakov, 2009). In this paper we tackle the problem of automatically identifying false friends in weakly comparable corpora by taking into account the distributional and frequency information collected from non-parallel texts.

Identifying false friends automatically has the same prerequisite as the problem of detecting cognates – identifying similarly (and identically) spelled words between two languages, which is far from trivial if one takes into account the specificity of inter-language variation of a specific language pair. In this contribution we focus on the problem of false friends on two quite similar languages with a high lexical overlap – Croatian and Slovene – which enables us to circumvent the problem of identifying similarly spelled words and use identical words only as the word pair candidate list for false friends.

Our approach to identifying false friends relies on two types of information extracted from corpora. The first one is the frequency of a false friend candidate pair in the corresponding corpora where the greater the difference in frequency, the more certain one can be that the words are used in different meanings. The second information source is the context from corresponding corpora where the context dissimilarity of the two words in question is calculated through a vector space model.

The paper is structured as follows: in Section 2 we give an overview of the related work. In Section 3 we describe the resources we use and in Section 4 we present the gold standards used for evaluation. Section 5 describes the experimental setup and Section 6 reports on the results. We conclude the paper with final remarks and ideas for future work.

2 Related Work

Automatic detection of false friends was initially limited to parallel corpora but has been extended to comparable corpora and web snippets (Nakov et al., 2007). The approaches to automatically identify false friends fall into two categories: those that only look at orthographic features of the source and the target word, and those that combine orthographic features with the semantic ones.

Orthographic approaches typically rely on combinations of a number of orthographic similarity measures and machine learning techniques to classify source and target word pairs to cognates, false friends or unrelated words and evaluate the different combinations against a manually compiled list of legitimate and illegitimate cognates. This has been attempted for English and French (Inkpen et al., 2005; Frunza and Inkpen, 2007) as well as for Spanish and Portuguese (Torres and Aluísio, 2011).

Most of the approaches that combine orthographic features with the semantic ones have been performed on parallel corpora where word frequency information and alignments at paragraph, sentence as well as word level play a crucial role at singling out false friends, which has been tested on Bulgarian and Russian (Nakov and Nakov, 2009). Work on non-parallel data, on the other hand, often treats false friend candidates as search queries, and considers the retrieved web snippets for these queries as contexts that are used to establish the degree of semantic similarity of the given word pair (Nakov and Nakov, 2007).

Apart from the web snippets, comparable corpora have also been used to extract and classify pairs of cognates and false friends between English and German, English and Spanish, and French and Spanish (Mitkov et al., 2007). In their work, the traditional distributional approach is compared with the approach of calculating n-nearest neighbors for each false friend candidate in the source language, translating the nearest neighbors via a seed lexicon and calculating the set intersection to the N nearest neighbors of the false friend candidate from the target language.

A slightly different setting has been investigated by Schultz et al. (2004) who built a medical domain lexicon from a closely related language pair (Spanish-Portuguese) and used the standard distributional approach to filter out false friends from cognate candidates by catching orthographically most similar but contextually most dissimilar word pairs.

The feature weighting used throughout the related work is mostly plain frequency with one case of using TF-IDF (Nakov and Nakov, 2007) whereas cosine is the most widely used similarity measure (Nakov and Nakov, 2007; Nakov and Nakov, 2009; Schulz et al., 2004) while Mitkov et al. (2007) use skew divergence which is very similar to Jensen-Shannon divergence.

The main differences between the work we report on in this paper and the related work are:

1. we identify false friends on a language pair with a large lexical overlap – hence we can look for false friends only among identically spelled words, such as *boja*, which means *buoy* in Slovene but *colour* in Croatian, and not among similarly spelled words, such as the Slovene adjective *bučen* (*made of pumpkins* and *noisy*) and its Croatian counterpart *bučan* (only *noisy*);

2. we inspect multiple association and similarity measure combinations on two different corpora pairs, which enables us to assess the stability of those parameters in the task at hand;

3. we work on two different corpora pairs which we have full control over (that is not the case with web snippets), and are therefore able to examine the impact of corpus type and corpus size on the task;

4. we use three categories for the identically spelled words:

   (a) we use the term *true equivalents* (TE) to refer to the pairs that have the same meaning and usage in both languages (e.g. adjective *bivši*, which means *former* in both languages),

   (b) the term *partial false friends* (PFF) describes pairs that are polysemous and are equivalent in some of the senses but false friends in others (e.g. verb *dražiti*, which can mean either *irritate* or *make more expensive* in Slovene but only *irritate* in Croatian), and

   (c) we use the term *false friends* (FF) for word pairs which represent different concepts in the two languages (e.g. noun *slovo*, which means *farewell* in Slovene and *letter of the alphabet* in Croatian)

By avoiding the problem of identifying relevant similarly spelled words prior to the identification of false friends, in this paper we focus only on the latter and avoid adding noise from the preceding task.

3 Resources Used

In this paper we use two types of corpora: Wikipedia corpora (hereafter WIKI) which have gained in popularity lately because of their simple construction and decent size and web corpora (hereafter WAC) which are becoming the standard for building big corpora.

We prepared the WIKI corpora from the dumps of the Croatian and Slovene Wikipedias by extracting their content, tokenizing and annotating them with morphosyntactic descriptions and lemma information. The web corpora of Croatian and Slovene were built in previous work of Ljubešić and Erjavec (2011). They were created by crawling the whole top-level Slovene and Croatian domains and applying generic text extraction, language identification, near-duplicate removal, linguistic filtering and morphosyntactic annotation and lemmatization.

In terms of content, it is to expect that web corpora are much richer genre-wise while articles in Wikipedia corpora all belong to the same genre. As far as topics are concerned, web corpora are believed to be more diverse but contain a less uniform topic distribution than Wikipedia corpora. Finally, it is to expect that Wikipedia corpora contain mostly standard language while web corpora contain a good portion of user-generated content and thereby non-standard language as well.

Some basic statistical information on the corpora is given in Table 1.

CORPUS	MWORDS	MTOKENS	DOC #
HR.WIKI	31.21	37.35	146,737
SL.WIKI	23.47	27.85	131,984
HRWAC	787.23	906.81	2,550,271
SLWAC	450.06	525.55	1,975,324

Table 1: Basic statistics about the corpora used

Both types of corpora are regularly used in today's NLP research and one of the tasks of this paper is to compare those two not only in relation to the specific task of false friends identification, but on a broader scale of exploiting their contextual and frequency information as well.

4 Gold Standards

The gold standards for this research were built from identically spelled nouns, adjectives and verbs that appeared with a frequency equal or higher than 50 in the web corpora for both languages.

The false friend candidates were categorized in the three categories defined in Section 2: false friends, partial false friends and true equivalents.

Manual classification was performed by three annotators, all of them linguists. Since identifying false friends is hard even for a well-trained linguist, all of them consulted monolingual dictionaries and corpora for both languages before making the final decision.

The first annotation session was performed by a single annotator only. Out of 8491 candidates, he managed to identify 117 FFs, 110 PFFs and 8264 (97.3%) TEs. All the identified FFs and PFFs as well as 380 TEs were then given to two more annotators, shrinking the dataset to be annotated by the other two annotators down to 607 entries, i.e. to only 7% of the initial dataset. The agreement between all three annotators on the smaller dataset is given in Table 2.

ANNOTATORS	INTERSECTION	KAPPA
A1 A2	0.766	0.549
A1 A3	0.786	0.598
A2 A3	0.743	0.501
average	0.765	0.546

Table 2: Inter-annotator agreement on building the gold standards

The obtained average kappa inter-annotator agreement is considered moderate and proves the problem to be quite complex, even for humans well trained in both languages with all the available resources at hand. Since we did not have sufficient resources for all the annotators to revise their divergent annotations, we proceeded by building the following two gold standards:

1. the first gold standard (GOLD1) contains only FFs and TEs on which all the three annotators agreed (60 FFs and 324 TEs) and

2. the second gold standard (GOLD2) contains all entries where at least the first and one of the other two annotators agreed (81 FFs, 33 PFFs and 351 TEs).

We consider GOLD1 to be simpler and cleaner while GOLD2 contains the full complexity of the task at hand.

5 Experimental Setup

We experimented with the following parameters: corpus type, corpus size, association measure for feature weighting, similarity measure for comparing context vectors and gold standard type.

We ran our experiments on two pairs of corpora:

1. one pair originating from local Wikipedia dumps (WIKI) and
2. one pair originating from the top-level-domain web corpora of the two languages (WAC)

We took under consideration the following association measures:

1. TF-IDF (TF-IDF) is well known from information retrieval but frequently applied on other problems as well; we consider context vectors to be information entities and calculate the IDF statistic for a term t and vector set V as follows:

$$IDF(t, V) = \log \frac{|V|}{|\{v \in V : t \in v\}|}$$

2. log-likelihood (LL) (Dunning, 1993) which has proven to perform very well in a number of experiments on lexicon extraction i.e. finding words with the most similar context, performing similarity well as TF-IDF and
3. discounted log-odds (LO) first used in lexicon extraction by Laroche and Langlais (2010), showing consistently better performance than LL; it is calculated from contingency table information as follows:

$$LO = \log \frac{(O_{11} + 0.5)(O_{22} + 0.5)}{(O_{12} + 0.5)(O_{21} + 0.5)}$$

The following similarity measures were taken into account:

1. the well-known cosine measure (COSINE),
2. the Dice measure (DICE), defined in (Otero, 2008) as DiceMin, which has proven to be very good in various tasks of distributional semantics (v_{1f} is the feature weight of feature f in vector v_1):

$$DICE(v_1, v_2) = \frac{2 * \sum_f min(v_{1f}, v_{2f})}{\sum_f v_{1f} + v_{2f}}$$

3. and the Jensen-Shannon divergence (JENSHAN) which shows consistent performance on various tasks:

$$JS(v_1, v_2) = \frac{KL(v_1|v_2)}{2} + \frac{KL(v_2|v_1)}{2}$$

$$KL(v_1|v_2) = \sum_f v_{1f} \log \frac{v_{1f}}{v_{1f} + v_{2f}}$$

We used the standard approach for extracting context and building context vectors and calculated the frequency distribution of three content words to the left and to the right of the headword without encoding their position. We did not perform any cross-lingual feature projection via a seed lexicon or similar, but relied completely on the lexical overlap between the two similar languages.

Apart from the context and its dissimilarity, there is another, very fundamental source of information that can be used to assess the difference in usage and therefore meaning – the frequency of the word pair in question in specific languages. That is why we also calculated pointwise mutual information (PMI) between candidate pairs.

$$PMI(w_1, w_2) = \log \frac{p(w_1, w_2)}{p(w_1) * p(w_2)}$$

We estimated the joint probability of the two words by calculating the maximum likelihood estimate of the identically spelled word on the merged corpora. We considered this measure to be a strong baseline. For a weak baseline we took a random ordering of pairs of words (RANDOM).

Since the result of the procedure of identifying false friends in this setting is a single ranked list of lemma pairs where the ranking is performed by contextual or frequency dissimilarity, the same evaluation method can be applied as to evaluating a single query response in information retrieval. That is why we evaluated the output of each setting with average precision (AP), which averages over all precisions calculated on lists of false friend candidates built from each positive example upwards.

As three categories were encoded in the GOLD2 gold standard, we weighted FFs with 1, TEs with 0 and PFFs with 0.5. In the GOLD1 gold standard FFs were, naturally, weighted with 1 and TEs with 0.

6 Results

In our initial set of experiments we ran a Cartesian product on the sets of corpora types, gold standards, association measures and similarity measures. The results of those experiments are given in Table 3.

WIKI			
GOLD1	COSINE	DICE	JENSHAN
TF-IDF	0.326	0.349	0.337
LL	0.333	0.401	0.355
LO	0.340	0.539	0.434
PMI			0.634
GOLD2	COSINE	DICE	JENSHAN
TF-IDF	0.376	0.392	0.380
LL	0.390	0.440	0.406
LO	0.442	0.561	0.470
PMI			0.581
WAC			
GOLD1	COSINE	DICE	JENSHAN
TF-IDF	0.777	0.757	0.739
LL	0.773	0.934	0.880
LO	0.973	0.324	0.903
PMI			0.629
GOLD2	COSINE	DICE	JENSHAN
TF-IDF	0.694	0.714	0.659
LL	0.714	0.828	0.782
LO	0.883	0.384	0.837
PMI			0.600
RANDOM GOLD1			0.267
RANDOM GOLD2			0.225

Table 3: Average precision obtained over corpora types, gold standards, association measures and similarity measures

The first observation is that the overall results on the WAC corpus pair are about twice as high as the results obtained on the WIKI corpus pair. Since the first is more than 20 times larger than the second, we assumed the amount of information available to be the main cause for such drastic difference.

We then analyzed the difference in the results obtained on the two gold standards. As expected, the results are better on PMI baselines, the RANDOM baseline and in the distributional approach on the WAC corpus pair. The reverse result was obtained with the distributional approach on the WIKI corpus pair and at this point we assumed that it is the result of chance since the results are quite low and close to each other.

6.1 The Baselines

All the results outperformed the weak RANDOM baseline. On the contrary, the strong PMI baseline, which uses only frequency information, proved to be a better method for identifying false friends in the WIKI corpus pair, while it was outperformed by distributional methods on the WAC corpus pair. An important observation regarding PMI in general is that its results relies solely on frequencies of words and having more information than necessary to make good frequency estimates for all the words analyzed cannot improve the results any further. This is the reason why the PMI scores on both corpora pairs regarding the specific gold standard are so close to each other (0.634 and 0.629 on GOLD1, 0.581 and 0.600 on GOLD2), regardless of the much larger size of the WAC corpora pair. This shows that both corpora pairs are large enough for good frequency estimates of the gold standard entries.

Since frequency was not directly encoded in the distributional approach, it seemed reasonable to combine the PMI results with those obtained by the distributional approach. We therefore performed linear combinations of the PMI baseline and various distributional results. They yielded no improvements except in the case of TF-IDF, which still performed worse than most other distributional approaches.

The conclusion regarding PMI is that if one does not have access to a large amount of textual data, pointwise mutual information or some other frequency-based method could be the better way to approach the problem of false friend identification. However, having a lot of data does give advantage to distributional methods. We will look into the exact amount of the data needed to outperform PMI in subsection 6.5.

6.2 Document Alignments on the WIKI Pair

Since PMI performed so well, especially on the WIKI corpus pair on which we have access to document alignments as well, we decided to perform another experiment in which we use that additional information. We calculated the joint probability $p(w_1, w_2)$ not by calculating the maximum likelihood estimate of the identically spelled words in a merged corpus but by taking into account the number of co-occurrences of the identically spelled words in aligned documents only. Naturally, this produced much lower joint probabilities than our initial PMI calculation.

The results of this experiment showed to be as low as the random baseline (0.189 on GOLD1 and 0.255 on GOLD2). The reason was that low-frequency lemmas, many of which are TEs, never occurred together in aligned documents giving those pairs the lowest possible score. When removing the entries that never co-occur, the results did rise slightly over the initial PMI score (0.669 on GOLD1 and 0.549 on GOLD2), but roughly half of the lemma pairs were excluded from the calculation.

To conclude, identifying false friends with a simple measure like pointwise mutual information in case of a limited amount of available data cannot benefit from the additional structure like the Wikipedia document alignments. Having much more data, which would be the case in larger Wikipedias, or applying a more sophisticated measure that would be resistant to scarce data, could prove to be beneficial and is considered a direction for future work.

6.3 Association and Similarity Measures

We continued our analysis by observing the interplay of association and similarity measures. First, we performed our analysis on the much better results obtained on the WAC corpus pair. DICE and LL turned out to be a once-again winning combination. TF-IDF underperformed when compared to LL, showing that LL is the superior association measure in this problem as well. JENSHAN showed a very high consistency, regardless of the association measure used, which is an interesting property, but it never obtained the highest score.

The big surprise was the LO association measure. On the WAC corpus pair it resulted in the overall best score when used with COSINE, but failed drastically when combined with DICE. The situation got even more puzzling once we compared these results with those obtained on the WIKI corpus pair where DICE and LO gave the best overall result. Laroche and Langlais (2010) report to get slightly better or identical results when using LO with COSINE in comparison to DICE.

Trying to find an explanation for such variable results of the LO association measure, we decided to analyze the strongest features in the context vectors of both LO and LL on both corpora pairs. We present our findings in Table 4 on the example of the word *gripa* which means *flu* in both languages. We analyzed the 50 strongest features and classified them in one of the following categories: typo, foreign name, rare term and expected term.

The presented data does shed light on the underlying situation, primarily on the LO association measure, and secondly on the difference between the corpora pairs. LL is a very stable association measure that, regardless of the noise present in the corpora, gave the highest weight to the features one would associate with the concept in question. On the contrary, LO is quite good at emphasizing the noise from the corpora. Since more noise is present in web corpora than in Wikipedia corpora, LO got very good results on the WIKI corpus pair but failed on the WAC corpus pair.

	WIKI			
	SL-LO	SL-LL	HR-LO	HR-LL
typo	0.24	0.00	0.56	0.16
foreign	0.06	0.00	0.22	0.08
rare	0.10	0.00	0.04	0.00
ok	0.60	1.00	0.18	0.76
	WAC			
	SL-LO	SL-LL	HR-LO	HR-LL
typo	0.62	0.00	0.72	0.12
foreign	0.20	0.00	0.26	0.00
rare	0.04	0.00	0.00	0.00
ok	0.14	1.00	0.02	0.88

Table 4: Results of the analysis of the 50 strongest features in the eight different LL and LO vectors

This still did not offer an explanation why LO performed as well as it did on the WAC corpus pair when it was paired with COSINE, or to a smaller extent with JENSHAN. The reason for such behavior lies in the primary difference between DICE and the remaining similarity measures: the latter take into account only the features defined in both vectors while DICE works on a union of the features. Transforming DICE in such a way that it takes into account only the intersection of the defined features did improve the results when using it with LO (from 0.324 and 0.384 to 0.575 and 0.591), but the results deteriorated when used with

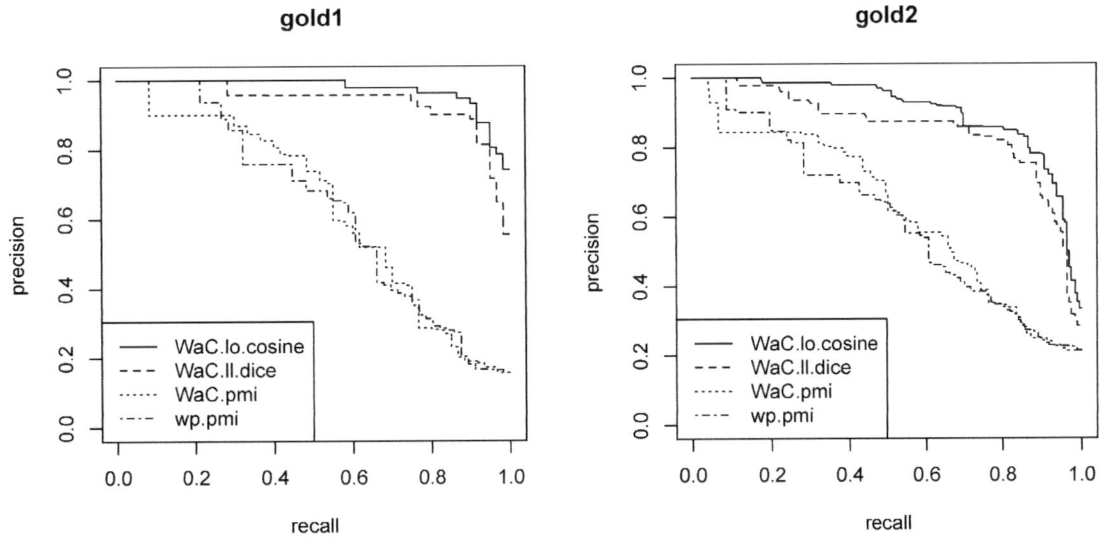

Figure 1: Precision-recall curve of chosen settings on both gold standards

LL (0.934 and 0.828 to 0.768 and 0.719).

We can conclude that LL is a much more stable association measure than LO, but LO performs extremely well as long as the corpora are not noisy or it is not combined with a similarity score that calculates the similarity on a union of the defined features.

6.4 Precision-Recall Curves

We visualized the results obtained with best performing and most interesting settings in Figure 1 with two precision-recall curves, one for each gold standard.

The PR curves stressed the similarity of the results of the PMI method on same gold standards between corpora pairs along the whole precision-recall trade-off spectrum. They also emphasized the significance of the higher quality of the results obtained by the distributional approach on the large WAC corpus pair.

Although somewhat unpredictable, the LO association measure, when coupled with the correct similarity measure, consistently outperformed LL on the whole spectrum on both gold standards.

6.5 Corpus Size

We performed a final set of experiments, which focused on experimenting with the parameter of corpus size. In general, we were interested in the learning curves on different corpora pairs with best performing settings. We also looked for the point where the distributional approach overtakes the frequency approach and a direct comparison between the two corpora pairs.

The learning curves, calculated on random portions of both corpora pairs on GOLD1, are presented in Figure 2. Both PMI learning curves proved our claim that with a sufficient amount of information required to make good frequency estimates, no further improvement can be achieved. On these datasets good estimates were obtained on 5 million words (both languages combined). The PMI learning curve on the WAC corpus pair was steady on the whole scale and we identified the point up to which PMI is more suitable for identifying false friends than distributional methods somewhere around 130 million words (both corpora combined) from where distributional methods surpass the ~ 0.63 plain frequency result.

The WIKI.LL.DICE and the WAC.LL.DICE curves on the left plot enabled us to compare the suitability of the two corpora pairs for the task of identifying false friends and distributional tasks in general. At lower corpus sizes the results were very close, but from 10 million words onwards, the WAC corpus pair outperformed the WIKI corpus pair, consistently pointing toward the conclusion that web corpora are more suitable for distributional approaches than Wikipedia corpora.

The performance of the two distributional approaches depicted on the second graph evened out

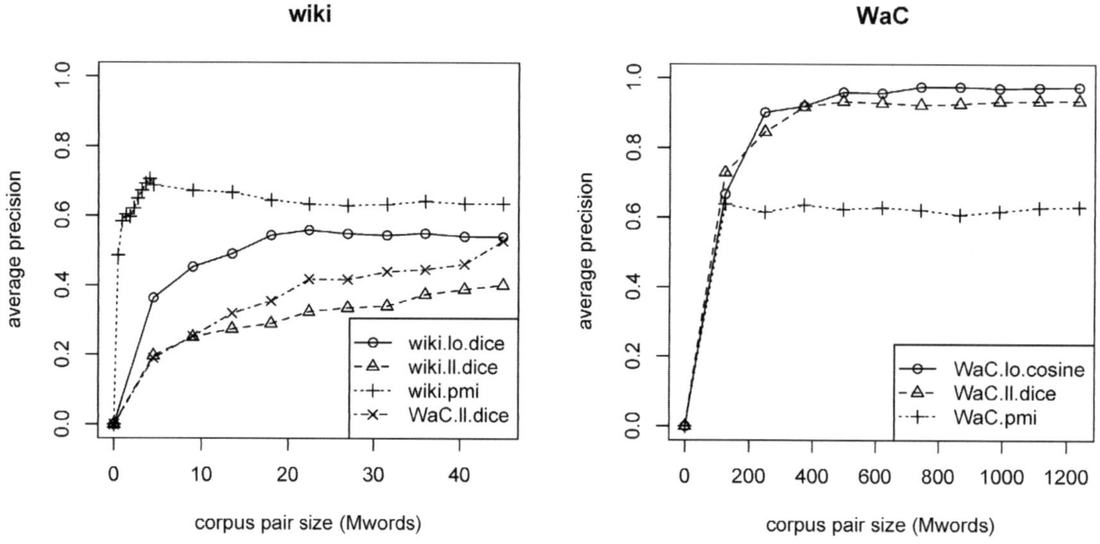

Figure 2: Learning curve on both corpora pairs on GOLD1

around the 500 million word mark, showing that around 250 million words per language should suffice for this task. Having lower-frequency entries in the gold standard would, naturally, call for more data. However, the criterion of 50 occurrences in 500+ million tokens web corpora we used for constructing our gold standards should cover most cases.

Finally, let us point out that the WIKI.LO.DICE curve on the left graph climbed much faster than the WIKI.LL.DICE curve, showing faster learning with the LO association measure in comparison to LL. An interesting observation is that the LO curve obtained its maximum slightly after the 20 million words mark, after which it started a slow decline. Although it could be surprising to see a learning curve declining, this is in line with our previous insights regarding the LO association measure not responding well to many new low-frequency features included in the vector space making the LO+DICE combination struggle. This is one additional reminder that the LO association measure should be used with caution.

7 Conclusion

In this paper we compared frequency-based and distributional approaches to identifying false friends from two frequently used types of corpora pairs – Wikipedia and web corpora. We have used the PMI method for frequency-based ranking and three association and three similarity measures for distributional-based ranking.

The PMI method has proven to be a very good method if one does not have more than 75 million words available per language, in which case it outperformed the more complex distributional approach. Good frequency estimates for PMI were obtained on 2.5 million words per language, after which introducing more data did not yield any further improvement.

Using document alignments from Wikipedia as an additional source for the frequency-based approach did not perform well because of the small size of the Wikipedias in question (slightly above 100,000 articles), often producing zero joint probabilities for non-false friends. A more thought-through approach that could resist data sparsity or using larger Wikipedias is one of our future research directions.

The DICE+LL similarity and association measures proved to be a very stable combination as is the case on the opposite task of translation equivalence extraction (Ljubešić et al., 2011).

The LO association measure gave excellent results, but only if it was paired with a similarity measure that takes into account only the intersection of the features or if the context vectors were calculated on very clean corpora since LO tends to overemphasize low frequency features. We would recommend using this association measure in distributional approaches, but only if one of the above criteria is satisfied.

The amount of data on which the distributional approach stopped benefitting from more data on this task was around 250 million words per language.

Overall, web corpora showed to be better candidates for distributional methods than Wikipedia corpora for two reasons: 1. the WAC learning curve is steeper, and 2. there are few languages which contain 75 million words per language that are necessary to outperform the frequency-based approach and even fewer for which there are 250 million words per language needed for the learning curve to even out.

Our two primary directions for future research are 1. preceding this procedure with identifying language-pair-specific similarly spelled words and 2. including additional language pairs such as Croatian and Czech or Slovene and Czech.

Acknowledgments

The research leading to these results has received funding from the European Union Seventh Framework Programme FP7/2007-2013 under grant agreement no. PIAP-GA-2012-324414 (project Abu-MaTran) and from the Slovene national research programme no. P6-0215.

We would like to thank Daša Berović and Jelena Tušek for their help in annotating the datasets.

References

Keith Allan, editor. 2009. *Concise Encyclopedia of Semantics*. Elsevier Science.

Rubén Chacón Beltrán. 2006. Towards a typological classification of false friends (Spanish-English). *Revista Española de Linguística Aplicada*, 19:29–39.

Ted Dunning. 1993. Accurate methods for the statistics of surprise and coincidence. *Comput. Linguist.*, 19(1):61–74.

Oana Frunza and Diana Inkpen. 2007. A tool for detecting French-English cognates and false friends. In *Proceedings of the 14th conference Traitement Automatique des Langues Naturelles, TALN'07,*, Toulouse.

Sylviane Granger and Helen Swallow. 1988. False friends: a kaleidoscope of translation difficulties. *Langage et l'Homme*, 23(2):108–120.

John Holmes and Rosinda Guerra Ramos. 1993. False friends and reckless guessers: Observing cognate recognition strategies. In Thomas Huckin, Margot Haynes, and James Coady, editors, *Second Language Reading and Vocabulary Learning*. Norwood, New Jersey: Ablex.

Diana Inkpen, Oana Frunza, and Grzegorz Kondrak. 2005. Automatic identification of cognates and false friends in French and English. In *Proceedings of the International Conference on Recent Advances in Natural Language Processing (RANLP 2005)*, pages 251–257.

Audrey Laroche and Philippe Langlais. 2010. Revisiting context-based projection methods for term-translation spotting in comparable corpora. In *Proceedings of the 23rd International Conference on Computational Linguistics*, COLING '10, pages 617–625, Stroudsburg, PA, USA. Association for Computational Linguistics.

Nikola Ljubešić and Tomaž Erjavec. 2011. hrWaC and slWac: Compiling Web Corpora for Croatian and Slovene. In Ivan Habernal and Václav Matousek, editors, *Text, Speech and Dialogue - 14th International Conference, TSD 2011, Pilsen, Czech Republic, September 1-5, 2011. Proceedings*, volume 6836 of *Lecture Notes in Computer Science*, pages 395–402. Springer.

Nikola Ljubešić, Darja Fišer, Špela Vintar, and Senja Pollak. 2011. Bilingual lexicon extraction from comparable corpora: A comparative study. In *First International Workshop on Lexical Resources, An ESSLLI 2011 Workshop, Ljubljana, Slovenia - August 1-5, 2011.*

Ruslan Mitkov, Viktor Pekar, Dimitar Blagoev, and Andrea Mulloni. 2007. Methods for extracting and classifying pairs of cognates and false friends. *Machine Translation*, 21(1):29–53.

Svetlin Nakov and Preslav Nakov. 2007. Cognate or false friend? Ask the Web. In *Proceedings of the RANLP'2007 workshop: Acquisition and management of multilingual lexicons.*

Svetlin Nakov and Preslav Nakov. 2009. Unsupervised extraction of false friends from parallel bi-texts using the web as a corpus. In *Proceedings of the 6th International Conference on Recent Advances in Natural Language Processing (RANLP'09)*, pages 292—298.

Stefan Schulz, Kornél Markó, Eduardo Sbrissia, Percy Nohama, and Udo Hahn. 2004. Cognate mapping - A heuristic strategy for the semi-supervised acquisition of a Spanish lexicon from a Portuguese seed lexicon. In *Proceedings of the 20th International Conference on Computational Linguistics.*

Lianet Sepúlveda Torres and Sandra Maria Aluísio. 2011. Using machine learning methods to avoid the pitfall of cognates and false friends in Spanish-Portuguese word pairs. In *Proceedings of the 8th Brazilian Symposium in Information and Human Language Technology, STIL'11.*

Named Entity Recognition in Estonian

Alexander Tkachenko
Institute of Computer Science
University of Tartu
Liivi 2, Tartu, Estonia
alex.tk.fb@gmail.com

Timo Petmanson
Institute of Computer Science
University of Tartu
Liivi 2, Tartu, Estonia
timo_p@ut.ee

Sven Laur
Institute of Computer Science
University of Tartu
Liivi 2, Tartu, Estonia
swen@math.ut.ee

Abstract

The task of Named Entity Recognition (NER) is to identify in text predefined units of information such as person names, organizations and locations. In this work, we address the problem of NER in Estonian using supervised learning approach. We explore common issues related to building a NER system such as the usage of language-agnostic and language-specific features, the representation of named entity tags, the required corpus size and the need for linguistic tools. For system training and evaluation purposes, we create a gold standard NER corpus. On this corpus, our CRF-based system achieves an overall F_1-score of 87%.

1 Introduction

Named Entity Recognition (NER) is the task of identification of information units in text such as person names, organizations and locations. It is an important subtask in many *natural language processing* (NLP) applications such as text summarization, information filtering, relation extraction and question answering. NER has been extensively studied for widely spoken languages such as English with the state-of-the-art systems achieving near-human performance (Marsh and Perzanowski, 1998), but no research has yet been done in regards to Estonian.

The main difference of Estonian, a Finno-Ugric language, compared to English is high morphological richness. Estonian is a synthetic language and has relatively high morpheme-per-word ratio. It has both agglutinative and fusional (inflective) elements: morphemes can express one or more syntactic categories of the word. Although Estonian is considered a subject-verb-object (SVO) language, all phrase permutations are legal and widely used. These factors make NLP for Estonian particularly complicated.

In this work, we address the problem of NER in Estonian using supervised learning approach. We explore common issues related to building a NER system such as the usage of language-agnostic and language-specific features, the representation of named entity tags, the required corpus size and the need for linguistic tools.

To train and evaluate our system, we have created a gold standard NER corpus of Estonian news stories, in which we manually annotated occurrences of locations, persons and organizations. Our system, based on Conditional Random Fields, achieves an overall cross-validation F_1-score of 87%, which is compatible with results reported for similar languages.

Related work. The concept of NER originated in the 1990s in the course of the Message Understanding Conferences (Grishman and Sundheim, 1996), and since then there has been a steady increase in research boosted by evaluation programs such as CoNLL (Tjong Kim Sang and De Meulder, 2003) and ACE (ACE, 2005). The earliest works mainly involved using hand-crafted linguistic rules (Grishman, 1995; Wakao et al., 1996). Rule-based systems typically achieve high precision, but suffer low coverage, are laborious to build and and not easily portable to new text domains (Lin et al., 2003). The current dominant approach for addressing NER problem is supervised machine learning (Tjong Kim Sang and De Meulder, 2003). Such systems generally read a large annotated corpus and induce disambiguation rules based on discriminative features. Frequently used techniques include Hidden Markov Models (Bikel et al., 1997), Maximum Entropy Models (Bender et al., 2003) and Linear Chain Conditional Random Fields (McCallum and Li, 2003). The downside of supervised learning is the need for a large, annotated training corpus.

Recently, some research has been done on NER for highly inflective and morphologically rich languages similar to Estonian. Varga and Simon (2007) report F_1-score of 95% for Hungarian in business news domain using a Maximum Entropy classifier. Notably, authors state that morphological preprocessing only slightly improves the overall performance. Konkol and Konopík (2011) also use Maximum Entropy based approach for NER in Czech achieving 79% F_1-score. Pinnis (2012) reports F-score of 60% and 65% for Latvian and Lithuanian languages respectively using CRF classifier with morphological preprocessing and some custom refinements. Küçük and others (2009) describe a rule-based NER system for Turkish language which achieves F_1-score of 79%. We observe that the reported results are notably inferior compared to well-studied languages such as English. This can be explained by the language complexity and the lack of required linguistic tools and annotated corpora.

2 The Corpus

Papers on NER for English language commonly use publicly available named entity tagged corpora for system development and evaluation (Tjong Kim Sang and De Meulder, 2003; Chinchor, 1998). As no such resources are available for the Estonian, we have built our corpus from scratch. Our corpus consists of 572 news stories published in the local online newspapers Delfi[1] and Postimees[2] between 1997 and 2009. Selected articles cover both local and international news on a range of topics including politics, economics and sports. The total size of the corpus is 184,638 tokens.

The raw text was preprocessed using the morphological disambiguator `t3mesta` (Kaalep and Vaino, 1998). The processing steps involve tokenization, lemmatization, part-of-speech tagging, grammatical and morphological analysis. The resulting dataset was then manually name entity tagged. Due to the limited resources, the corpus was first tagged by one of the authors and then examined by the other, after which conflicting cases were resolved. Following the MUC guidelines (Chinchor, 1998), we distinguish three types of entities: person names (PER), locations (LOC) and organizations (ORG). Words that do not fall into any of these categories were tagged as *other* (O). We assume that named entities do not overlap. In case a named entity is contained within another named entity, only the top-level entity is annotated. Table 1 and Figure 1 give an overview of named entity occurrences in the corpus.

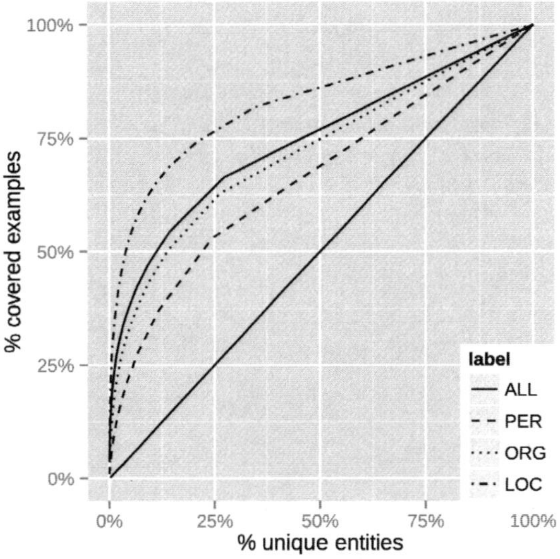

Figure 1: Cumulative number of examples covered by unique entities, starting with the most frequent.

	PER	LOC	ORG	Total
All	5762	5711	3938	15411
Unique	3588	1589	1987	7164

Table 1: Number of named entities in the corpus.

The corpus is organized closely following CoNLL03 formatting conventions (Tjong Kim Sang and De Meulder, 2003). In a data file, each line corresponds to a word with empty lines representing sentence boundaries. Each line contains four fields: the word itself, its lemma, its grammatical attributes[3] and its named entity tag. Named entity tags are encoded using a widely accepted BIO annotation scheme (Ramshaw and Marcus, 1995). Figure 2 demonstrates an example sentence.

The corpus is freely available for research purposes and is accessible at the repository of public language resources of Tartu University (Laur et al.,

[1] `http://delfi.ee`

[2] `http://postimees.ee`

[3] Definition of the attributes can be found at `http://www.cl.ut.ee/korpused/morfliides/seletus.php?lang=en`

11.	11.+0	_O_ ?	O
juunil	juuni+l	_S_ sg ad	O
laastas	laasta+s	_V_ s	O
tromb	tromb+0	_S_ sg n	O
Raplamaal	Rapla_maa+l	_H_ sg ad	B-LOC
Lõpemetsa	Lõpe_metsa+0	_H_ sg g	B-LOC
küla	küla+0	_S_ sg n	I-LOC
.	.	_Z_	O

Figure 2: An example sentence in the corpus: On the 11th of June, a tornado devastated Lypemetsa village in Rapla county.

2013).

3 System Overview

Two important components in the design of a NER system are features and a learning algorithm. Features encode characteristic attributes of words relevant for the classification task. Possible examples of features are word lemma, part of speech, occurrence in some dictionary. The task of a learning algorithm is to study the features over a large collection of annotated documents and identify rules that capture entities of a particular type.

3.1 Features

In our system, we have implemented the following groups of features:

Base-Line Features. This group includes features based mostly on the word's orthography: (1) word itself in lowercase; (2) word prefixes and suffixes of lengths 3-4; (3) word type: is-capitalized, all-capitalized, is-number, is-alphanumeric, contains-dash, contains-apostrophe, contains-digit, contains-dot, contains-capitalized-letter, is-punctuation-mark; (4) word parts before and after a dash in case of compound words; (5) whether the word is first in the sentence.

Morphological Features. These features are based on information provided by morphological disambiguator `t3mesta`: word lemma, POS-tag, word case, word ending, constituent morphemes.

Dictionary-based Features. We composed a large dictionary of entities covering common person names and surnames, local and international organizations and geographical locations. The dictionary contains entities in both Estonian and English. The lists of Estonian entities were obtained from multiple public on-line resources. A large collection of entities in English was downloaded from the web site of the Illinois Named Entity Tagger (Ratinov and Roth, 2009). Table 2 gives an overview of dictionary size and content. The dictionary covers 21% of the unique entities in the corpus, out of which 41% are unambiguous, meaning that the entity matches exactly one category in the dictionary.

Collected entities were preprocessed with a morphological disambiguator `t3mesta`. Words were replaced with their lemmas and turned to lower case. For a dictionary lookup we employed a leftmost longest match approach.

Dictionary Type	Size
Common Estonian first names (KeeleWeb, 2010)	5538
Common first and second names in English (Ratinov and Roth, 2009)	9348
Person full names in English (Ratinov and Roth, 2009)	877037
Estonian locations (Maa-amet, 2013)	7065
International locations in Estonian (Päll, 1999)	6864
Locations in English (Ratinov and Roth, 2009)	5940
Estonian organisations (Kaubandus-Tööstuskoda, 2010)	3417
International organisations (Ratinov and Roth, 2009)	329
Total	903279

Table 2: Dictionaries and numbers of entries.

WordNet Features. Estonian Wordnet is a knowledge base containing more than 27000 different concepts (sets of synonymous words) (Kerner et al., 2010). Wordnet encodes various semantic relationships between the concepts, which can be used as valuable information in NER tasks.

Based on the lemmas and their part-of-speech, we used Wordnet relations to encode hyperonymy, be in a state, belongs to a class and synset id information as extra features.

Global features. Global features enable to aggregate context from word's other occurrences in the same document (Chieu and Ng, 2003). We implemented global features as described in (Ratinov and Roth, 2009). For each occurrence $w_1, \ldots, w_N$ of the word w the set of features $c(w_i)$ is generated: (1) word is capitalized in document at any position, but the beginning of a sentence; (2) preceding word is a proper name; (3) following word is a proper name; (4) preceding word's presence in gazetteers; (5) following word's presence in gazetteers. Then, a set of features of the word w is extended with the aggregated context $\bigcup_{i=1}^{N} c(w_i)$.

3.2 Learning Algorithm

In this work, we use conditional random fields model (CRFs). CRFs are widely used for the task of NER due to their sequential nature and ability to handle a large number of features. Our choice is also substantiated by our earlier experiments on Estonian NER, where CRFs have demonstrated superior performance over a Maximum Entropy classifier (Tkachenko, 2010). We use CRFs implemented in the Mallet software package (McCallum, 2002).

4 Experiments and Results

In this section, we conduct a number of experiments to investigate the system behavior with respect to different factors.

We assess system performance using standard precision, recall and F_1 measure (Tjong Kim Sang and De Meulder, 2003). Scores for individual entity types are obtained by averaging results of 10-fold cross-validation on the full dataset. When splitting the data, document bounds are taken into account so that content of a single document fully falls either into training or test set. In this way, we minimize terminology transfer between samples used for training and testing. To summarize the results of an experiment with a single number, we report the weighted average of a corresponding measure over all entity types.

4.1 Named Entity Tag Representation

The choice of NE tag representation scheme has been shown to have significant effect on NER system performance (Ratinov and Roth, 2009). In this experiment, we set out to determine which scheme works best for the Estonian language. We consider two frequently used schemes – BIO (Ramshaw and Marcus, 1995) and BILOU. BIO format identifies each token as either the beginning, inside or outside of NE. BILOU format additionally distinguishes the last token of multi-token NEs as well as unit-length NEs. Hence, given NEs of three types (per, loc, org), the BIO scheme will produce 7 and BILOU 13 distinct tags.

Table 3 compares system performance using BIO and BILOU schemes. BILOU outperforms BIO in both precision and recall achieving a modest, but statistically significant 0.3 ppt improvement in F_1-score. This agrees with related research for the English language (Ratinov and Roth, 2009). In the following experiments we use a superior BILOU scheme.

Scheme	P (%)	R (%)	F_1 (%)
BIO	87.0	86.3	86.7
BILOU	**87.5**	**86.6**	**87.0**

Table 3: End system performance using BIO and BILOU tag representation schemes. BILOU outperforms BIO (p-value 0.04).

4.2 Feature Utility Analysis

	Feature group	P (%)	R (%)	F_1 (%)
1)	Baseline	83.3	76.8	79.9
2)	1) + Morphological	85.3	84.0	84.7
3)	2) + Dictionary	86.3	85.1	85.7
4)	2) + WordNet	85.4	84.2	84.8
5)	2) + Global	85.7	84.7	85.2
6)	All Features	**87.5**	**86.6**	**87.0**

Table 4: System performance using different groups of features.

Table 4 illustrates system performance using groups of features introduced in Section 3.1. We note that for each token we have included features from its immediate neighbors in the window of size 2. *Morphological* features demonstrate a major effect, increasing F_1-score by 4.8 ppt. Further inclusion of *Dictionary*, *WordNet* and *Global* features improves F_1-score by 1.0, 0.1 and 0.5 ppt respectively. By combining all groups of features, we achieve an overall F_1-score of 87%. Results for individual types of named entities are presented in Table 5. It is worth mentioning, that we have also attempted to do automatic feature selection using χ^2-test and by discarding infrequent features. However, both methods resulted in a significant loss of performance.

NE type	P (%)	R (%)	F_1 (%)
PER	**90.2**	**91.6**	**90.9**
ORG	80.0	74.7	77.1
LOC	89.4	89.6	89.5
ALL	87.5	86.6	87.0

Table 5: End-system performance.

4.3 Corpus Size

In this experiment, we study our system's learning capacity with respect to the amount of the training material. For this purpose, we repeat a 10-

fold cross-validation experiments with an increasing number of documents. In Figure 3, we observe the steepest gain in performance up to 300 documents, which further starts to flatten out. This indicates that our corpus is of an appropriate size for the task at hand, and that our system design is feasible.

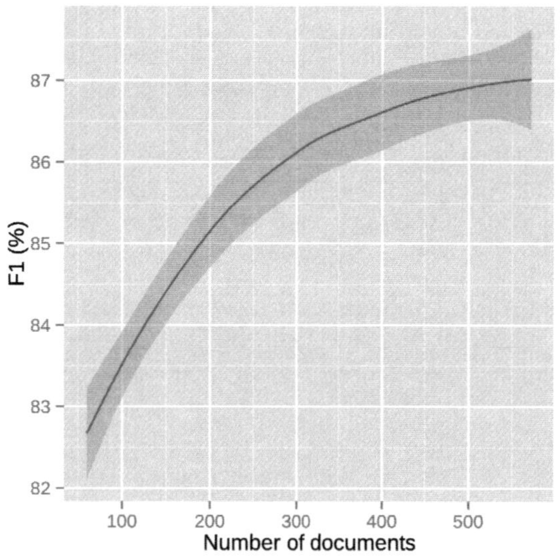

Figure 3: End-system smoothed F_1-score with increasing number of documents in the cross-validation corpus. Shaded area depicts 95% confidence interval.

4.4 NER without Morphological Analysis

In the previous section, we have shown that extending the baseline feature set with morphological features significantly boosts system performance. However, morphological analysis was performed with a commercial tool which may not be available due to licensing restrictions. It is, therefore, interesting to explore system performance without using such language specific features. In this experiment, we omit all the features produced by morphological analyzer. Since we still want to use *dictionary* and *global* features, we need to address an issue of word form normalization. For this purpose, we have built a simple statistical lemmatizer by analyzing lemmas and their inflected forms in Estonian Reference Corpus (Kaalep et al., 2010). As a result, we have achieved F_1-score of 84.8% – a 2.2 ppt decrease compared to the best result (see Table 6).

We conclude that even for highly inflective languages such as Estonian simple techniques for word form normalization, such as our lemmatizer, enable to achieve performance not much inferior than sophisticated linguistic tools.

lemmatizer	P (%)	R (%)	F_1 (%)
custom	86.4	83.3	84.8
t3mesta	**87.5**	**86.6**	**87.0**

Table 6: Performance comparison of NER systems using `t3mesta` and our custom-built lemmatizer.

5 Conclusions

In this work, we have addressed design challenges in building a robust NER system for Estonian. Our experiments indicate that a supervised learning approach using a rich set of features can effectively handle the complexity of the language. We demonstrated the importance of the features based on linguistic information, external knowledge and context aggregation. We observed that the choice of tag representation scheme affects system performance with BILOU outperforming a widely used BIO scheme. We also showed that an acceptable performance in NER can be achieved without using sophisticated language-specific linguistic tools, such as morphological analyzer. Last, but not least, we have built a first gold standard corpus for NER in Estonian and made it freely available for future studies. On this corpus, our system achieves an overall cross-validation F_1-score of 87%.

Acknowledgments

We would like to thank Filosoft[4] for kindly providing us morphological disambiguator `t3mesta`.

References

ACE. 2005. Automatic content extraction 2005 evaluation. Webpage: http://www.itl.nist.gov/iad/mig//tests/ace/ace05/.

Oliver Bender, Franz Josef Och, and Hermann Ney. 2003. Maximum entropy models for named entity recognition. In *Proceedings of the seventh conference on Natural language learning at HLT-NAACL*, volume 4, pages 148–151. Association for Computational Linguistics.

Daniel M Bikel, Scott Miller, Richard Schwartz, and Ralph Weischedel. 1997. Nymble: a high-performance learning name-finder. In *Proceedings*

[4] http://www.filosoft.ee

of the fifth conference on Applied natural language processing, pages 194–201. Association for Computational Linguistics.

Hai Leong Chieu and Hwee Tou Ng. 2003. Named entity recognition with a maximum entropy approach. In *In Proceedings of the Seventh Conference on Natural Language Learning*, pages 160–163.

Nancy Chinchor. 1998. Muc-7 named entity task definition, version 3.5. In *Proc. of the Seventh Message Understanding Conference.*

Ralph Grishman and Beth Sundheim. 1996. Message understanding conference-6: A brief history. In *Proceedings of COLING*, volume 96, pages 466–471.

Ralph Grishman. 1995. The NYU system for MUC-6 or where's the syntax? In *Proceedings of the 6th conference on Message understanding*, pages 167–175. Association for Computational Linguistics.

Heiki-Jaan Kaalep and Tarmo Vaino. 1998. Kas vale meetodiga õiged tulemused? Statistikale tuginev eesti keele morfoloogiline ühestamine. *Keel ja Kirjandus*, pages 30–38.

Heiki-Jaan Kaalep, Kadri Muischnek, Kristel Uiboaed, and Kaarel Veskis. 2010. The Estonian Reference Corpus: its composition and morphology-aware user interface. In *Proceedings of the 2010 conference on Human Language Technologies–The Baltic Perspective: Proceedings of the Fourth International Conference Baltic HLT 2010*, pages 143–146. IOS Press.

Eesti Kaubandus-Tööstuskoda. 2010. List of Estonian organizations. Available at `http://www.koda.ee/?id=1916`.

KeeleWeb. 2010. List of common Estonian first names. Available at `http://www.keeleveeb.ee/`.

Kadri Kerner, Heili Orav, and Sirli Parm. 2010. Growth and revision of Estonian WordNet. *Principles, Construction and Application of Multilingual Wordnets*, pages 198–202.

Michal Konkol and Miloslav Konopík. 2011. Maximum entropy named entity recognition for Czech language. In *Text, Speech and Dialogue*, pages 203–210. Springer.

Dilek Küçük et al. 2009. Named entity recognition experiments on Turkish texts. In *Flexible Query Answering Systems*, pages 524–535. Springer.

Sven Laur, Alexander Tkachenko, and Timo Petmanson. 2013. Estonian NER corpus. Available at `http://metashare.ut.ee/repository/search/?q=Estonian+NER+corpus`.

Winston Lin, Roman Yangarber, and Ralph Grishman. 2003. Bootstrapped learning of semantic classes from positive and negative examples. In *Proceedings of ICML-2003 Workshop on The Continuum from Labeled to Unlabeled Data*, volume 1, page 21.

Maa-amet. 2013. List of Estonian locations. Available at `http://www.maaamet.ee/index.php?lang_id=1&page_id=505`.

Elaine Marsh and Dennis Perzanowski. 1998. Muc-7 evaluation of IE technology: Overview of results. In *Proceedings of the seventh message understanding conference (MUC-7)*, volume 20.

Andrew McCallum and Wei Li. 2003. Early results for named entity recognition with conditional random fields, feature induction and web-enhanced lexicons. In *Proceedings of the seventh conference on Natural language learning at HLT-NAACL*, volume 4, pages 188–191. Association for Computational Linguistics. TEST.

Andrew Kachites McCallum. 2002. Mallet: A machine learning for language toolkit. Available at `http://mallet.cs.umass.edu/`.

Mārcis Pinnis. 2012. Latvian and Lithuanian named entity recognition with TildeNER. *Seed*, 40:37.

Peeter Päll. 1999. Maailma kohanimed. Eesti Keele Sihtasutus. Available at `http://www.eki.ee/knab/mkn_ind.htm`.

Lance A Ramshaw and Mitchell P Marcus. 1995. Text chunking using transformation-based learning. In *Proceedings of the Third ACL Workshop on Very Large Corpora*, pages 82–94. Cambridge MA, USA.

Lev Ratinov and Dan Roth. 2009. Design challenges and misconceptions in named entity recognition. In *Proceedings of the Thirteenth Conference on Computational Natural Language Learning*, pages 147–155.

Erik F Tjong Kim Sang and Fien De Meulder. 2003. Introduction to the CoNLL-2003 shared task: Language-independent named entity recognition. In *Proceedings of the seventh conference on Natural language learning at HLT-NAACL*, volume 4, pages 142–147. Association for Computational Linguistics.

Alexander Tkachenko. 2010. Named entity recognition for the Estonian language. Master's thesis, University of Tartu.

Dániel Varga and Eszter Simon. 2007. Hungarian named entity recognition with a maximum entropy approach. *Acta Cybernetica*, 18(2):293–301.

Takahiro Wakao, Robert Gaizauskas, and Yorick Wilks. 1996. Evaluation of an algorithm for the recognition and classification of proper names. In *Proceedings of the 16th conference on Computational linguistics-Volume 1*, pages 418–423. Association for Computational Linguistics.

On Named Entity Recognition in Targeted Twitter Streams in Polish

Jakub Piskorski
Linguistic Engineering Group
Polish Academy of Sciences
Jakub.Piskorski@ipipan.waw.pl

Maud Ehrmann
Department of Computer Science
Sapienza University of Rome
ehrmann@di.uniroma1.it

Abstract

This paper reports on some experiments aiming at tuning a rule-based NER system designed for detecting names in Polish online news to the processing of targeted Twitter streams. In particular, one explores whether the performance of the baseline NER system can be improved through the incremental application of knowledge-poor methods for name matching and guessing. We study various settings and combinations of the methods and present evaluation results on five corpora gathered from Twitter, centred around major events and known individuals.

1 Introduction

Recently, Twitter emerged as an important social medium providing most up-to-date information and comments on current events of any kind. This results in an ever-growing interest of various organizations in tools for real-time monitoring of Twitter streams to collect their business-specific information therefrom for analysis purposes. Since monitoring the entire Twitter stream appears to be unfeasible due to the high volume of published tweets, one usually monitors targeted Twitter streams, i.e., streams of tweets potentially satisfying specific information needs.

Applications for monitoring Twitter streams usually require named entity recognition (NER) capacity. However, due to the nature of Twitter messages, i.e., being short, noisy, written in an informal style, lacking punctuation and capitalization, containing misspellings, non-standard abbreviations, and non grammatically correct sentences, the application of even basic NLP tools (trained on formal texts) on tweets usually results in poor performances. In the case of well-formed texts such as online news, exploitation of contextual clues is crucial to named entity identification and classification (e.g., '*Mayor of*' in the left context of a capitalized token is a reliable pattern to classify it as city name). Such external evidence is often missing in tweets, and entity names are frequently incomplete, abbreviated or glued with other words. Furthermore, deployment of supervised ML-based techniques for NER from tweets is challenging due to the dynamic nature of Twitter.

In this paper, we report on experiments aiming at tuning a rule-based NER system, initially designed for detecting names in Polish online news, to the processing of targeted Twitter streams. In particular, we explore whether the performance of the baseline NER system can be improved through the utilization of knowledge-poor methods (based on string distance metrics) for name matching and name guessing. In comparison to English, Polish is a free-word order and highly inflective language, with particularly complex declension paradigm of proper names, which makes NER for Polish a more difficult task.

The remaining part of the paper is structured as follows. First, Section 2 provides information on related work. Next, Section 3 describes the baseline NER system and the knowledge-poor enhancements. Subsequently, Section 4 presents the evaluation results. Finally, Section 5 gives a summary and an outlook as regards future research.

2 Related Work

The problem of NER has gained lot of attention in the last two decades and a vast bulk of research on development of NER from formal texts exists (Nadeau and Sekine, 2007). Although most of the reported work focused on NER for major languages, efforts on NER for Polish have also been reported. (Piskorski, 2005) describes a rule-based NER system for Polish that covers the classical named-entity types, i.e., persons, locations, organizations, as well as numeral and temporal expressions. (Marcińczuk and Piasecki, 2007) and (Marcińczuk and Piasecki, 2010) report on a memory-based learning and Hidden Markov Model approach resp. to automatic extraction of information on events in the reports of Polish Stockholders, which involves NER. Also in (Lubaszewski, 2007) and (Lubaszewski, 2009) some general-purpose information extraction tools for Polish are addressed. Efforts related to creation of a dictionary of Warsaw urban proper names oriented towards NER is reported in (Savary et al., 2009; Marciniak et al., 2009). (Graliński et al., 2009) present *NERT*, another rule-based NER system for Polish which covers similar types of NEs as (Piskorski, 2005). Finally, some efforts on CRF-based NER methods for Polish are reported in (Waszczuk et al., 2010) and (Marcińczuk and Janicki, 2012).

While NER from formal texts has been well studied, relatively little work on NER for Twitter was reported. (Locke and Martin, 2009) presented a SVM-based classifier for classifying persons, locations and organizations in Twitter. (Ritter et al., 2011) described an approach to segmentation and classification of a wider range of names in tweets based on CRFs (using POS and shallow parsing features) and Labeled LDA resp. (Liu et al., 2011) proposed NER (segmentation and classification) approach for tweets, which combines KNN and CRFs paradigms. The reported precision/recall figures are significantly lower than the state-of-the-art results for NER from well-formed texts and oscillate around 50-80%. Better results were reported in case of extracting names from targeted tweets (person names from tweets on live sport events) (Choudhury and Breslin, 2011). (Nebhi, 2012) presented a rule-based NER system for detecting persons, organizations and locations which exploits an external global knowledge base on entities to disambiguate NE type. (Liu et al., 2012) proposed a factor graph-based approach to jointly conducting NER and NEN (Named Entity Normalization), which improves F-measure performance of NER and accuracy of NEN when run sequentially. An Expectation-Maximization approach to NE disambiguation problem was reported by (Davis et al., 2012). Finally, (Li et al., 2012) presented an unsupervised system for extracting (no classification) NEs in targeted Twitter streams, which exploits knowledge gathered from the web and exhibits comparable performance to the supervised approaches mentioned earlier.

Most of the above mentioned work on NER in tweets focused on English. To our best knowledge no prior work on NER in tweets in Polish has been reported, which makes our effort a pioneering contribution in this specific field. Our work also contributes to NER from targeted Twitter streams.

3 Named Entity Extraction from Targeted Tweets in Polish

The objective of this work is to explore various linguistically lightweight strategies to adapt an existing news-oriented rule-based NER system for Polish to the processing of tweets in targeted Twitter streams. Starting from the adaptation of a NER rule-based system to the processing of tweets (Section 3.1), we incrementally refine the approach with, first, the introduction of a string similarity-based name matching step (Section 3.2) and, second, the exploitation of corpus statistics and knowledge-poor method for name guessing (Section 3.3).

3.1 NER Grammar for Polish

The starting point of our explorations is an existing NER system for Polish, modeled as a cascade of finite-state grammars using the ExPRESS formalism (Piskorski, 2007). Similarly to rule-based approaches to NER for many other Indo-European languages, the grammars consist of a set of extraction patterns for person, organization and location names. The patterns exploit both internal (e.g., company designators) and external clues (e.g., titles and functions of a person, etc.) for name detection and classification; a simple extraction pattern for person names can be illustrated as follows:

```
PER :> ( ( gazetteer & [TYPE: "firstname",
                        SURFACE: #F] )
         ( gazetteer & [TYPE: "initial",
                        SURFACE: #I] ) ?
         ( surname-candidate & [SURFACE: #L] )
       ):name
  -> name: person & [NAME: #FULL-NAME]
  & #full_name := ConcWithBlanks(#F,#I,#L).
```

This rule first matches a sequence consisting of: a first name (through a gazetteer look-up), an optional initial (gazetteer look-up as well) and, finally, a sequence of characters considered as surname candidate (e.g., capitalized tokens), which was detected by a lower-level grammar[1] and is represented as a structure of type *surname-candidate*. The right-hand side of the extraction

[1]Lower-level grammar extract small-scale structures which might constitute parts of named entities.

pattern specifies the output structure of type *person* with one attribute called NAME, whose value is simply a concatenation of the values of the variables #F, #I and #L assigned to the surface forms of the matched first name, initial and surname candidate respectively.

Overall the grammar contains 15 extraction patterns for person names, 10 for location names, and 10 for organization names. It relies on a huge gazetteer of circa 294K entries, which is an extended version of the gazetteer described in (Savary and Piskorski, 2011) and includes, i.a., 39K inflected forms of both Polish and foreign first names, 86K inflected forms of surnames, 5K of organisation names (only partially inflected), 10K of inflected location names (e.g., city names, country names, rivers, etc.). No morphological analyzer for Polish is used and only a tiny fraction of the extraction patterns relies on morphological information (encoded in the gazetteer). In this original grammar, the patterns are divided into sure-fire patterns and less reliable patterns (whose precision is expected to be lower). The latter ones are patterns that rely solely on gazetteer information (simple look-up), which might have ambiguous interpretation, e.g., patterns that only match first names in text. When applied on conventional online news, the performance of this original NER grammar oscillates around 85% in terms of F-measure.

In order to process tweets, we slightly modified this grammar, mostly by simplifying it. Since mentions of entities in tweets frequently occur as single tokens (e.g., external evidence as in classical news is often missing), we did not keep the distinction between sure-fire and less-reliable patterns. Furthermore, the original NER grammar 'included' a mechanism (encoded directly in pattern specification) to lemmatize the recognized names as well as to extract various attributes such as titles (e.g., '*Pan*' (Mr.)) and position (e.g., '*Prezydent*' (president)) for persons. As we are mainly interested in the detection and classification of NEs while processing tweets, these functionalities were not needed and the grammar simply extracts names and their type. This 'reduced' NER grammar constitutes the baseline approach, and will be referred to as BASE in the remaining part of the paper. It is worth mentioning that we tested as well a version of the grammar with lower-cased lexical resources, but due to poor results (mainly due to high ambiguity of lower-case lexical entries) we did not conduct further explorations in this direction.

3.2 String distance-based Name Matching

In tweets, names are often abbreviated (e.g., '*Parl. Europ.*' and '*PE*' are abbreviations of '*Parlament Europejski*'), glued to other words (e.g., '*prezydent Komorowski*' is sometimes written as '*prezydentKomorowski*') and misspelled variants are frequent (e.g., '*Donlad Tusk*' is a frequent misspelling of '*Donald Tusk*'). The NER grammar 'as is' would fail to recognize the particular names in the aforementioned examples. Therefore, in order to improve the recall of the 'tweet grammar', we perform a second run deploying string distance metrics (in the entire targeted Twitter stream) for matching new mentions of names previously recognized by the NER grammar (see Section 3.1). Furthermore, due to the highly inflective character of Polish, we also expect to capture with string distance metrics non-nominative mentions of names (e.g., '*Rzeczpospolitej* - genitive/dative/locative form of '*Rzeczpospolita*' - the name of a Polish daily newspaper), which the NER grammar might have failed to recognize.

Inspired by the work reported in (Piskorski et al., 2009) we explored the performance of several string distance metrics. First, we tested the baseline *Levenshtein* edit distance metric given by the minimum number of character-level operations (insertion, deletion, or substitution) needed to transform one string into another (Levenshtein, 1965). Next, we used an extension thereof, namely *Smith-Waterman* (SW) metric (Smith and Waterman, 1981), which additionally allows for variable cost adjustment to the cost of a gap and variable cost of substitutions (mapping each pair of symbols from alphabet to some cost). We used a variant of this metric, where the *Smith-Waterman* score is normalized using the *Dice coefficient* (the average length of strings compared).

Subsequently, we explored variants of the *Jaro* metric (Jaro, 1989; Winkler, 1999). It considers the number and the order of the common characters between the two strings being compared. More precisely, given two strings $s = a_1 \dots a_K$ and $t = b_1 \dots b_L$, we say that a_i in s is *common* with t if there is a $b_j = a_i$ in t such that $i - R \leq j \leq i + R$, where $R = \lfloor \max(|s|, |t|)/2 \rfloor - 1$. Furthermore, let $s' = a'_1 \dots a'_{K'}$ be the characters in

s which are common with t (with preserved order of appearance in s) and let $t' = b'_1 \dots b'_{L'}$ be defined analogously. A *transposition* for s' and t' is defined as any position i such that $a'_i \neq b'_i$. Let us denote the number of transpositions for s' and t' as $T_{s',t'}$. The *Jaro* similarity is then calculated as:

$$J(s,t) = \frac{1}{3} \cdot (\frac{|s'|}{|s|} + \frac{|t'|}{|t|} + \frac{|s'| - \lfloor T_{s',t'}/2 \rfloor}{|s'|})$$

A *Winkler* variant of *Jaro* metric boosts this similarity for strings with agreeing initial characters and is calculated as:

$$JW(s,t) = J(s,t) + \delta \cdot boost_p(s,t) \cdot (1 - J(s,t))$$

where δ denotes the common prefix adjustment factor (default value is 0.1) and $boost_p(s,t) = \min(|lcp(s,t)|, p)$. Here $lcp(s,t)$ denotes the longest common prefix between s and t. Further, p stands for the upper bound of $|lcp(s,t)|^2$, i.e., up from a certain length of $lcp(s,t)$ the 'boost value' remains the same.

The *q-gram* metric (Ukkonen, 1992) is based on the intuition that two strings are similar if they share a large number of character-level q-grams. We used a variant thereof, namely *skip-gram* metric (Keskustalo et al., 2003), which exhibited better performance than any other variant of character-level q-grams based metrics. It is based on the idea that in addition to forming bigrams of adjacent characters, bigrams that skip characters are considered. *Gram classes* are defined that specify what kind of skip-grams are created, e.g. $\{0,1\}$ class means that normal bigrams are formed, and bigrams that skip one character. In particular, we tested $\{0,1\}$ and $\{0,2\}$ classes. Due to the nature of Twitter we expected skip-grams to be particularly useful in our experiments.

Considering the declension paradigm of Polish we also considered the basic *CommonPrefix* metric introduced in (Piskorski et al., 2009), which is based on the longest common prefix. It is calculated as:

$$CP(s,t) = (|lcp(s,t)|)^2 / |s| \cdot |t|$$

Finally, we evaluated the performance of *longest common sub-strings* distance metric, which recursively finds and removes the longest common sub-string in the two strings compared. Let $lcs(s,t)$ denote the first longest common sub-string for s and t and let s_{-p} denote a string obtained by removing from s the first occurrence of p in s. The *LCS* metric is calculated as:

$$LCS(s,t) = \begin{cases} 0 \text{ if } |lcs(s,t)| \leq 2 \\ |lcs(s,t)| + LCS(s_{-lcs(s,t)}, t_{-lcs(s,t)}) \\ \text{otherwise} \end{cases}$$

The string distance-based name matching described in this section will be referred to as MATCH-X, with X standing for the name of the string distance metric being used.

3.3 Name Clustering

Since contextual clues for recognizing names in formal texts are often missing in tweets, we additionally developed a rudimentary name guesser to boost the recall. Let us also observe that using string distance metrics described in Section 3.2 to match all not yet captured mentions of previously recognized names might not be easy due the fact that the process of creating abbreviations in Twitter is very productive, e.g., '*Rzeczpospolita*' appears abbreviated as ' *Rzepa*', *Rzp.* or '*RP*, which are substantially different from the original name.

The main idea beyond the name guesser is based on the following assumption: given a targeted Twitter stream, if a capitalized word n-gram has a couple of 'similar' word n-grams in the same stream, most of which are not recognized as valid word forms, then such a group of n-grams word are most likely named mentions of the same entity (e.g., person, organization or location, etc.). To be more precise, the name guesser works as follows.

1. Compute $S = \{s_1, s_2, ...s_k\}$ - a set of word uni- and bigrams (cluster seeds) in the Twitter stream[3], where $frequency(s_i) \geq \phi^4$ and $character - length(s_i) \geq 3$ for all $s_i \in S$.

2. Create an initial set of singleton 'name' clusters: $C = \{C_1, C_2, \dots, C_k\}$ with $C_i = \{s_i\}$.

3. Build clusters of simmilar n-grams around the selected uni- and bigrams

[2]Here p is set to 6.

[3]The vast majority of names annotated in our test corpus are either word unigrams or bigrams (see Section 4.1.)

[4]ϕ We explored various values of this parameter, which is described in Section 4.2

using the string distance metric m: Assign each word n-gram w in the Twitter stream to at most one cluster C_j with $j \in \arg\min_{x \in \{1,2,\dots,k\}} dist_m(s_x, w)$[5], and $dist_m(s_j, w) \leq maxDist$, where $maxDist$ is a predefined constant.

4. Iteratively merge most-simmilar clusters in C: If $\exists C_x, C_y \in C$ with $DIST(C_x, C_y) \leq DIST(C_i, C_j)$ for $i, j \in \{1, \dots, |C|\}$[6] and $DIST(C_x, C_y) \leq maxDist$ then $C = C \setminus \{C_x, C_y\} \cup (C_x \cup C_y)$.

5. Discard 'small' clusters:
$C = \{C_x \in C : |C_x| \geq 3\}$

6. Discard clusters containing high number of n-grams, whose parts are valid word forms, but not proper names: $C = \{C_x \in C : \Sigma_{w \in C_x} \frac{WordForm^*(w)}{|C_x|} \leq 0.3\}$, where $WordForm^*(w) = 1$ if all the words constituting the word n-gram w are valid word forms, but not proper names, and $WordForm^*(w) = 0$ otherwise, e.g., $WordForm^*$(Jan Grzyb) $= 0$ since *Grzyb* (eng. mushroom) can be interpreted as a valid word form, which is not a proper name, whereas *Jan* has only proper name interpretation.

7. Use the n-grams in the remaining clusters in C (each of them is considered to contain named mentions of the same entity) to match names in the Twitter stream through simple lexicon look-up.

For computing similarity of n-grams and merging clusters we used the *longest common substrings* (*LCS*) metric which performed on average best (in terms of F-measure) in the context of name matching (see Section 3.2 and 4). For checking whether tokens constitute valid word forms we exploited *PoliMorf* (Woliński et al., 2012), a freely available morphological dictionary of Polish, consisting of circa 6.7 million word forms, including proper names. Proper names are distinguished from other entries in the aforementioned resource.

The name guesser sketched above will be referred to as CLUSTERING. Instead of building the name clusters around n-grams, whose frequency exceeds certain threshold, we also tested building clusters around least frequent n-grams (i.e., whose frequency is ≤ 3), which will be referred to as CLUSTERING-INFRQ. The name guesser runs either independently or on top of the NER grammar described in Section 3.1 in order to detect 'new' names in the unconsumed part of the tweet collection, i.e., names recognized by the grammar are preserved. It is important to emphasize that the clustering-based name guesser only detects names without classifying them.

4 Experiments

4.1 Dataset

We have gathered tweet collections using Twitter search API[7] focusing on some major events in 2012/2013 and on famous individuals, namely: (a) Boston marathon bombings, (b) general comments on Donald Tusk, the prime minister of Poland, (c) discussion on the public comments of Antoni Macierewicz (a politician of the Law and Justice opposition party in Poland) on the Polish president crash in Smoleńsk (Russia) in 2010, (d) debate on the controversial firing of the journalist Cezary Gmyz from one of the major Polish newspapers *Rzeczpospolita* and, (e) a collection of random tweets in Polish. Each tweet collection was extracted using simple queries, e.g., *"zamach* AND *(Boston* OR *Bostonie)"* ("attack" AND "'Boston"' either in nominative of locative form) for collecting tweets on the Boston bombings. From each collection a subset of randomly chosen tweets was selected for evaluation purposes. We will refer to the latter as the *test corpus*, whereas the entire tweet collections will be referred to as the *stream corpus*.

In the stream corpus, we computed for each tweet: (a) the *text-like fraction* of its body, i.e., the fraction of the body which contains text, and (b) the *lexical validity*, i.e., the percentage of tokens in the text-like part of the body of the tweet which are valid word forms in Polish[8]. Figure 1 and 2 show the histograms for text-like fraction and lexical validity of the tweets in each collection in the stream corpus. We can observe that large portion of the tweets contains significant text-like part, which is

[5] We denote the distance between two strings x and y measured with the string distance metric m as $dist_m(x, y)$

[6] $DIST(C_x, C_y) = \Sigma_{s \in C_x} \Sigma_{t \in C_y} \frac{dist_m(s,t)}{|C_x| \cdot |C_y|}$ (average distance between strings in the two clusters)

[7] https://dev.twitter.com

[8] For computing lexical validity we used *PoliMorf* (Woliński et al., 2012), already mentioned in the previous section.

also lexically valid. Interestingly, the random collection exhibits lower lexical validity, which is due to more colloquial language used in the tweets in this collection.

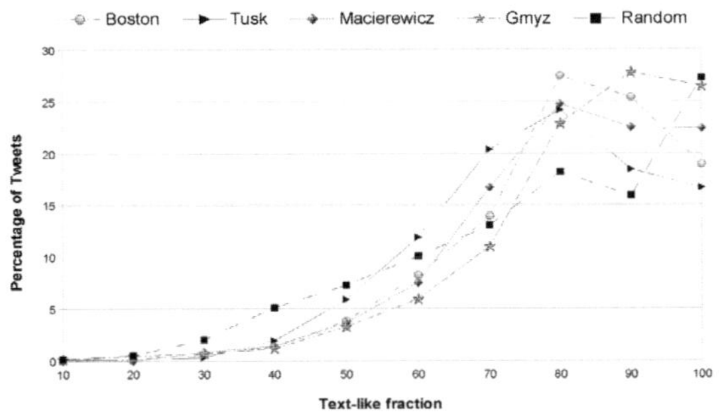

Figure 1: Text-like fraction of the tweets in each collection.

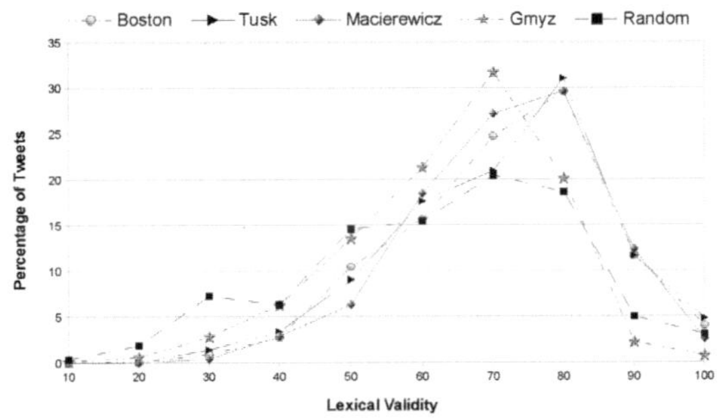

Figure 2: Lexical validity of the tweets in each collection.

We built the *test corpus* by randomly selecting tweets whose text-like fraction of the body was $\geq 80\%$, additionally checking the language and removing duplicates. These tweets were afterwards manually annotated with person, location and organization names, according to the following guidelines: consideration of unigram entities, non-inclusion of titles, functions and alike, non-inclusion of spurious punctuation marks and exclusion of names starting with '@', since their recognition as names is trivial.

The test corpus statistics are provided in Table 1. We provide in brackets the number of tweets in the corresponding tweet collections in the entire stream corpus. In this *test corpus*, 86,7% of the annotated names are word unigrams, whereas bigrams constitute 12,7% of the annotated names and 3- and 4-grams account only for a tiny fraction (0,6%); this is in line with the characteristics of the Twitter language, which favours quick and simple expressions. For each collection, we computed the name diversity as the ratio between entity occurrences and unique entities, as well as the average number of entities per tweet[9]. Targeted stream corpora show a medium name diversity (except for *Boston* and *Gmyz* collections, centred on a very specific location and person name resp.) and a high rate of entity per tweet (around 2.2), in contrast with *random* corpus which shows a high name diversity (0.79) for a low average number of entity per tweets. Reported to the limited number of characters in tweets (140), the important significant number of entity per tweet in targeted streams accounts, on the one hand, for the usefulness of working on targeted streams and, on the other, for the importance of NER in tweets.

Corpus	#tweets	name diversity	#names per tweet	#PER	#LOC	#ORG
Boston	198 (2953)	0.24	2.16	34	298	96
Tusk	232 (1186)	0.36	2.42	393	88	80
Macierewicz	303 (931)	0.32	2.17	494	60	104
Gmyz	310 (672)	0.24	2.09	471	18	159
Random	286 (7806)	0.79	0.36	59	19	27

Table 1: Test corpus statistics.

4.2 Evaluation

In our experiments we evaluated the performance of (i) the NER grammar (BASE), a combination thereof with (ii) different name matching strategies (MATCH) and (iii) different variants of the name guesser (CLUSTERING, CLUSTERING-INFRQ) and, finally, (iv) the combinations of all techniques. Within the MATCH configuration, we experimented all string distance metrics presented in 3.2 but since Jaro, Jaro-Winkler and Smith-Waterman metrics performed on average worse than the others, we did not consider them in further experiments. We selected the best performing metric, *LCS* [10], as the one used by the name guesser (CLUSTERING) in subsequent experiments. As a complement, we measured the performance of the name guesser alone to compare it with BASE. Furthermore, name matching and

[9]In the limit of our reference corpora, i.e. entities of type person, location and organization.

[10]Skip-grams was the other metric which exhibited similar performance

name guessing algorithms were using the tweet collections in the stream corpus (as quasi 'Twitter stream window') in order to gather knowledge for matching/guessing 'new' names in the test corpus.

We measured the performance of the different configurations in terms of Precision (P), Recall (R) and F-measure (F), according to two different schemes: *exact match*, where entity types and both boundaries should match perfectly, and *fuzzy match*, which allows for one name boundary returned by the system to be different from the reference, i.e., either too short or too long on the left or on the right, but not on both. Furthermore, since the clustering-based name guesser described in 3.3 does not classify names, for any settings with this technique we only evaluated name detection performance, i.e., no distinction between name types was made. The overall summary of the results for the entire pool of tweet collections, is presented in Table 3.

In the context of the CLUSTERING algorithm we explored various settings as regards the minimum frequency of an n-gram to be considered as cluster seed (ϕ parameter - see Section 3.3). More precisely, we tested values in the range of 1 to 30 for all corpora and system settings which included CLUSTERING, and compared the resulting P/R and F figures. An example of a curve with P/R values (exact match) of BASE-CLUSTERING algorithm applied on the 'Boston' corpus with varying values of ϕ is given in Figure 3. One can observe and hypothesize that the frequency threshold does not impact much the performance. Suchlike curves for other settings were of a similar nature. Therefore we decided to set the ϕ to 1 in all settings reported in Table 3.

4.3 Results analysis

The performance of the NER grammars is surprisingly good, both in case of exact and fuzzy match evaluation. Except for *random* corpus (which shows rather low performance with 55% precision and 39% recall), precision figures oscillate around 85-95%, whereas recall is somewhat worse (60-75%), as was to be expected. The low recall for 'Gmyz' corpus is due to the non-matching of a frequently occurring person name. Precision and recall figures for each entity type for BASE are given in Table 2. In general, recognition of organization names appears to be more difficult (lower recall), especially in the random corpus.

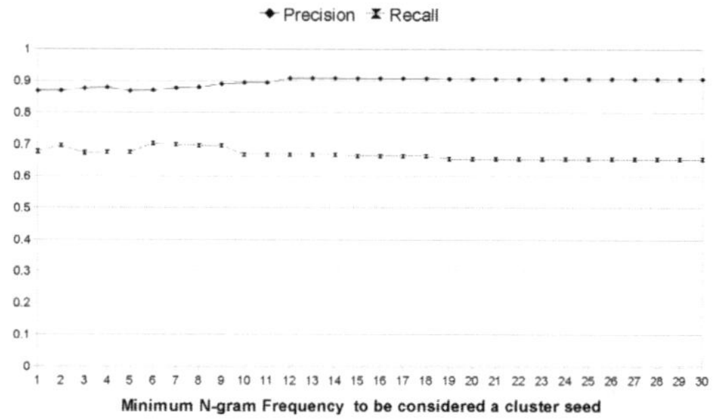

Figure 3: Precision and Recall figures for BASE-CLUSTERING applied on 'Boston' corpus, with different frequency thresholds of n-grams to be considered cluster seeds.

Corpus	PER		ORG		LOC	
	P	R	P	R	P	R
Boston	31.6	35.3	87.9	30.2	94.3	71.8
Tusk	87.6	71.2	82.4	35.0	89.9	70.5
Gmyz	85.5	32.5	82.8	15.1	88.9	44.4
Macierewicz	93.6	80.2	71.2	35.6	83.7	60.0
Random	56.7	55.9	0	0	53.3	42.1

Table 2: Precision/recall figures for person, organization and location name recognition (exact match) with BASE.

Extending BASE with MATCH yields some improvements in terms of recall (including *random* corpus), whereas precision either oscillates around the figures achieved by BASE, or deteriorates. In case of 'Gmyz' corpus, we can observe significant gain in both recall and precision through using the name matching step. With regard to the other corpora, the reason for not obtaining a significant gain could be due to two reasons: (a) the n-grams identified as similar to the names recognized by BASE are already covered by BASE with some patterns (e.g., inflected forms of many entities are stored in the gazetteer), or (b) using string distance metrics in the MATCH step might not be the best method to capture mentions of a recognized entity, as exemplified in Table 4, where the mentions of a newspaper *Rzeczpospolita* (captured by BASE) may be significantly different, e.g., in terms of the character length.

Regarding the results for CLUSTERING-INFRQ, running it alone, yielded poor results for all corpora, only in case of the'Gmyz' corpus a gain could be observed. CLUSTERING performed better than CLUSTERING-INFRQ for all corpora.

Deploying BASE with CLUSTERING on top of it results in up to 1.5-6% (exact match) and 4-

Method	Boston			Tusk			Gmyz			Macierewicz			AVERAGE		
EXACT MATCH															
	P	R	F	P	R	F	P	R	F	P	R	F	P	R	F
BASE	85.6	59.6	70.2	87.7	65.9	75.3	85.3	28.5	42.8	90.5	71.3	79.8	87.3	56.3	67.0
BASE-MATCH-LEV	80.8	62.9	70.7	87.4	66.5	75.5	90.9	63.6	**74.8**	90.2	72.3	80.3	87.3	66.3	75.3
BASE-MATCH-SW	70.9	62.1	66.3	76.6	67.5	71.8	78.0	59.1	68.0	89.4	73.1	80.4	78.7	65.5	71.6
BASE-MATCH-J	67.7	62.1	64.8	79.3	68.1	73.3	60.9	48.3	53.9	60.0	73.3	65.9	67.0	63.0	64.5
BASE-MATCH-JW	63.2	62.1	62.7	75.5	68.3	71.7	48.2	48.9	48.6	58.0	74.0	65.0	61.2	63.3	62.0
BASE-MATCH-SKIP(0,1)	80.9	62.1	70.3	87.6	66.5	75.6	91.3	63.0	74.5	90.3	72.2	80.2	87.5	66.0	75.2
BASE-MATCH-SKIP(0,2)	80.9	62.1	70.3	87.7	66.3	75.5	**91.5**	**63.0**	74.6	**90.6**	72.2	80.4	**87.7**	65.9	75.2
BASE-MATCH-CP	80.2	59.6	68.4	87.7	66.0	75.3	83.5	58.6	68.9	90.2	71.4	79.7	85.4	63.9	73.1
BASE-MATCH-LCS	80.7	63.6	71.1	86.8	67.0	75.7	82.3	59.0	68.7	90.2	72.9	80.7	85	65.6	74.1
CLUSTERING	66.2	10.0	17.4	60.6	33.2	42.9	61.3	36.0	45.3	52.9	33.4	41.0	60.3	28.2	36.7
CLUSTERING-INFRQ	37.5	1.4	2.7	27.3	1.1	2.1	60.7	31.5	41.5	54.8	28.6	37.6	45.1	15.7	21.0
BASE-CUSTERING	86.8	67.8	76.1	**91.1**	72.7	80.9	80.6	61.0	69.4	86.3	74.6	80.0	86.2	69.0	76.6
BASE-CLUSTERING-INFRQ	89.7	65.0	75.3	89.4	69.3	78.1	81.2	58.5	68.0	89.9	74.2	81.3	87.6	66.8	75.7
BASE-MATCH-CLUSTERING	87.6	**75.9**	**81.4**	90.2	**73.8**	**81.2**	74.1	62.8	68.0	86.1	**76.3**	80.9	84.5	**72.2**	**77.9**
BASE-MATCH-CLUSTERING-INFRQ	**90.0**	73.4	80.8	88.6	70.4	78.5	74.3	60.3	66.6	89.6	75.8	**82.1**	85.6	70.0	77.0
FUZZY MATCH															
Method	**Boston**			**Tusk**			**Gmyz**			**Macierewicz**			**AVERAGE**		
	P	R	F	P	R	F	P	R	F	P	R	F	P	R	F
BASE	86.6	60.3	71.1	92.2	69.3	79.1	88.0	29.5	44.2	95.0	74.8	83.7	90.5	58.5	69.5
BASE-MATCH-LEV	81.7	63.6	71.5	92.3	70.2	79.8	93.6	65.4	77.0	94.9	76.1	84.5	90.6	68.8	78.2
BASE-MATCH-SW	73.3	64.3	68.5	80.8	71.3	75.8	91.4	67.6	77.7	94.2	77.1	84.8	84.9	70.1	76.7
BASE-MATCH-J	70.5	64.7	67.5	85.5	73.4	79.0	86.2	68.4	76.2	63.4	77.5	69.8	76.4	71.0	73.1
BASE-MATCH-JW	65.8	64.7	65.3	81.9	74.0	77.7	68.2	69.1	68.7	61.4	78.4	68.9	69.3	71.6	70.2
BASE-MATCH-SKIP(0,1)	81.8	62.9	71.1	92.3	70.1	79.6	94.0	64.8	76.7	95.1	76.0	84.5	90.8	68.5	78.0
BASE-MATCH-SKIP(0,2)	81.8	62.9	71.1	92.2	69.7	79.4	94.2	64.8	76.8	95.0	75.7	84.3	90.8	68.3	77.9
BASE-MATCH-CP	81.1	60.3	69.2	92.2	69.3	79.1	93.8	65.9	77.4	95.0	75.2	84.0	90.5	67.7	77.4
BASE-MATCH-LCS	81.6	64.3	71.9	92.4	71.3	80.5	93.1	66.7	77.7	94.9	76.7	84.9	90.5	69.8	78.8
CLUSTERING	83.1	12.6	21.9	96.4	52.8	68.2	89.2	52.3	66.0	87.7	55.5	68.0	89.1	43.3	56.0
CLUSTERING-INFRQ	87.5	3.3	6.3	68.2	2.7	5.1	91.1	47.2	62.2	94.2	49.1	64.5	85.3	25.6	34.5
BASE-CLUSTERING	93.1	72.7	81.6	**96.9**	77.4	86.0	94.5	71.4	81.4	91.7	79.3	85.1	94.1	75.2	83.5
BASE-CLUSTERING-INFRQ	**95.5**	69.2	80.2	95.9	74.3	83.7	**96.4**	69.4	80.7	**96.9**	79.9	87.6	**96.2**	73.2	83.1
BASE-MATCH-CLUSTERING	93.3	**80.8**	**86.6**	96.5	**79.0**	**86.9**	92.9	**78.7**	**85.2**	91.8	81.3	86.2	93.6	**80.0**	**86.2**
BASE-MATCH-CLUSTERING-INFRQ	95.1	77.6	85.5	96.0	76.3	85.0	94.5	76.7	84.7	96.6	**81.8**	**88.6**	95.6	78.1	86.0

Table 3: Precision, Recall and F-measure figures for exact (top) and fuzzy match (bottom). The best results are highlighted in bold.

CEZARY GMYZ zwolniony z "**Rzeczpospolitej**". To efekt spotkania z Zarządem i Radą Nadzorczą wydawcy dziennika http://t.co/QspE3edh
@agawaa ...usiłujesz czepić sie szczegółu, gdy istota sprawy jest taka: **Rzepa**/Gmyz pitolili bez sensu.
Konflikt w **Rzepie**? Ta cała sytuacja na to wskazuje. Gmyz się nie wycofuje, a **Rzepa** jak najbardziej.
@volanowski Nowa linia: Gmyz wyrzucony z **Rzepy** czyli PO we wszystkich sprawach smoleńskich jest cacy i super. Ludzie na to nie pójda.
@TomaszSkory Być może "**Rz**" i Gmyz płacą teraz właśnie za "skróty myślowe" swoich informatorów. Dlaczego RMF nie płaci za "skróty" swoich?
Gmyz wyleciał z **RP**, a Ziemkiewicz stracił Subotnik? Nie lepiej było nieco zejść z 3.50 zł, czy chodzi o coś zupełnie innego?
Gmyz wyrzucony z "**Rzeczpospolitej**". "Dzisiaj zwolniono mnie dyscyplinarnie": Cezary Gmyz stracił pracę w "**Rzeczp**... http://t.co/ObZIxXML

Table 4: Examples of various ways of referring to a newspaper *Rzeczpospolita* in tweets.

10% (fuzzy match) gain in F-measure compared to BASE (mainly thanks to gain in recall), except 'Gmyz' corpus, where the gain is higher. The average gain over the four targeted corpora against the best combination of BASE-MATCH in F-measure is 1.3%. We observed comparable improvement for the *random* corpus. It turned out CLUSTERING often contributes to the recognition of names glued to other words and/or character sequences.

Combining BASE with MATCH-LCS and CLUSTERING/CLUSTERING-INFRQ yields further improvements against the other settings. In particular, the gain in F-measure of BASE-MATCH-CLUSTERING against BASE, measured over the four targeted corpora, is 10.9% and 16.7% for exact and fuzzy match respectively (mainly due to gain in recall).

Considering the nature of Twitter messages the average F-measure score over the four targeted corpora for BASE-MATCH-CLUSTERING, amounting to 77.9% (exact match) and 86.2% (fuzzy match) can be seen as a fairly good result. Although the difference in some of the corresponding scores for exact and fuzzy match appear substantial, it is worth mentioning that CLUSTERING algorithm often guesses name candidates that are either preceded or followed by some characters not belonging to the name itself, which is penalized in exact-match evaluation. This problem could be alleviated through deployment of heuristics to trim such 'unwanted' characters. Another source of false positives extracted by CLUSTERING is the fact that this method might, beyond person, organization and location types, recognize any kind of NEs, which, even not very frequent, is penalized since they are not present in our reference corpus.

In general, considering the shortness of names in Twitter, the major type of errors in all settings are either added or missed entities, but more rarely overlapping problems. One of the main source of errors is due to the fact that single-token names, which are frequent in tweets, often exhibit type ambiguity. Once badly recognized, these errors are propagated over the next processing steps.

5 Conclusions and Outlook

In this paper we have reported on experiments on tuning an existing finite-state based NER grammar for processing formal texts to NER from targeted Twitter streams in Polish through combining it with knowledge-poor techniques for string distance-based name matching and corpus statistics-based name guessing. Surprisingly, the NER grammar alone applied on the four test corpora (including circa 2300 proper names) yielded P, R, and F figures for exact (fuzzy) matching proper names (including: person, organization and locations) of 87.3% (90.5%), 56.3% (58.5) and 67% (69.5%) resp., which can be considered fairly reasonable result, though some variations across tweet collections could be observed (depending on the topic and how people 'tweet' about). The integration of the presented knowledge-poor techniques for name matching/guessing resulted in P, R and F figures for exact (fuzzy) matching names of 84.5% (93.6%), 72.2% (80.0) and 77.9% (86.2%) resp. (setting with best F-measure scores), which constitutes a substantial improvement against the grammar-based approach. We can observe that satisfactory-performing NER from targeted Twitter streams in Polish can be achieved in a relatively straightforward manner.

As future work to enhance our experiments, we envisage to: (a) enlarge the pool of test corpora, (b) carry out a more thorough error analysis, (c) test a wider range of string distance metrics (Cohen et al., 2003), (d) study the applicability of the particular NER grammar rules w.r.t. their usefulness in NER in targeted Twitter streams and (e), compare our approach with an unsupervised ML-approach, e.g. as in (Li et al., 2012).

Acknowledgments

The authors gratefully acknowledge the support of the ERC Starting Grant MultiJEDI No. 259234 and the Polish National Science Centre grant N N516 481940 'Diversum'.

References

Smitashree Choudhury and John Breslin. 2011. Extracting Semantic Entities and Events from Sports Tweets. In *Proceedings of the* 1st *Workshop on Making Sense of Microposts (#MSM2011)*, pages 22–32.

William W. Cohen, Pradeep Ravikumar, and Stephen E. Fienberg. 2003. A Comparison of String Distance Metrics for Name-matching Tasks. In *Proceedings of the IJCAI-2003 Workshop on Information Integration on the Web (IIWeb-03)*, pages 73–78.

Alexandre Davis, Adriano Veloso, Altigran S. da Silva, Wagner Meira, Jr., and Alberto H. F. Laender. 2012. Named Entity Disambiguation in Streaming Data. In *Proceedings of the* 50th *Annual Meeting of the Association for Computational Linguistics: Long Papers - Volume 1*, ACL '12, pages 815–824, Stroudsburg, PA, USA. Association for Computational Linguistics.

Filip Graliński, Krzysztof Jassem, Michał Marcińczuk, and Paweł Wawrzyniak. 2009. Named entity recognition in machine anonymization. In *Recent Advances in Intelligent Information Systems*, pages 247–260, Warsaw. Exit.

Mathew Jaro. 1989. Advances in record linking methodology as applied to the 1985 census of Tampa Florida. *Journal of the American Statistical Society*, 84(406):414–420.

Heikki Keskustalo, Ari Pirkola, Kari Visala, Erkka Leppänen, and Kalervo Järvelin. 2003. Non-adjacent Digrams Improve Matching of Cross-lingual Spelling Variants. In *Proceedings of SPIRE, LNCS 22857, Manaus, Brazil*, pages 252–265.

Vladimir Levenshtein. 1965. Binary Codes for Correcting Deletions, Insertions, and Reversals. *Doklady Akademii Nauk SSSR*, 163(4):845–848.

Chenliang Li, Jianshu Weng, Qi He, Yuxia Yao, Anwitaman Datta, Aixin Sun, and Bu-Sung Lee. 2012. TwiNER: Named Entity Recognition in Targeted Twitter Stream. In *Proceedings of the* 35th *International ACM SIGIR Conference on Research and Development in Information Retrieval*, SIGIR '12, pages 721–730, New York, NY, USA. ACM.

Xiaohua Liu, Shaodian Zhang, Furu Wei, and Ming Zhou. 2011. Recognizing Named Entities in Tweets. In *Proceedings of the* 49th *Annual Meeting of the Association for Computational Linguistics: Human Language Technologies - Volume 1*, pages 359–367, Stroudsburg, PA, USA. Association for Computational Linguistics.

Xiaohua Liu, Ming Zhou, Furu Wei, Zhongyang Fu, and Xiangyang Zhou. 2012. Joint Inference of Named Entity Recognition and Normalization for Tweets. In *Proceedings of the* 50th *Annual Meeting of the Association for Computational Linguistics: Long Papers - Volume 1*, ACL '12, pages 526–535, Stroudsburg, PA, USA. Association for Computational Linguistics.

Brian Locke and James Martin. 2009. *Named Entity Recognition: Adapting to Microblogging.* Senior Thesis, University of Colorado.

Wiesław Lubaszewski. 2007. Information extraction tools for polish text. In *Proc. of LTC'07, Poznań, Poland*, Poznań. Wydawnictwo Poznanskie.

Wiesław Lubaszewski. 2009. *Słowniki komputerowe i automatyczna ekstrakcja informacji z tekstu.* AGH Uczelniane Wydawnictwa Naukowo-Dydaktyczne, Kraków.

Michał Marcińczuk and Maciej Janicki. 2012. Optimizing CRF-Based Model for Proper Name Recognition in Polish Texts. In A. Gelbukh, editor, *CICLing 2012, Part I*, volume 7181 of *Lecture Notes in Computer Science (LNCS)*, pages 258––269. Springer, Heidelberg.

Michał Marcińczuk and Maciej Piasecki. 2007. Pattern extraction for event recognition in the reports of polish stockholders. In *Proceedings of IMCSIT–AAIA'07, Wisła, Poland*, pages 275–284.

Michał Marcińczuk and Maciej Piasecki. 2010. Named Entity Recognition in the Domain of Polish Stock Exchange Reports. In *Proceedings of Intelligent Information Systems 2010, Siedlce, Poland*, pages 127–140.

Małgorzata Marciniak, Joanna Rabiega-Wiśniewska, Agata Savary, Marcin Woliński, and Celina Heliasz. 2009. Constructing an Electronic Dictionary of Polish Urban Proper Names. In *Recent Advances in Intelligent Information Systems*. Exit.

David Nadeau and Satoshi Sekine. 2007. A Survey of Named Entity Recognition and Classification. *Lingvisticae Investigationes*, 30(1):3–26.

Kamel Nebhi. 2012. Ontology-Based Information Extraction from Twitter. In *Proceedings of the COLING 2012 IEEASM Workshop*, Mumbai, India.

Jakub Piskorski, Karol Wieloch, and Marcin Sydow. 2009. On Knowledge-poor Methods for Person Name Matching and Lemmatization for Highly Inflectional Languages. *Information Retrieval*, 12(3):275–299.

Jakub Piskorski. 2005. Named-Entity Recognition for Polish with SProUT. In *LNCS Vol 3490: Proceedings of IMTCI 2004, Warsaw, Poland.*

Jakub Piskorski. 2007. ExPRESS – Extraction Pattern Recognition Engine and Specification Suite. In *Proceedings of FSMNLP 2007.*

Alan Ritter, Sam Clark, Mausam, and Oren Etzioni. 2011. Named Entity Recognition in Tweets: An Experimental Study. In *Proceedings of the 2011 Conference on Empirical Methods in Natural Language Processing (EMNLP 2011)*, pages 1524–1534, Edinburgh, Scotland, UK. Association for Computational Linguistics.

Agata Savary and Jakub Piskorski. 2011. Language Resources for Named Entity Annotation in the National Corpus of Polish. *Control and Cybernetics*, 40(2):361–391.

Agata Savary, Joanna Rabiega-Wiśniewska, and Marcin Woliński. 2009. Inflection of Polish Multi-Word Proper Names with Morfeusz and Multiflex. *LNAI*, 5070.

T. Smith and M. Waterman. 1981. Identification of Common Molecular Subsequences. *Journal of Molecular Biology*, 147:195–197.

Esko Ukkonen. 1992. Approximate String Matching with q-grams and Maximal Matches. *Theoretical Computer Science*, 92(1):191–211.

Jakub Waszczuk, Katarzyna Głowińska, Agata Savary, and Adam Przepiórkowski. 2010. Tools and Methodologies for Annotating Syntax and Named Entities in the National Corpus of Polish. In *Proceedings of the International Multiconference on Computer Science and Information Technology (IMCSIT 2010): Computational Linguistics – Applications (CLA'10)*, pages 531–539.

William Winkler. 1999. The State of Record Linkage and Current Research Problems. Technical report, Statistical Research Division, U.S. Bureau of the Census, Washington, DC.

Marcin Woliński, Marcin Miłkowski, Maciej Ogrodniczuk, Adam Przepiórkowski, and Łukasz Szałkiewicz. 2012. PoliMorf: A (not so) new open morphological dictionary for Polish. In *Proceedings of the Eighth International Conference on Language Resources and Evaluation, LREC 2012*, pages 860–864.

Recognition of Named Entities Boundaries in Polish Texts

Michał Marcińczuk and **Jan Kocoń**
Institute of Informatics, Wrocław University of Technology
Wybrzeże Wyspiańskiego 27
Wrocław, Poland
{michal.marcinczuk,jan.kocon}@pwr.wroc.pl

Abstract

In the paper we discuss the problem of low recall for the named entity (NE) recognition task for Polish. We discuss to what extent the recall of NE recognition can be improved by reducing the space of NE categories. We also present several extensions to the binary model which give an improvement of the recall. The extensions include: new features, application of external knowledge and post-processing. For the partial evaluation the final model obtained 90.02% recall with 91.30% precision on the corpus of economic news.

1 Introduction

Named entity recognition (NER) aims at identifying text fragments which refer to some objects and assigning a category of that object from a predefined set (for example: *person*, *location*, *organization*, *artifact*, *other*). According to the ACE (Automatic Content Extraction) English Annotation Guidelines for Entities (LDC, 2008) there are several types of named entities, including: proper names, definite descriptions and noun phrases. In this paper we focus on recognition of proper names (PNs) in Polish texts.

For Polish there are only a few accessible models for PN recognition. Marcińczuk and Janicki (2012) presented a hybrid model (a statistical model combined with some heuristics) which obtained 70.53% recall with 91.44% precision for a limited set of PN categories (first names, last names, names of countries, cities and roads) tested on the CEN corpus[1] (Marcińczuk et al., 2013). A model for an extended set of PN categories (56 categories) presented by Marcińczuk et al. (2013) obtained much lower recall of 54% with 93% precision tested on the same corpus. Savary and Waszczuk (2012) presented a statistical model which obtained 76% recall with 83% precision for names of people, places, organizations, time expressions and name derivations tested on the National Corpus of Polish[2] (Przepiórkowski et al., 2012).

There are also several other works on PN recognition for Polish where a rule-based approach was used. Piskorski et al. (2004) constructed a set of rules and tested them on 100 news from the *Rzeczpospolita* newspaper. The rules obtained 90.6% precision and 85.3% recall for person names and 87.9% precision and 56.6% recall for company names. Urbańska and Mykowiecka (2005) also constructed a set of rules for recognition of person and organization names. The rules were tested on 100 short texts from the Internet. The rules obtained 98% precision and 89% recall for person names and 85% precision and 73% recall for organization names. Another rule-based approach for an extended set of proper names was presented by Abramowicz et al. (2006). The rules were tested on 156 news from the *Rzeczpospolita* newspaper, the *Tygodnik Powszechny* newspaper and the news web portals. The rules obtained 91% precision and 93% recall for country names, 55% precision and 73% recall for city names, 87% precision and 70% recall for road names and 82% precision and 66% recall for person names.

The accessible models for PN recognition for Polish obtain relatively good performance in terms of precision. However, in some NLP tasks like recognition of semantic relations between PNs (Marcińczuk and Ptak, 2012), coreference resolution (Kopeć and Ogrodniczuk, 2012; Broda et al., 2012a), machine translation (Graliński et al., 2009a) or sensitive data anonymization (Graliński et al., 2009b) the recall is much more important than the fine-grained categorization of PNs.

[1] Home page: http://nlp.pwr.wroc.pl/cen.

[2] Home page: http://nkjp.pl

Unfortunately, the only model recognising wide range of PN categories obtains only 54% recall. Therefore, our goal is to evaluate to what extent the recall for this model can be improved.

2 Evaluation methodology

In the evaluation we used two corpora annotated with 56 categories of proper names: KPWr[3] (Broda et al., 2012b) and CEN (already mentioned in Section 1). The KPWr corpus consists of 747 documents containing near 200K tokens and 16.5K NEs. The CEN corpus consists of 797 documents containing 148K tokens and 13.6K NEs. Both corpora were tagged using the morphological tagger WCRFT (Radziszewski, 2013).

We used a 10-fold cross validation on the KPWr corpus to select the optimal model. The CEN corpus was used for a cross-corpus evaluation of the selected model. In this case the model was trained on the KPWr corpus and evaluated on the CEN corpus. We presented results for strict and partial matching evaluation (Chinchor, 1992). The experiments were conducted using an open-source framework for named entity recognition called Liner2[4] (Marcińczuk et al., 2013).

3 Reduction of NE categories

In this section we investigate to what extent the recall of NE recognition can be improved by reducing the number of NE categories. As a reference model we used the statistical model presented by Marcińczuk and Janicki (2012). The model uses the Conditional Random Fields method and utilize four types of features, i.e. orthographic (18 features), morphological (6 features), wordnet (4 features) and lexicon (10 features) — 38 features in total. The model uses only local features from a window of two preceding and two following tokens. The detailed description of the features is presented in Marcińczuk et al. (2013). We did not used any post-processing methods described by Marcińczuk and Janicki (2012) (unambiguous gazetteer chunker, heuristic chunker) because they were tuned for the specific set of NE categories.

We have evaluated two schemas with a limited number of the NE categories. In the first more common (Finkel et al., 2005) schema, all PNs are divided into four MUC categories, i.e. *person*, *organization*, *location* and *other*. In the other schema, assuming a separate phases for PN recognition and classification (Al-Rfou' and Skiena, 2012), we mapped all the PN categories to a single category, namely NAM.

For the MUC schema we have tested two approaches. In the first approach we trained a single classifier for all the NE categories and in the second approach we trained four classifiers — one for each category. This way we have evaluated three models: **Multi-MUC** — a cascade of four classifiers, one classifier for every NE category; **One-MUC** — a single classifier for all MUC categories; **One-NAM** — a single classifier for NAM category.

Model	P	R	F
Multi-MUC	76.09%	57.41%	65.44%
One-MUC	70.66%	65.39%	67.92%
One-NAM	80.46%	78.59%	79.52%

Table 1: Strict evaluation of the three NE models

For each model we performed the 10-fold cross-validation on the KPWr corpus and the results are presented in Table 1. As we expected the highest performance was obtained for the One-NAM model where the problem of PN classification was ignored. The model obtained recall of 78% with 80% precision. The results also show that the local features used in the model are insufficient to predict the PN category.

4 Improving the binary model

In this section we present and evaluate several extensions which were introduced to the One-NAM model in order to increase its recall. The extensions include: new features, application of external resources and post processing.

4.1 Extensions

4.1.1 Extended gazetteer features

The reference model (Marcińczuk and Janicki, 2012) uses only five gazetteers of PNs (*first names*, *last names*, names of *countries*, *cities* and *roads*). To include the other categories of PNs we used two existing resources: a gazetteer of proper names called NELexicon[5] containing ca. 1.37 million of forms and a gazetteer of PNs extracted from the National Corpus of Polish[6] containing 153,477

[3]Home page: `http://nlp.pwr.wroc.pl/kpwr`.
[4]`http://nlp.pwr.wroc.pl/liner2`

[5]`http://nlp.pwr.wroc.pl/nelexicon`.
[6]`http://clip.ipipan.waw.pl/Gazetteer`

forms. The categories of PNs were mapped into four MUC categories: *person*, *location*, *organization* and *other*. The numbers of PNs for each category are presented in Table 2.

Category	Symbol	Form count
person	per	455,376
location	loc	156,886
organization	org	832,339
other	oth	13,612
TOTAL		1,441,634

Table 2: The statistics of the gazetteers.

We added four features, one for every category. The features were defined as following:

$$gaz(n,c) = \begin{cases} B & \text{if } n\text{-th token starts a sequence of words} \\ & \text{found in gazetteer } c \\ I & \text{if } n\text{-th token is part of a sequence of} \\ & \text{words found in gazetteer } c \text{ excluding} \\ & \text{the first token} \\ 0 & \text{otherwise} \end{cases}$$

where $c \in \{per, loc, org, oth\}$ and n is the token index in a sentence. If two or more PNs from the same gazetteer overlap, then the first and longest PN is taken into account.

4.1.2 Trigger features

A trigger is a word which can indicate presence of a proper name. Triggers can be divided into two groups: *external* (appear before or after PNs) and *internal* (are part of PNs). We used a lexicon of triggers called PNET (Polish Named Entity Triggers)[7]. The lexicon contains 28,000 inflected forms divided into 8 semantic categories (*bloc*, *country*, *district*, *geogName*, *orgName*, *persName*, *region* and *settlement*) semi-automatically extracted from Polish Wikipedia[8]. We divided the lexicon into 16 sets — two for every semantic category (with *internal* and *external* triggers). We defined one feature for every lexicon what gives 16 features in total. The feature were defined as following:

$$trigger(n,s) = \begin{cases} 1 & \text{if } n\text{-th token base is found} \\ & \text{in set } s \\ 0 & \text{otherwise} \end{cases}$$

[7] `http://zil.ipipan.waw.pl/PNET.`

[8] `http://pl.wikipedia.org`

4.1.3 Agreement feature

An agreement of the morphological attributes between two consecutive words can be an indicator of phrase continuity. This observation was used by Radziszewski and Pawlaczek (2012) to recognize noun phrases. This information can be also helpful in PN boundaries recognition. The feature was defined as following:

$$agr(n) = \begin{cases} 1 & \text{if } number[n] = number[n-1] \\ & \text{and } case[n] = case[n-1] \\ & \text{and } gender[n] = gender[n-1] \\ 0 & \text{otherwise} \end{cases}$$

The `agr(n)` feature for a token n has value 1 when the n-th and $n-1$-th words have the same case, gender and number. In other cases the value is 0. If one of the attributes is not set, the value is also 0.

4.1.4 Unambiguous gazetteer look-up

There are many proper names which are well known and can be easily recognized using gazetteers. However, some of the proper names present in the gazetteers can be also common words. In order to avoid this problem we used an *unambiguous gazetteer look-up* (Marcińczuk and Janicki, 2012). We created one gazetteer containing all categories of PNs (see Section 4.1.1) and discarded all entries which were found in the SJP dictionary[9] in a lower case form.

4.1.5 Heuristics

We created several simple rules to recognize PNs on the basis of the orthographic features. The following phrases are recognized as proper names regardless the context:

- **a camel case word** — a single word containing one or more internal upper case letters and at least one lower case letter, for example *RoboRally* — a name of board game,
- **a sequence of words in the quotation marks** — the first word must be capitalised and shorter than 5 characters to avoid matching ironic or apologetic words and citations,
- **a sequence of all-uppercase words** — we discard words which are roman numbers and ignore all-uppercase sentences.

[9] `http://www.sjp.pl/slownik/ort.`

4.1.6 Names propagation

The reference model does not contain any document-based features. This can be a problem for documents where the proper names occur several times but only a few of its occurrences are recognised by the statistical model. The other may not be recognized because of the unseen or unambiguous contexts. In such cases the global information about the recognized occurrences could be used to recognize the other unrecognized names. However, a simple propagation of all recognized names might cause loss in the precision because of the common words which are also proper names. To handle this problem we defined a set of patterns and propagate only those proper names which match one of the following pattern: (1) a sequence of two or more capitalised words; (2) all-uppercase word ended with a number; or (3) all-uppercase word ended with hyphen and inflectional suffix.

4.2 Evaluation

Table 3 contains results of the 10-fold cross validation on the KPWr corpus for the One-NAM model, One-NAM with every single extension and a complete model with all extensions. The bold values indicate an improvement comparing to the base One-NAM model. To check the statistical significance of precision, recall and F-measure difference we used Student's t-test with a significance level $\alpha = 0.01$ (Dietterich, 1998). The asterisk indicates the statistically significant improvement.

Model	P	R	F
One-NAM	80.46%	78.59%	79.52%
Gazetteers	**80.60%**	**78.71%**	**79.64%**
Triggers	**80.60%**	78.58%	**79.58%**
Agreement	**80.73%**	**78.90%**	**79.80%**
Look-up	80.18%	**79.56%***	**79.87%**
Heuristics	79.98%	**79.20%***	**79.59%**
Propagate	80.46%	78.59%	79.52%
Complete	80.33%	**80.61%***	**80.47%***

Table 3: The 10-fold cross validation on the KPWr corpus for *One-NAM* model with different extensions.

Five out of six extensions improved the performance. Only for the name propagation we did not observe any improvement because the KPWr corpus contains only short documents (up to 300 words) and it is uncommon that a name will appear more than one time in the same fragment. However, tests on random documents from the Internet showed the usefulness of this extension.

For the unambiguous gazetteer look-up and the heuristics we obtained a statistically significant improvement of the recall. In the final model we included all the presented extensions. The final model achieved a statistically significant improvement of the recall and the F-measure.

To check the generality of the extensions, we performed the cross-domain evaluation on the CEN corpus (see Section 2). The results for the 56nam, the One-NAM and the Improved One-NAM models are presented in Table 4. For the strict evaluation, the recall was improved by almost 4 percentage points with a small precision improvement by almost 2 percentage points.

Evaluation	P	R	F
56nam model (Marcińczuk et al., 2013)			
Strict	93%	54%	68%
One-NAM model			
Strict	85.98%	81.31%	83.58%
Partial	91.12%	86.65%	88.83%
Improved One-NAM model			
Strict	86.61%	85.05%	85.82%
Partial	91.30%	90.02%	90.65%

Table 4: The cross-domain evaluation of the basic and improved One-NAM models on CEN.

5 Conclusions

In the paper we discussed the problem of low recall of models for recognition of a wide range of PNs for Polish. We tested to what extent the reduction of the PN categories can improve the recall. As we expected the model without PN classification obtained the best results in terms of precision and recall.

Then we presented a set of extensions to the One-NAM model, including new features (morphological agreement, triggers, gazetteers), application of external knowledge (a set of heuristics and a gazetteer-based recogniser) and post-processing (proper names propagation). The final model obtained 90.02% recall with 91.30% precision on the CEN corpus for the partial evaluation what is a good start of further NE categorization phase.

Acknowledgments

This work was financed by Innovative Economy Programme project POIG.01.01.02-14-013/09.

References

Witold Abramowicz, Agata Filipowska, Jakub Piskorski, Krzysztof Węcel, and Karol Wieloch. 2006. Linguistic Suite for Polish Cadastral System. In *Proceedings of the LREC'06*, pages 53–58, Genoa, Italy.

Rami Al-Rfou' and Steven Skiena. 2012. SpeedRead: A fast named entity recognition pipeline. In *Proceedings of COLING 2012*, pages 51–66, Mumbai, India, December. The COLING 2012 Organizing Committee.

Bartosz Broda, Lukasz Burdka, and Marek Maziarz. 2012a. Ikar: An improved kit for anaphora resolution for polish. In Martin Kay and Christian Boitet, editors, *COLING (Demos)*, pages 25–32. Indian Institute of Technology Bombay.

Bartosz Broda, Michał Marcińczuk, Marek Maziarz, Adam Radziszewski, and Adam Wardyński. 2012b. KPWr: Towards a Free Corpus of Polish. In Nicoletta Calzolari, Khalid Choukri, Thierry Declerck, Mehmet Uğur Doğan, Bente Maegaard, Joseph Mariani, Jan Odijk, and Stelios Piperidis, editors, *Proceedings of LREC'12*. ELRA.

Nancy Chinchor. 1992. MUC-4 Evaluation Metrics. In *Proceedings of the Fourth Message Understanding Conference*, pages 22–29.

Thomas G. Dietterich. 1998. Approximate statistical tests for comparing supervised classification learning algorithms. *Neural Computation*, 10(7):1895–1924.

Jenny Rose Finkel, Trond Grenager, and Christopher D. Manning. 2005. Incorporating Non-local Information into Information Extraction Systems by Gibbs Sampling. In The Association for Computer Linguistics, editor, *Proceedings of the 43nd Annual Meeting of the Association for Computational Linguistics (ACL 2005)*, pages 363–370.

Filip Graliński, Krzysztof Jassem, and Michał Marcińczuk. 2009a. An Environment for Named Entity Recognition and Translation. In L Màrquez and H Somers, editors, *Proceedings of the 13th Annual Conference of the European Association for Machine Translation*, pages 88–95, Barcelona, Spain.

Filip Graliński, Krzysztof Jassem, Michał Marcińczuk, and Paweł Wawrzyniak. 2009b. Named Entity Recognition in Machine Anonymization. In M A Kłopotek, A Przepiórkowski, A T Wierzchoń, and K Trojanowski, editors, *Recent Advances in Intelligent Information Systems.*, pages 247–260. Academic Pub. House Exit.

Mateusz Kopeć and Maciej Ogrodniczuk. 2012. Creating a coreference resolution system for polish. In Nicoletta Calzolari (Conference Chair), Khalid Choukri, Thierry Declerck, Mehmet Uğur Doğan, Bente Maegaard, Joseph Mariani, Jan Odijk, and Stelios Piperidis, editors, *Proceedings of the Eight International Conference on Language Resources and Evaluation (LREC'12)*, Istanbul, Turkey, may. European Language Resources Association (ELRA).

LDC. 2008. ACE (Automatic Content Extraction) English Annotation Guidelines for Relations (Version 6.2).

Michał Marcińczuk and Maciej Janicki. 2012. Optimizing CRF-Based Model for Proper Name Recognition in Polish Texts. In Alexander F. Gelbukh, editor, *CICLing (1)*, volume 7181 of *Lecture Notes in Computer Science*, pages 258–269. Springer.

Michał Marcińczuk, Jan Kocoń, and Maciej Janicki. 2013. Liner2 - A Customizable Framework for Proper Names Recognition for Polish. In Robert Bembenik, Łukasz Skonieczny, Henryk Rybiński, Marzena Kryszkiewicz, and Marek Niezgódka, editors, *Intelligent Tools for Building a Scientific Information Platform*, volume 467 of *Studies in Computational Intelligence*, pages 231–253. Springer.

Michał Marcińczuk and Marcin Ptak. 2012. Preliminary study on automatic induction of rules for recognition of semantic relations between proper names in polish texts. In Petr Sojka, Ales Horák, Ivan Kopecek, and Karel Pala, editors, *Text, Speech and Dialogue — 15th International Conference, TSD 2012, Brno, Czech Republic, September 3-7, 2012. Proceedings*, volume 7499 of *Lecture Notes in Artificial Intelligence (LNAI)*. Springer-Verlag, September.

Jakub Piskorski, Peter Homola, Małgorzata Marciniak, Agnieszka Mykowiecka, Adam Przepiórkowski, and Marcin Woliński. 2004. Information Extraction for Polish Using the SProUT Platform. In Mieczyslaw A. Kłopotek, Slawomir T. Wierzchoń, and Krzysztof Trojanowski, editors, *Intelligent Information Processing and Web Mining, Proceedings of the International IIS: IIPWM'04 Conference*, Advances in Soft Computing, Zakopane. Springer-Verlag.

Adam Przepiórkowski, Mirosław Bańko, Rafał L. Górski, and Barbara Lewandowska-Tomaszczyk, editors. 2012. *Narodowy Korpus Języka Polskiego [Eng.: National Corpus of Polish]*. Wydawnictwo Naukowe PWN, Warsaw.

Adam Radziszewski and Adam Pawlaczek. 2012. Large-Scale Experiments with NP Chunking of Polish. In Petr Sojka, Aleš Horák, Ivan Kopeček, and Karel Pala, editors, *TSD*, volume 7499 of *Lecture Notes in Computer Science*, pages 143–149. Springer Berlin Heidelberg.

Adam Radziszewski. 2013. A Tiered CRF Tagger for Polish. In Robert Bembenik, Łukasz Skonieczny, Henryk Rybiński, Marzena Kryszkiewicz, and Marek Niezgódka, editors, *Intelligent Tools for Building a Scientific Information Platform*, volume 467 of *Studies in Computational Intelligence*, pages 215–230. Springer Berlin Heidelberg.

Agata Savary and Jakub Waszczuk. 2012. Narzędzia do anotacji jednostek nazewniczych. In Adam Przepiórkowski, Mirosław Bańko, Rafał L. Górski, and Barbara Lewandowska-Tomaszczyk, editors, *Narodowy Korpus Języka Polskiego*. Wydawnictwo Naukowe PWN. Creative Commons Uznanie Autorstwa 3.0 Polska.

Dominika Urbańska and Agnieszka Mykowiecka. 2005. Multi-words Named Entity Recognition in Polish texts. In Radovan Grabík, editor, *SLOVKO 2005 – Third International Seminar Computer Treatment of Slavic and East European Languages, Bratislava, Slovakia*, pages 208–215. VEDA.

Adapting the PULS Event Extraction Framework to Analyze Russian Text

Lidia Pivovarova,[1,2] **Mian Du,**[1] **Roman Yangarber**[1]
[1] Department of Computer Science
University of Helsinki, Finland
[2]St. Petersburg State University, Russia

Abstract

This paper describes a plug-in component to extend the PULS information extraction framework to analyze Russian-language text. PULS is a comprehensive framework for information extraction (IE) that is used for analysis of news in several scenarios from English-language text and is primarily monolingual. Although monolinguality is recognized as a serious limitation, building an IE system for a new language from the bottom up is very labor-intensive. Thus, the objective of the present work is to explore whether the base framework can be extended to cover additional languages with limited effort, and to leverage the pre-existing PULS modules as far as possible, in order to accelerate the development process. The component for Russian analysis is described and its performance is evaluated on two news-analysis scenarios: epidemic surveillance and cross-border security. The approach described in the paper can be generalized to a range of heavily-inflected languages.

1 Introduction

1.1 Problem Statement

PULS[1] is a framework for information extraction from text (IE), designed for decision support in various domains and scenarios. To date, work on PULS has mostly concentrated on English-language text, though some effort has gone into adapting PULS to other languages, (Du et al., 2011). This paper describes a component that is used to extend PULS to analyze Russian-language text, and demonstrates its performance on two IE scenarios: infectious epidemics and cross-border security. The epidemics scenario is built to provide an early warning system for professionals and organizations responsible for tracking epidemic threats around the world. Because information related to outbreaks of infectious disease often appears in news earlier than it does in official sources, text mining from the Web for medical surveillance is a popular research topic, as discussed in, e.g., (Collier et al., 2008; Huttunen et al., 2002; Rortais et al., 2010; Zamite et al., 2010). Similarly, in the security scenario, the system tracks cross-border crime, including illegal migration, smuggling, human trafficking, as well as general criminal activity and crisis events; text mining for this scenario has been previously reported by (Ameyugo et al., 2012; Atkinson et al., 2011). The new component monitors open-source media in Russian, searching for incidents related to the given scenarios. It extracts information from plain, natural-language text into structured database records, which are used by domain specialists for daily event monitoring. The structure of the database records (called *templates*) depends on the scenario. For the epidemics scenario the system extracts the fields: disease name, location of the incident, date, number of victims, etc. In the security domain, the template contains the type of event, date and location, the perpetrator, number of victims (if any), goods smuggled, etc.

Monolinguality is a serious limitation for IE, since end-users are under growing pressure to cover news from multiple languages, (Piskorski et al., 2011). The Russian-language component that we describe here is an experiment in extending PULS to multi-lingual coverage. Our aim is to explore whether a such an extension can be built with limited effort and resources.

1.2 Prior work on IE from Russian

IE in Russian has been the topic of several recent studies. For example, (Piskorski et al., 2011) uses

[1]http://puls.cs.helsinki.fi

Russian among other languages to study information fusion across languages. Extraction techniques are used for ontology learning in (Bocharov et al., 2010) and (Schumann, 2012). The University of Sheffield's GATE system, (Bontcheva et al., 2003), which supports multi-lingual IE, has been adapted to Russian as part of the MUSE-3 project, (though little is published on functionality available in Russian). HP Labs have recently started adaptation of their information extraction solutions to Russian, (Solovyev et al., 2012).

Much literature devoted to Russian-language information extraction is published only in Russian; a brief review can be found in (Khoroshevsky, 2010). The majority of existing applications for Russian IE, and Natural Language Processing (NLP) in general, are commercially based, and are either published in Russian only, or not at all. One major player in Russian text mining is Yandex, the leading Russian search engine. Yandex uses IE to support its main search service, e.g., to underline addresses and persons in search results, and in a service called "Press Portraits,"[2] which builds profiles for various personalities found in the news. A profile may include the profession, biographical facts, news that s/he is involved in, and related people—using information automatically extracted from on-line Russian media. Yandex also recently unveiled an open-source toolkit Tomita, for developing IE systems based on context-free grammars.

Dictum, a company that builds applications for NLP and sentiment analysis in Russian, provides a toolkit for Russian morphological, syntactic and semantic analysis. Their *Fact Extraction* component[3] finds persons, organizations, locations, etc., and creates simple facts about persons: corporate posts, date of birth, etc.

RCO, a company focused on research and development of text analysis solutions, provides the RCO Fact Extractor tool[4], which performs fact extraction from unstructured text. One common usage scenario is setting up a list of target objects (persons, companies) and extracting all events where these objects are mentioned as participants. The tool also includes a module that allows the user to adjust search patterns.

With the exception of Tomita and AOT (see Section 3), few resources are available in open-source.

2 The Baseline English System

The PULS news-tracking pipeline consists of three main components: a Web-crawler that tries to identify potentially relevant articles using a broad keyword-based Web search; a rule-based Information Extraction system that uses patterns acquired through semi-supervised learning, that determines exactly what happened in the article, creating a structured record that is stored in the database; and a relevance classifier that determines the relevance of the selected articles—and events that they describe—to the particular use-case scenario and the users' needs. This paper will mostly focus on the IE component, as other two components are language-independent.

The IE system contains modules for lower-level—morphological and syntactic—analysis, as well as higher-level—semantic—analysis, and produces filled templates on output, extracted from an input document, (Du et al., 2011).

PULS follows a classic IE processing pipeline:

- Pre-processing,
- Lexical markup,
- Shallow syntactic analysis/chunking,
- Semantic pattern matching
- Reference resolution and logical inference

Pre-processing includes tokenization, part-of-speech tagging, processing of punctuation, numeric expressions, etc.

Lexical markup is tagging of lexical units found in text with semantic information found in a dictionary and/or ontology. PULS uses several domain-independent and domain-specific lexicons and ontologies. The ontology is a network of concepts organized in a hierarchy by several relations, among which the "is-a" relation is the most common. One key factor that enables the addition of new languages efficiently is that the ontology is language-independent. The system uses the lexicons to map words into concepts. A lexicon consists of word-forms and some common multi-word expressions (MWEs), which appear in text and represent some ontology concept. We assume that *within a given domain* each word or

[2] http://news.yandex.ru/people
[3] http://dictum.ru/en/object-extraction/blog
[4] http://www.rco.ru/eng/product.asp

MWE in the lexicon represents exactly one concept, (Yarowsky, 1995). A concept may be represented by more than one word or MWE.[5] Each scenario has its own scenario-specific ontology and lexicons; the Epidemics ontology consists of more than 4000 concepts (which includes some disease names). Diseases are organized in a hierarchy, e.g., "hepatitis" is a parent term for "hepatitis A". The Security ontology consists of 1190 concepts.

The domain-specific lexicon is a collection of terms that are significant for a particular scenario, mapped to their semantic types/concepts. The Security and Epidemics scenarios use a common location lexicon, that contains approximately 2500 names of countries, cities and provinces. Locations are organized according the "part-of" relation: cities are part-of provinces, which are part-of states, etc.

Syntactic analysis is implemented as a cascade of lower-level patterns. PULS uses shallow analysis (chunking), which does not try to build complete syntactic tree for a sentence but recognizes local grammatical structures—in particular, the noun and verb groups. This phase also identifies other common constructions needed for IE, (names, dates, etc.). As a result of the syntactic analysis, each sentence is represented as a set of fragments.

The pattern base is the main component of the IE system, responsible for finding factual information in text. A pattern is a set of semantic, syntactic and morphological constraints designed to match pieces of natural-language text. When a pattern fires it triggers an action, which creates an abstract logical entity based on the text matched by the pattern. The entity is added to an internal pool of entities found in the document so far. Facts produced by the system are based on the entities in this pool. The patterns are arranged in a cascade such that the results produced by one pattern are used by subsequent patterns to form more complex entities.

Patterns operate on a sentence-by-sentence basis. To link information in the surrounding sentences PULS uses concept-based reference resolution and logical inference rules. The reference resolution component is a set of rules for merging mentions of the same object and events.

Inference rules work on a logical level (rather than text), operating on entities found at the preceding stages of analysis. These entities can be used to fill slots in an event description, for example, to find event time and location, or to perform logical inference. For example, if the event type is *human-trafficking* and a concept related to *organ-transplantation* is mentioned in the sentence, an inference rule may specialize the event type to *human-trafficking-organs*.

3 Russian Morphology and Syntax

To speed development, we use pre-existing tools for tokenization, morphological and syntactic analysis in Russian. The range of freely-available, open-source tools for Russian is quite narrow, especially for syntactic analysis. Significant efforts for overcoming this situation have been the focus of the recent "Dialogue" series of conferences[6], which organized workshops on Russian morphology, (Astaf'eva et al., 2010), and syntax, (Toldova et al., 2012). Workshops take the form of competitions, where the participants tackle shared tasks. Eight teams participated in the latest workshop, devoted to syntax. However, only one—AOT[7]—offers their toolkit under the GNU LGPL license.

The AOT toolkit, (Sokirko, 2001) is a collection of modules for NLP, including libraries for morphological, syntactic, and semantic analysis, language generation, tools for working with dictionaries, and GUIs for visualization of the analysis. Due to its open availability and high quality of linguistic analysis, AOT is currently a *de-facto* standard for open-source Russian-language processing.

The AOT morphological analyzer, called "*Lemm*", analyzes text word by word; its output for each word contains: an index, the surface form, the base lemma, part of speech, and morphological tags. Lemm works on the morphological level only, and leaves all morphological ambiguity intact, to be resolved by later phases.

Lemm uses a general-purpose Russian morphological dictionary, which can be edited and extended (e.g., with neologisms, domain-specific terms, etc.). To add a new lemma into the dictionary, one needs to specify its inflectional

[5]By default, words that appear only in the general-purpose dictionary, and do not appear in any domain-specific lexicon, are automatically identified with a concept having an identical name.

[6]Dialogue—International Conference of Computational Linguistics (http://www.dialog-21.ru/en/)

[7]The AOT project ("Automatic Processing of Text" in Russian)—www.aot.ru

paradigm. For Russian IE, we had to add to the dictionary certain words and terms that designate scenario-specific concepts, for example "мигрант" (*migrant*) and "гастарбайтер" (*gastarbaiter*), which have become common usage in recent Russian-language media.

The syntactic analyzer in AOT, "*Synan*", uses a hybrid formalism, a mix of dependency trees and constituent grammars. The output for a sentence contains two types of syntactic units: binary parent-child relations, and "groups", which are token sequences *not* analyzed further but treated as an atomic expression. This approach is theoretically natural, since certain syntactic units may not have a clear root, for example, complex name expressions ("Aleksey Sokirko") or numeric expressions ("forty five"). To make it compatible with the overall PULS structure, we transform all Synan output into dependency-tree form; groups simply become linked chains. Synan attempts to produce a complete, connected parse structure for the entire sentence; in practice, it produces a set of fragments, consisting of relations and groups. In the process, it resolves morphological ambiguity, when possible.

To unify the results of Lemm and Synan, we built a special "wrapper," (Du et al., 2011). The wrapper takes every binary (syntactic) relation in the Synan output, finds the items corresponding to the relation's parent and child in Lemm's output, and resolves their morphological ambiguity (if any) by removing all other morphological readings. If the lemma for parent or child is null—as, e.g., when the corresponding element is a group—we infer information from Lemm output for the element that is missed in Synan. If a word does not participate in any relation identified by Synan, its analysis is based only on Lemm output, *preserving* all unresolved morphological ambiguity—to be potentially resolved at a later stage, typically by scenario-specific patterns. Finally, the wrapper assembles the resulting analysis for all words into a set of tree fragments.

4 Russian Information Extraction

4.1 Ontology and Dictionaries

The ontology, a network of semantic classes, is language-independent, and in Russian IE, we used the pre-existing domain ontologies for the epidemics and security domains, with minor modifications. Most of the changes centered on removing vestiges of English language-specific information, e.g., by making explicit the distinctions among certain concepts that may be confounded in English due to ambiguity of English lexical units. For example, in English, the word "convict" means both the verb and the convicted person (patient nominalization), so it may be tempting to represent them by the same concept. In Russian, as in many other languages, these are different concepts as well as distinct lexemes.

A Russian domain-specific lexicon was added to the system. Russian IE uses a shared lexicon for epidemics and security. The lexicon contains not only translations of the corresponding English words, but also includes MWEs that appear in Russian media and correspond to the domain-specific concepts. The current Russian domain-specific lexicon contains approximately 1000 words and MWEs. Constructing the multiword lexicon for Russian is more complicated than for English because Russian has a rich morphology and complex grammatical agreement. For example, to find a simple *Adjective+Noun* collocation in text, the system needs to check that the adjective agrees with the noun in gender, case, and number. To resolve this problem, we built a special set of low-level patterns, which match MWEs. These patterns are subdivided into several classes, according to their syntactic form: *Adjective+Noun*, *Noun+Noun*, *Verb+Noun*, *Verb+Preposition+Noun*, etc. The grammatical constraints are coded only once for each class of pattern, and apply to all patterns in the class. For example, in the *Noun+Noun* class, the second noun must be in genitive case (a genitive modifier of the head noun), e.g., "цироз печени" (*cirrhosis of the liver*), or in the instrumental case, e.g., "торговля людьми" (*human trafficking*). This simplifies adding new MWEs into the dictionary.

We use the multilingual GeoNames database, (www.geonames.org) as the source of geographic information in Russian. The disease dictionary is mapped into Russian using the International Classification of Diseases.[8] The system also identifies common animal diseases: anthrax, African swine fever, rabies, etc.

4.2 Pattern Bases

The pattern base is the main component of the IE system for extracting higher-level logical objects.

[8]ICD10: http://www.who.int/classifications/icd/en/

	Syntactic variant	Example		Syntactic variant	Example
I	Verb + Object (active clause)	арестовали мигранта *[someone] arrested a migrant*	II	Object + Verb (reverse word order)	мигранта арестовали (same meaning)
III	Participle + Object (passive clause)	арестован мигрант *migrant is arrested [by someone]*	IV	Object + Participle (reverse word order)	мигрант арестован (same meaning)
V	Noun + Object (nominalization)	арест мигранта *arrest of a migrant*	VI	(reverse word order is rare, unlikely in news)	—

Table 1: Examples of syntactic variants for a single pattern Russian

Patterns are language-dependent and domain-dependent, which means that patterns must capture the lexical, syntactic and stylistic features of the analyzed text. It was not possible to directly translate or map the English pattern base into Russian for at least two reasons.

The first reason is technical. PULS's English pattern base has over 150 patterns for the epidemics domain, and over 300 patterns for security.[9] These patterns were added to the system through an elaborate pattern-acquisition process, where semi-supervised pattern acquisition for English text was used, (Greenwood and Stevenson, 2006; Yangarber et al., 2000), to bootstrap many pattern candidates from raw text based on a small set of seed patterns; the candidates were subsequently checked manually and included in the system. Many of these patterns are typically in "base-form", i.e., simple active clauses; the English system takes each active-clause, "subject-verb-object" pattern, and generalizes it to multiple syntactic variants, including passive clauses, relative clauses, etc. Thus we created the Russian domain-specific patterns directly in PULS's pattern-specification language. A pattern consists of a regular expression trigger and action code.

The second reason is theoretical. Unlike English, Russian is a heavily inflected, free word-order language. In English, the active "subject-word-object" clause has only one form, whereas in Russian all six permutations of the three elements are possible, depending on the information structure and pragmatic focus. This means that we would need 6 pattern variants to match a single active clause, and many more to process other clausal types. The free word-order makes it difficult to generate syntactic clausal variants; it also complicates the bootstrapping of patterns from seeds.

Therefore, for Russian we used a different strategy, close to that used by (Tanev et al., 2009) for Romance languages. In this approach, the patterns first create "shallow", incomplete events where only 1–2 slots are filled. Then, the inference rule mechanism attempts to fill the remaining slots and complete the events. The majority of Russian patterns currently consist of two elements (such as verb and object, or verb and subject), so that only two word-order variants are possible. Currently, the Russian patterns match five syntactic constructions. These are listed in Table 1, along with examples from the security scenario. All example phrases have the same meaning ("migrant was arrested") but different syntactic form. The active clause and the passive clause in Russian may have either V–O word order—types I and III—or O–V,—types II and IV. The difference between the active and the passive variants is in the grammatical features only, which are marked by flexions.

Types I, III, and V in the table can be captured by one simple pattern:

class(ARREST) noungroup(MIGRANT)

This pattern matches when a content phrase—belonging to *any* part of speech (noun, verb, or participle)—whose semantic head is the concept *"ARREST"* governs (i.e., in this case, precedes) a noun group headed by the concept *"MIGRANT"*. The pattern primitives—*class*, *noungroup* and others—build on top of the POS, syntactic, and morphological tags that are returned by the AOT wrapper. Types II and IV show variants of the pattern in reverse order. Note that the patterns use general ontology classes—shared with English—rather than literal words.[10]

When a pattern fires, the system checks the constraints on grammatical features (e.g., case and number agreement) on the matched phrases or words. We introduce three types of constraints: accusative object-case agreement for type I and

[9]The difference is partly due to the fact that the security scenario has several event types—illegal migration, human-trafficking, smuggling, general crisis—and sub-types, while epidemics deals with one event type.

[10]NB: in practice, the patterns are more complex because they allow various sentence modifiers to appear between verb and object, which is a standard extension to this basic form of the pattern.

Concept	Event type
organ-transplant	*Human-Trafficking-Organs*
border-guard	*Migration-Illegal-Entry*
customs-officer	*Smuggling*

Table 2: Examples of concepts found in context that trigger rules to specialize the event type

II, for nominative subject-case agreement for type III and IV, and and genitive-case nominalization agreement for type V. If the constraints are satisfied, the event is created—that is, the same event structure for any of the five pattern types.

For the security scenario the system currently has 23 such "basic" patterns. Most of them initially produce an event of a general class *CRISIS* and fire when the text mentions that someone was arrested, sentenced, jailed, etc. If additional security-related concepts are found in text nearby, inference rules will fill additional slots in the event template, and specialize the type of the event. The Russian security scenario uses *exactly the same* set of inference rules as does the English Security Scenario. Example rules are shown in Table 2. For example, when an inference rule finds in the context of an event a semantic concept that is a sub-type of the type given in the left column, the *Type* of the event is specialized to the corresponding value in the right column, Table 2.

For the epidemics scenario, the system currently uses only 7 patterns. Two produce an underspecified event, when the text mentions that someone has become sick. The actual disease name is again found by inference rules from nearby context; if no disease is mentioned, the event is discarded. Two additional patterns work "in reverse": they match in cases when the text mentions an outbreak or case of a disease. Then the inference rules try to find who is suffering from disease and the number of victims. The inference rules are again fully shared between English and Russian. Some of the patterns are "negative"—they match such statements as "there is no threat of epidemic", which appear often in official reports.

In addition, the Russian pattern base contains 41 lower-level patterns, common for the security and epidemics domains. These include, for example, patterns to match date expressions, to analyze collective-partitive noun groups (*"a group of migrants"*, *"a team of doctors"*, and so on), which have general applicability.

Slot	*English system*			*Russian system*		
	rec	pre	F	rec	pre	F
Event Type	67	72	**69.41**	70	57	62.83
Suspect	46	52	**48.81**	52	44	47.67
Total	27	71	**46.47**	44	37	40.20
Countries	56	55	**55.49**	48	40	43.63
Time	29	29	**29.00**	29	22	25.02
All	53	58	**53.31**	55	45	49.09

Table 3: Border Security scenario evaluation

Event type	*English test suite*	*Russian test suite*
CRISIS	19	28
HUMAN-TRAFFICKING	4	4
ILLEGAL-MIGRATION	34	34
SMUGGLE	10	2
Total	67	68

Table 4: Distribution of event types in the test suites for the Security scenario

5 Evaluation

5.1 Security

For evaluation, we used a test corpus of 64 Russian-language documents. Several assessors annotated 65 events, and approximately one third of the documents contained events. We compared the Russian-language IE system with the English-language system. The English test suite consists of 50 documents with 70 events.

Evaluation results for the security domain are presented in table 3, with scores given for the main slots: *Event Type* (one of *Migration*, *Human Trafficking*, *Smuggling*, and *Crisis*), *Suspect*, *Total* (number of suspects), *Countries* (a list of one or more countries involved in event), and *Time* (event date). The table shows that currently the Russian system achieves a lower overall score than the English system—the F-measure for all slots is 4–5% lower, with precision being consistently lower than recall for the Russian system.

Note that the development of a correct and well-balanced test suite is in itself a challenging task, and hence the evaluation numbers may be biased. In the test suites used for these experiments, shown in table 4, the English security scenario includes more events of type *SMUGGLE* than the Russian validation suite, and both validation suites contain few events of type *HUMAN-TRAFFICKING*.

5.2 Epidemic Surveillance

For evaluation, we used a test corpus of 75 Russian documents. We asked several assessors to

Slot name	*English system*			*Russian system*		
	r	p	F	r	p	F
Disease	74	74	74.00	93	81	**86.58**
Country	65	67	65.98	91	86	**88.42**
Total	68	79	**73.09**	30	78	43.33
Time	56	58	**56.98**	38	52	43.91
Status	77	75	75.99	93	81	**86.58**
All Slots	68	69	68.83	70	71	**70.44**

Table 5: Epidemics scenario evaluation.

correct events found by the system and add missing events in case they were not found by system. Assessors annotated 120 events. We compare the Russian-language IE system with the English-language system. The PULS English validation suite for Epidemics currently consists of 60 documents with 172 events.

Evaluation results are shown in table 5, where the scores are given for the main slots: *Disease*, *Country*, *Total* (number of victims), *Status* ("dead" or "sick") and *Time*. Results for the Russian system are somewhat better than for English. This is due in part to the bias in the process which we used to select documents for the test suite: the assessors marked documents in which the system found events, rather than searching and annotating documents from scratch. (This aspect of the evaluation will be corrected in future work.) The events that the system found could be relevant, spurious, or erroneous; in case the system missed an event, the assessor's job was to add it to the gold-standard answers. Note that in general the amount of irrelevant documents processed by PULS is much larger than the amount of relevant documents (only about 1% of all documents that contain keywords relevant to epidemics contain useful events). Thus it is impractical to ask assessors to read raw documents. As a consequence, the scores for the main slots, such as *Disease* or *Country*, may be overstated: the majority of documents mention only one disease, and since an event was found by the system in most documents selected for the test suite, the *Disease* slot is usually filled correctly. The results for the auxiliary slots, e.g., *Time*, *Total*, are closer to our expectation.

5.3 Comparison of Languages and Scenarios

In general, the epidemics scenario performs much better than security, both in Russian and English. This is due to fact that the task definition for epidemics is simpler, better formalized, and deals with one type of event only. As noted in (Huttunen et al., 2002), event representation in text may have different structure depending on the scenario: the "classic" IE scenarios, such as the MUC Management Succession or Terror Attacks, describe events that occur at a specific point in time, whereas other scenarios, such as *Natural Disasters* or *Disease Outbreaks* describe a process that is spread out in time and space. Consequently, events in the latter ("nature") scenarios are more complex, may have hierarchical structure, and may even overlap in text. From the theoretical point of view it would be interesting to compare how the *events representation*, (Pivovarova et al., 2013), differs in different languages. Moreover, such differences can be important in cross-language information summarization, (Ji et al., 2013).

Event Type	**English**	**Russian**
Epidemic Surveillance		
DISEASE	31	5
HARM	825	412
Total	**856**	**417**
Border Security		
CRISIS	694	476
HUMAN-TRAFFICKING	10	12
ILLEGAL-MIGRATION	32	31
SMUGGLE	7	19
Total	**743**	**538**

Table 6: Number of events found by IE systems in parallel English-Russian news corpus.

We use a freely-available *comparable* news corpus, (Klementiev and Roth, 2006), to investigate the difference of event representation in English and Russian. The corpus contains 2327 BBC messages from the time period from 1 January 2001 to 10 May 2005, and their approximate translations from the *Lenta.ru* website; the translations may be quite different from their English sources and are stylistically similar to standard Russian news. We processed the corpora with the security and epidemics IE systems, using the respective language; the results are presented in the Table 6.

The table shows that for both scenarios the English system finds more events than the Russian, which probably means that coverage of the Russian IE is lower. We have yet to conduct a thorough evaluation of the events found. It is also clear from the table that specific events are much more rare than general events; for the security scenario, the majority of events have type CRISIS, which is a general type that indicates some incident related to crime; in the epidemics scenario, the majority of events have type HARM, i.e., which is a gen-

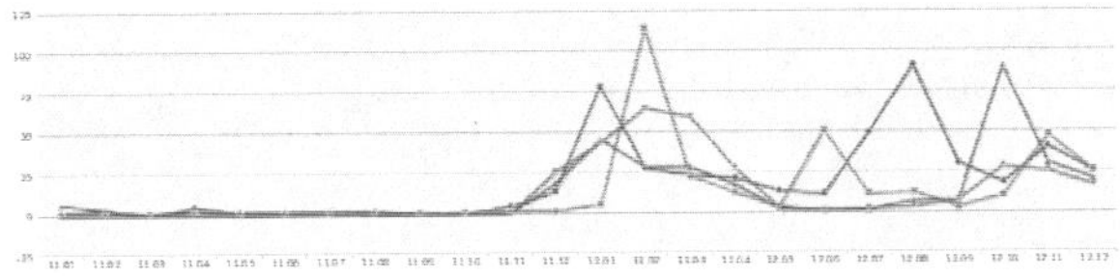

Figure 3: Monthly frequency of events for the four top-reported diseases in Russia

eral type indicating that there are victims (e.g., humans) suffering from some cause, not only harm caused by infections. The distributions of event types are similar in English and Russian corpora, which may hint that a lack of specific events may be a property of the scenarios, irrespective of the language. This agrees with the expectation that the majority of retrieved documents are not relevant.

6 Discussion

The Russian-language processing pipeline presented above is compatible with the working, pre-existing PULS IE system. It is worth noting again, that the output of the Russian-language analysis has the same form as that of the English-language PULS event extraction, that is, all fills for the template slots are output in *English* (except in the case of person names). This is made possible by the shared, language-independent ontology. An important benefit of this sharing is that the end-user is not required to understand Russian in order to determine whether the extracted facts and documents are relevant to her/his need. Thus, the slot fills may be presented in English, as shown in Figure 1. The document text, however, may be presented in Russian; users who can read Russian can see the original article text where event elements are indicated (by highlighting or underlining).

Figure 2 shows a summary-style list of events found from the news stream. The user can see events extracted from documents in a mix of languages (identified by the language tag in the left-most column). The database representation for events is shared and independent of the language; this permits the user get a grasp of current situation in the domain of interest, in more than one language.

We checked the impact of the Russian component on the system's coverage over the geographic area of the former USSR, which includes regions (outside Russia) where Russian may be used as a *lingua franca*, and may be common in press. Figure 3 shows the total number of events found in Russia, using both the Russian- and English-language IE systems for the four most frequently reported diseases. The check was conducted on news streams over 2011–2012. The number of events increases dramatically after deploying the Russian component, at the end of 2011 (near the middle of the timeline).

6.1 Conclusion

We have presented a "plug-in" extension to PULS, an English-language IE system, to cover Russian-language text. We currently handle two scenarios: Security and Epidemic Surveillance. The amount of effort needed to develop the Russian component was modest compared to the time and labour spent on the English-language IE system. The Russian system demonstrates a comparable level of performance to the baseline English IE: F-measure is about 4% lower for the Security scenario and 2% higher for the Epidemic Surveillance. We believe that this success is due to two main factors: first, the re-use of as many existing modules and knowledge bases as possible from the pre-existing English-language system; second, the use of shallow, permissive patterns in Russian in combination with logical inference rules.

In future research, we plan to further expand the pattern sets and lexicons, to analyze more kinds of syntactic and lexical phenomena in Russian. We plan to compare structural differences between the Security and Epidemics scenarios and their representation in Russian and English, to find language-dependent and language-independent features of the event representations. We plan to use cross-lingual analysis to obtain advances in two directions: first, pre-IE automatic pattern and paraphrase acquisition for free-word-order languages; second, post-IE aggregation of extracted information to improve overall quality by use of cross-document context, (Chen and Ji, 2009; Yangarber and Jokipii, 2005; Yangarber, 2006).

Acknowledgements

We thank Peter von Etter and Mikhail Novikov for help with the implementation; students of the Department of Information Systems, St. Petersburg State University, for annotating evaluation data. Work was funded in part by Frontex, Project on Automated Event Extraction, and the ALGODAN Center of Excellence of the Academy of Finland.

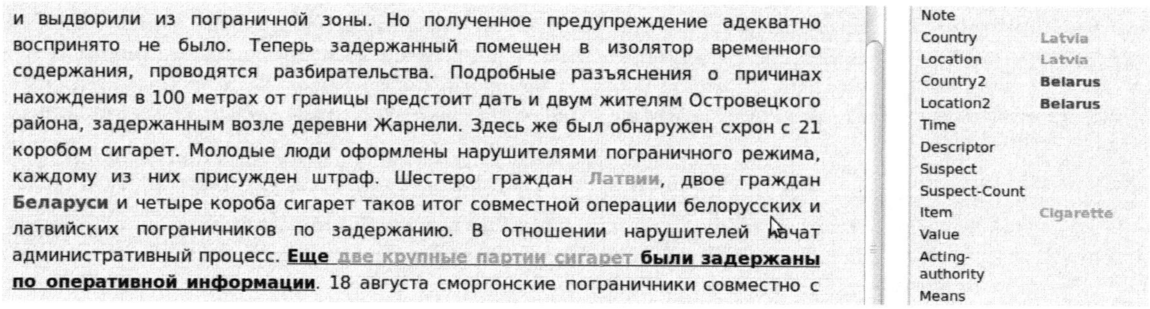

Figure 1: Document view and template view: a Smuggling event from the Security domain

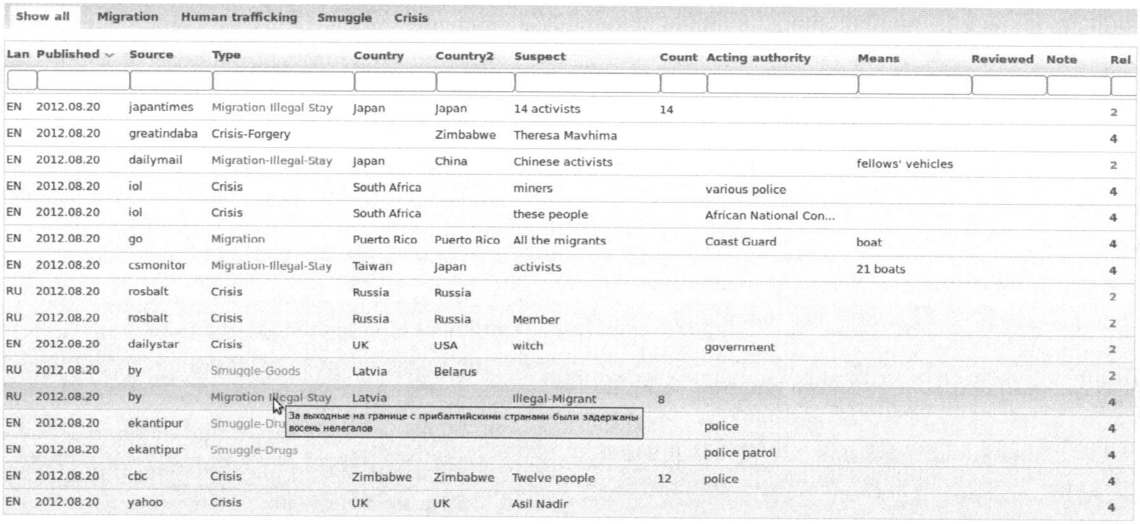

Show all | Migration | Human trafficking | Smuggle | Crisis

Lan	Published	Source	Type	Country	Country2	Suspect	Count	Acting authority	Means	Reviewed	Note	Rel
EN	2012.08.20	japantimes	Migration Illegal Stay	Japan	Japan	14 activists	14					2
EN	2012.08.20	greatindaba	Crisis-Forgery		Zimbabwe	Theresa Mavhima						4
EN	2012.08.20	dailymail	Migration-Illegal-Stay	Japan	China	Chinese activists			fellows' vehicles			2
EN	2012.08.20	iol	Crisis	South Africa		miners		various police				4
EN	2012.08.20	iol	Crisis	South Africa		these people		African National Con...				4
EN	2012.08.20	go	Migration	Puerto Rico	Puerto Rico	All the migrants		Coast Guard	boat			4
EN	2012.08.20	csmonitor	Migration-Illegal-Stay	Taiwan	Japan	activists			21 boats			4
RU	2012.08.20	rosbalt	Crisis	Russia	Russia							2
RU	2012.08.20	rosbalt	Crisis	Russia	Russia	Member						2
EN	2012.08.20	dailystar	Crisis	UK	USA	witch		government				2
RU	2012.08.20	by	Smuggle-Goods	Latvia	Belarus							2
RU	2012.08.20	by	Migration Illegal Stay	Latvia		Illegal-Migrant	8					4
EN	2012.08.20	ekantipur	Smuggle-Dru					police				4
EN	2012.08.20	ekantipur	Smuggle-Drugs					police patrol				4
EN	2012.08.20	cbc	Crisis	Zimbabwe	Zimbabwe	Twelve people	12	police				4
EN	2012.08.20	yahoo	Crisis	UK	UK	Asil Nadir						4

Figure 2: Summary view: a list of events in the Security domain. The tool-tip under the mouse shows a snippet of the original text, from which the event was extracted.

References

Ameyugo, G., Art, M., Esteves, A. S., and Piskorski, J. (2012). Creation of an EU-level information exchange network in the domain of border security. In *European Intelligence and Security Informatics Conference (EISIC)*. IEEE.

Astaf'eva, I., Bonch-Osmolovskaya, A., Garejshina, A., Grishina, J., D'jachkov, V., Ionov, M., Koroleva, A., Kudrinsky, M., Lityagina, A., Luchina, E., Sidorova, E., Toldova, S., Lyashevskaya, O., Savchuk, S., and Koval', S. (2010). NLP evaluation: Russian morphological parsers. In *Proceedings of Dialog Conference*, Moscow, Russia.

Atkinson, M., Piskorski, J., van der Goot, E., and Yangarber, R. (2011). Multilingual real-time event extraction for border security intelligence gathering. In Wiil, U. K., editor, *Counterterrorism and Open Source Intelligence*, pages 355–390. Springer Lecture Notes in Social Networks, Vol. 2.

Bocharov, V., Pivovarova, L., Rubashkin, V., and Chuprin, B. (2010). Ontological parsing of encyclopedia information. *Computational Linguistics and Intelligent Text Processing*.

Bontcheva, K., Maynard, D., Tablan, V., and Cunningham, H. (2003). GATE: A Unicode-based infrastructure supporting multilingual information extraction. In *Proceedings of Workshop on Information Extraction for Slavonic and other Central and Eastern European Languages*, Borovets, Bulgaria.

Chen, Z. and Ji, H. (2009). Can one language bootstrap the other: a case study on event extraction. In *Proceedings of the NAACL-HLT Workshop on Semi-Supervised Learning for Natural Language Processing*.

Collier, N., Doan, S., Kawazoe, A., Goodwin, R. M., Conway, M., Tateno, Y., Ngo, Q.-H., Dien, D., Kawtrakul, A., Takeuchi, K., Shigematsu, M., and Taniguchi, K. (2008). BioCaster: detecting public health rumors with a Web-based text mining system. *Bioinformatics*, 24(24).

Du, M., von Etter, P., Kopotev, M., Novikov, M., Tarbeeva, N., and Yangarber, R. (2011). Building support tools for Russian-language information extraction. In Habernal, I. and Matoušek, V., editors, *Text, Speech and Dialogue*, volume 6836 of *Lecture Notes in Computer Science*. Springer Berlin / Heidelberg.

Greenwood, M. and Stevenson, M. (2006). Improving semi-supervised acquisition of relation extraction patterns. In *Proceedings of Workshop on Information Extraction Beyond The Document, COLING-ACL*, volume 3808, pages 29–35. Springer, Lecture Notes in Artificial Intelligence, Sydney, Australia.

Huttunen, S., Yangarber, R., and Grishman, R. (2002). Diversity of scenarios in information extraction. In *Proceedings of the Third International Conference on Language Resources and Evaluation (LREC 2002)*, Las Palmas de Gran Canaria, Spain.

Ji, H., Favre, B., Lin, W.-P., Gillick, D., Hakkani-Tur, D., and Grishman, R. (2013). Open-domain multi-document summarization via information extraction: Challenges and prospects. In *Multi-source, Multilingual Information Extraction and Summarization*. Springer.

Khoroshevsky, V. F. (2010). Ontology driven multilingual information extraction and intelligent analytics. In *Web Intelligence and Security: Advances in Data and Text Mining Techniques for Detecting and Preventing Terrorist Activities on the Web*. IOS Press.

Klementiev, A. and Roth, D. (2006). Weakly supervised named entity transliteration and discovery from multilingual comparable corpora. In *Proceedings of the 21st International Conference on Computational Linguistics and the 44th annual meeting of the Association for Computational Linguistics*, Sydney, Australia.

Piskorski, J., Belyaeva, J., and Atkinson, M. (2011). Exploring the usefulness of cross-lingual information fusion for refining real-time news event extraction: A preliminary study. In *Proceedings of RANLP: 8th Conference on Recent Advances in Natural Language Processing*, Hissar, Bulgaria.

Pivovarova, L., Huttunen, S., and Yangarber, R. (2013). Event representation across genre. In *Proceedins of the 1st Workshop on Events: Definition, Detection, Coreference, and Representation*, NAACL HLT, Atlanta, Georgia.

Rortais, A., Belyaeva, J., Gemo, M., van der Goot, E., and Linge, J. P. (2010). Medisys: An early-warning system for the detection of (re-)emerging food- and feed-borne hazards. *Food Research International*, 43(5):1553–1556.

Schumann, A.-K. (2012). Towards the automated enrichment of multilingual terminology databases with knowledge-rich contexts–experiments with russian eurotermbank data. In *CHAT 2012: The Second Workshop on Creation, Harmonization and Application of Terminology Resources*, Madrid, Spain.

Sokirko, A. (2001). *Semantic dictionaries in automatic text analysis, based on DIALING system materials*. PhD thesis, Russian State University for the Humanities, Moscow.

Solovyev, V., Ivanov, V., Gareev, R., Serebryakov, S., and Vassilieva, N. (2012). Methodology for building extraction templates for Russian language in knowledge-based IE systems. Technical Report HPL-2012-211, HP Laboratories.

Tanev, H., Zavarella, V., Linge, J., Kabadjov, M., Piskorski, J., Atkinson, M., and Steinberger, R. (2009). Exploiting machine learning techniques to build an event extraction system for Portuguese and Spanish. *Linguamatica*, 2.

Toldova, S. J., Sokolova, E. G., Astaf'eva, I., Gareyshina, A., Koroleva, A., Privoznov, D., Sidorova, E., Tupikina, L., and Lyashevskaya, O. N. (2012). NLP evaluation 2011–2012: Russian syntactic parsers. In *Proceedings of Dialog Conference*, Moscow, Russia.

Yangarber, R. (2006). Verification of facts across document boundaries. In *Proceedings of the International Workshop on Intelligent Information Access (IIIA-2006)*, Helsinki, Finland.

Yangarber, R., Grishman, R., Tapanainen, P., and Huttunen, S. (2000). Automatic acquisition of domain knowledge for information extraction. In *Proceedings of the 18th International Conference on Computational Linguistics (COLING 2000)*, Saarbrücken, Germany.

Yangarber, R. and Jokipii, L. (2005). Redundancy-based correction of automatically extracted facts. In *Proceedings of HLT-EMNLP: Conference on Empirical Methods in Natural Language Processing*, Vancouver, Canada.

Yarowsky, D. (1995). Unsupervised word sense disambiguation rivaling supervised methods. In *Proceedings of the 33rd Annual Meeting of the Association for Computational Linguistics*, Cambridge, MA. ACM Press.

Zamite, J., Silva, F., Couto, F., and Silva, M. (2010). MEDCollector: Multisource epidemic data collector. In Khuri, S., Lhotská, L., and Pisanti, N., editors, *Information Technology in Bio- and Medical Informatics, ITBAM 2010*. Springer Berlin.

Semi-automatic Acquisition of Lexical Resources and Grammars for Event Extraction in Bulgarian and Czech

Hristo Tanev
Joint Research Centre
European Commission
via Fermi 2749, Ispra
Italy
hristo.tanev@jrc.ec.europa.eu

Josef Steinberger
University of West Bohemia
Faculty of Applied Sciences
Department of Computer Science and Engineering
NTIS Centre Univerzini 8, 30614 Plzen
Czech Republic
jstein@kiv.zcu.cz

Abstract

In this paper we present a semi-automatic approach for acqusition of lexico-syntactic knowledge for event extraction in two Slavic languages, namely Bulgarian and Czech. The method uses several weakly-supervised and unsupervised algorithms, based on distributional semantics. Moreover, an intervention from a language expert is envisaged on different steps in the learning procedure, which increases its accuracy, with respect to unsupervised methods for lexical and grammar learning.

1 Introduction

Automatic detection and extraction of events from online news provide means for tracking the developments in the World politics, economy and other important areas of life.

Event extraction is a branch of information extraction, whose goal is the automatic retrieval of structured information about events described in natural language texts. Events include interactions among different entities, to each of which an event-specific semantic role can be assigned. This role reflects the way in which the entity participates in the event and interacts with the other entities. For example, in the fragment "Three people were injured in a building collapse", the phrase "three people" may be assigned a semantic role $injured - victim$. The list of semantic roles depends on the adopted event model.

The event extraction technology may decrease the information overload, it allows automatic conversion of unstructured text data into structured one, it can be used to pinpoint interesting news articles, also extracted entities and their corresponding semantic roles can provide brief summaries of the articles.

Using lexico-syntactic knowledge is one of the promising directions in modeling the event-specific semantic roles (Hogenboom et al., 2011). While for English linear patterns seem to work quite well (Tanev et al., 2008), for other languages,where word ordering is more free, cascaded grammars proved to improve the results (Zavarella et al., 2008). In particular, Slavic languages are more free-order than English; consequently, using cascaded grammars may be considered a relevant approach.

In this paper we present an ongoing effort to build event extraction cascaded grammars for Bulgarian and Czech in the domain of violent news. To achieve this goal we put forward a semi-automatic approach for building of event extraction grammars, which uses several weakly-supervised algorithms for acquisition of lexical knowledge, based on distributional semantics and clustering. Moreover, the lexical knowledge is learned in the form of semantic classes, which then can be used as a basis for building of a domain-specific ontology.

To the best of our knowledge, there are no previous attempts to perform event extraction for Slavic languages, apart from the work presented in (Turchi et al., 2011).

The importance of Czech and Bulgarian languages comes from the geopolitical positions of the countries where they are spoken: Czech Republic is in a central geographical position between Eastern and Western Europe; Bulgaria is on the borders of the European Union, on a crossroad between Europe and Asia, surrounded by different cultures, languages and religions. These geopolitical factors contribute to the importance of the news from Czech Republic and Bulgaria and consequently make automatic event extraction from these news an useful technology for political analysts.

The paper has the following structure: In section 2 we make a short overview of the related approaches; in section 3 we describe our method for lexical and grammar learning; section 4 presents our experiments and evaluation for Bulgarian and Czech languages and section 5 discusses the outcome of the experiments and some future directions.

2 Related Work

There are different approaches for event extraction. Most of the work up to now has aimed at English (see among the others (Naughton et al., 2006) and (Yangarber et al., 2000)), however (Turchi et al., 2011) presented automatic learning of event extraction patterns for Russian, English and Italian.

Our work is based on weakly supervised algorithms for learning of semantic classes and patterns, presented in (Tanev et al., 2009) and (Tanev and Zavarella, 2013); these approaches are based on distributional semantics. There are different other methods which use this paradigm: A concept and pattern learning Web agent, called NELL (Never Ending Language Learning) is presented in (Carlson et al., 2010). Parallel learning of semantic classes and patterns was presented in (Riloff and Jones, 1999). However these approaches do not try to derive grammars from the acquired resources, but stop at purely lexical level.

Relevant to our approach are the grammar learning approaches. A survey of supervised and unsupervised approaches is presented in (D'Ulizia et al., 2011). The supervised ones require annotation of big amounts of data which makes the development process long and laborious. On the other hand, unsupervised methods try to generalize all the training data by using different heuristics like the minimal description length. Since for event extraction only specific parts of the text are analyzed, in order to use unsupervised grammar acquisition methods for learning of event extraction grammars, one should collect the exact phrases which describe the events. In practice, this would transform the unsupervised methods into supervised ones. With respect to the state-of-the art grammar inference approaches, our method allows for more interaction between the grammar expert and the learning system. Moreover, our learning starts from lexical items and not from annotated texts, which decreases the development efforts.

3 Semi-automatic Learning of Lexica and Grammars

The event extraction grammar, exploited in our approach is a cascaded grammar which on the first levels detects references to entities, like people, groups of people, vehicles, etc. On the upper levels our cascaded grammar detects certain events in which these entities participate: In the domain of violent news, people may get killed, wounded, kidnapped, arrested, etc. If we consider as an example the following Bulgarian text: "Група протестиращи бяха арестувани вчера по време на демонстрации в центъра на столицата" ("A group of protesters were arrested yesterday during demonstrations in the centre of the capital"), our grammar will detect first that "Група протестиращи" ("A group of protesters") refers to a group of people and then, it will find that "Група протестиращи бяха арестувани" ("A group of protesters were arrested") refers to an arrest event where the aforementioned group of people is assigned the semantic role *arrested*.

In order to build such a grammar, we acquire semi-automatically the following resources:

1. a dictionary of words which refer to people and other entities in the required domain-specific context, e.g. "войник", "voják" ("soldier" in Bulgarian and Czech), "жена" , "žena" ("woman" in Bulgarian and Czech), etc.

2. a list of modifiers and other words which appear in phrases referring to those entities, e.g. "цивилен", "civilní" ("civil" in Bulgarian and Czech), "НАТО" ("NATO"), etc.

3. grammar rules for parsing entity-referring phrases. For example, a simple rule can be: $PERSON\_PHRASE \rightarrow PER$ $connector$ ORG
where PER and ORG are words and multiwords, referring to people and organizations, $connector \rightarrow$ "от" for Bulgarian or $connector \rightarrow$ "" (empty string) for Czech. This rule can parse phrases like "войник от НАТО" or "voják NATO" ("NATO soldier")

4. a list of words which participate in event patterns like "арестуван", "zadržen" ("arrested" in Bulgarian and Czech) or "убит", "zabit" ("killed" in Bulgarian and Czech).

5. a set of grammar rules which parse event-description phrases. For example, a simple rule can be:
   $KILLING \rightarrow PER\ connector\ KILLED\_PARTICIPLE$
   where $connector \rightarrow$ "беше" for Bulgarian or $connector \rightarrow$ "byl" for Czech.
   This rule will recognize phrases like "Войник от НАТО беше убит" or "Voják NATO byl zabit" ("A NATO soldier was killed" in Bulgarian and Czech")

In order to acquire this type of domain lexica and a grammar, we make use of a semi-automatic method which acquires in parallel grammar rules and dictionaries. Our method exploits several state-of-the-art algorithms for expanding of semantic classes, distributional clustering, learning of patterns and learning of modifiers, described in (Tanev and Zavarella, 2013). The semantic class expansion algorithm was presented also in (Tanev et al., 2009). These algorithms are multilingial and all of them are based on distributional semantics. They use a non-annotated text corpus for training.

We integrated these algorithms in a semi-automatic schema for grammar learning, which is still in phase of development. Here is the basic schema of the approach:

1. The user provides a small list of seed words, which designate people or other domain-specific entities, e.g." soldiers","civilians", "fighters" (We will use only English-language examples for short, however the method is multilingual and consequently applicable for Czech and Bulgarian).

2. Using the multilingual semantic class expansion algorithm (Tanev et al., 2009) other words are learned (e.g. "policemen", "women", etc.), which are likely to belong to the same semantic class. First, the algorithm finds typical contextual patterns for the seed words from not annotated text. For example, all the words, referring to people tend to appear in linear patterns like *[PEOPLE] were killed*, *thousands of [PEOPLE]* , *[PEOPLE] are responsible*, etc. Then, other words which tend to participatre in the same contextual patterns are extracted from the unannotated text corpus. In such a way the algorithm learns additional words like "policemen", "killers", "terrorists", "women", "children", etc.

3. Since automatic approaches for learning of semantic classes always return some noise in the output, a manual cleaning by a domain expert takes place as a next step of our method.

4. Learning modifiers: At this step, for each semantic class learned at the previous step (e.g. *PEOPLE*, we run the modifier learning algorithm, put forward by (Tanev and Zavarella, 2013) , which learns domain-specific syntactic modifiers. Regarding the class *PEOPLE*), the modifiers will be words like " Russian", "American", "armed", "unarmed", "masked", etc. The modifier learning algorithm exploits the principle that the context distribution of words from a semantic class is most likely similar to the context distribution of these words with syntactic modifiers attached. The algorithm uses this heuristic and does not use any morphological information to ensure applications in multilingual settings.

5. Manual cleaning of the modifier list

6. Adding the following grammar rule at the first level of the cascaded grammar, which uses the semantic classes and modifiers, learned at the previous steps:
   $Entity(class : C) \rightarrow (LModif(class : C))*\ Word(class : C)\ (RModif(class : C))*$
   This rule parses phrases, like "masked gunmen from IRA", referring to an entity from a semantic class C, e.g. *PERSON*. It should consist of a sequence of 0 or more left modifiers for this class, e.g. "masked", a word from this class ("gunmen" in this example) and a sequence of 0 or more right modifiers ("from IRA" in the example").

7. Modifiers learned by the modifier learning algorithm do not cover all the variations in the structure of the entity-referring phrases, since sometimes the structure is more complex and cannot be encoded through a list of lexical patterns. Consider, for example, the following phrase "soldiers from the special forces of the Russian Navy". There is a little

chance that our modifier learning algorithm acquires the string "from the special forces of the Russian Navy", on the other hand the following two grammar rules can do the parsing:
$RIGHT\_PEOPLE\_MODIFIER \rightarrow$ $``from'' MILITARY\_FORMATION$
$MILITARY\_FORMATION \rightarrow$ $LeftModMF * \; MFW \; RightModMF*$
where $MILITARY\_FORMATION$ is a phrase which refers to some organization (in the example, shown above, the phrase is "the special forces of the Russian Navy"), MFW is a term which refers to a military formation ("the special forces") and $LeftModMF$ and $RightModMF$ are left and right modifiers of the military formation entity (for example, a right modifier is"of the Russian Navy").

In order to learn such more complex structure, we propose the following procedure:

(a) The linguistic expert chooses semantic classes, for which more elaborated grammar rules should be developed. Let's take for example the class *PEOPLE*.

(b) Using the context learning sub-algorithm of the semantic class expansion, used in step 2, we find contextual patterns which tend to co-occur with this class. Apart from the patterns shown in step 2, we also learn patterns like *[PEOPLE] from the special forces*, *[PEOPLE] from the Marines*, *[PEOPLE] from the Russian Federation*, *[PEOPLE] from the Czech Republic*, *[PEOPLE] with guns*, *[PEOPLE] with knives*, *[PEOPLE] with masks*, etc.

(c) We generalize contextual patterns, in order to create grammar rules. In the first step we create automatically syntactic clusters separately for left and right contextual patterns. Syntactic clustering puts in one cluster patterns where the slot and the content-bearing words are connected by the same sequence of stop words. In the example, shown above, we will have two syntactic clusters of patterns: The first consists of patterns which begin with *[PEOPLE] from the* and the second contains the patterns, which start with *[PEOPLE] with*. These clusters can be represented via grammar rules in the following way:
RIGHT_PEOPLE_MODIFIER $\rightarrow$ *"from the" X*
X $\rightarrow$ *(special forces | Marines | Russian Federation | Czech Republic)*
RIGHT_PEOPLE_MODIFIER $\rightarrow$ *"with" Y*
Y $\rightarrow$ *(knives | guns | masks)*

(d) Now, several operations can be done with the clusters of words inside the grammar rules:

- Words inside a cluster can be clustered further on the basis of their semantics. In our system we use bottom up agglomerative clustering, where each word is represented as a vector of its context features. Manual cleaning and merging of the clusters may be necessary after this automatic process. If words are not many, only manual clustering can also be an option. In the example above "special forces" and "Marines" may form one cluster, since both words designate the class *MILITARY_FORMATION* and the other two words designate countries and also form a separate semantic class.
- In the grammar introduce new non-terminal symbols, corresponding to the newly learnt semantic classes. Then, in the grammar rules substitute lists of words with references to these symbols. (Still we do modification of the grammar rules manually, however we envisage to automate this process in the future). For example, the rule

  X $\rightarrow$ *(special forces | Marines | Russian Federation | Czech Republic)*
  will be transformed into
  X $\rightarrow$ *(MILITARY_FORMATION | COUNTRY)*
  MILITARY_FORMATION $\rightarrow$ *(special forces | Marines)*
  COUNTRY $\rightarrow$ *(Russian Federation*

PEOPLE → *(NUMBER* от *(from))?* $PEOPLE_a$ Example: "двама от българските войници" *("two of the Bulgarian soldiers")* $PEOPLE_a$ → *PEOPLE*$_b$ *((*от *(from)* | на *(of)* | в *(in)) (ORG* | *PLACE))** Example: "служители на МВР" *("staff from the MVR (Ministry of the Internal Affairs)")* $PEOPLE_b$ → *LeftPM* PEOPLE_W RightPM** Example: "неизвестни нападатели с качулки" *("unknown attackers with hoods")*

Table 1: Rules for entity recognition for the Bulgarian language

| Czech Republic)

- Clusters can be expanded by using the semantic class expansion algorithm, introduced before, followed by manual cleaning. In our example, this will add other words for *MILITARY_FORMATION* and *COUNTRY*. Consequently, the range of the phrases, parsable by the grammar rules will be augmented.

(e) The linguistic expert may choose a subset of the semantic classes, obtained on the previous step, (e.g. the the semantic class *MILITARY_FORMATION*) to be modeled further via extending the grammar with rules about their left and right modifiers. Then, the semantic class is recursively passed to the input of this grammar learning procedure.

8. Learning event patterns: In this step we learn patterns like *[PEOPLE]* "бяха арестувани" or *[PEOPLE] "byl zadržen" ([PEOPLE] were/was arrested* in Bulgarian and Czech). The pattern learning algorithm collects context patterns for one of the considered entity categories (e.g. *[PEOPLE]*. This is done through the context learning sub-algorithm described in step 2. Then, it searches for such context patterns, which contain words, having distributional similarity to words, describing the target event (e.g. "арестувани", "zadržen" ("arrested")).

   For example, if we want to learn patterns for *arrest* events in Bulgarian, the algorithm first learns contexts of *[PEOPLE]*. These contexts are *[PEOPLE]* бяха убити (*[PEOPLE] were killed*), хиляди [PEOPLE] (*thousands of [PEOPLE]*), *[PEOPLE]* бяха заловени (*[PEOPLE] were captured*), etc. Then, we pass to the semantic expansion algorithm (see step 2) seed words which express the event arrest, namely "задържани", "арестувани" ("apprehended", "arrested"), etc. Then, it will discover other similar words like "заловени" ("captured"). Finally, the algorithm searches such contextual patterns, which contain any of the seed and learnt words. For example, the pattern [PEOPLE] бяха заловени (*[PEOPLE] were captured*) is one of the newly learnt patterns for *arrest* events.

9. Generalizing the patterns: In this step we apply a generalization algorithm, described in step 7 to learn grammar rules which parse events. For example, two of the learned rules for parsing of arrest events in Bulgarian are:

   ARREST → *PEOPLE* "бяха" *("were") ARREST_PARTICIPLE*
   ARREST_PARTICIPLE → *(* "арестувани" ("arrested") | "заловени"("captured") | "закопчани" ("handcuffed") *)*

The outcome of this learning schema is a grammar and dictionaries which recognize descriptions of different types of domain-specific entities and events, which happened with these entities. Moreover, the dictionaries describe semantic classes from the target domain and can be used further for creation of a domain ontology.

4 Experiments and Evaluation

In our experiments, we applied the procedure shown above to learn grammars and dictionaries for parsing of phrases, referring to people, groups of people and violent events in Bulgarian and Czech news. We used for training 1 million news titles for Bulgarian and Czech, downloaded from

KILLING → KILL_VERB (a (and) | i (and) | jeden (one) | jeden z (one of))? [PEOPLE]
KILL_VERB → (zabit (killed) | zabila | zahynul (died) | zabiti | ubodal (stabbed) | ubodala | ...)
KILLING → KILL_ADJ [PEOPLE]
KILL_ADJ → (mrtvou (dead) | mrtvého (dead) | ...)
KILLING → [PEOPLE] KILL_VERB$_a$
KILL_VERB$_a$ *→ (zahynul (died) | zamřel (died) | ...)*
KILLING → [PEOPLE] byl (was) KILL_VERB$_b$
KILL_VERB$_b$ *→ (zabit (killed) | ...)*

Table 2: Rules for parsing of killing events and their victims in Czech

the Web and a small number of seed terms, referring to people and actions. We had more available time to work for the Bulgarian language, that is why we learned more complex grammar for Bulgarian. Both for Czech and Bulgarian, we learned grammar rules parsing event description phrases with one participating entity, which is a person or a group of people. This is simplification, since often an event contains more than one participant, in such cases our grammar can detect the separate phrases with their corresponding participants, but currently it is out of the scope of the grammar to connect these entities. The event detection rules in our grammar are divided into semantic classes, where each class of rules detects specific type of events like *arrest, killing, wounding*, etc. and also assigns an event specific semantic role to the participating entity, e.g. *victim, perpetrator, arrested, kidnapped.*

In order to implement our grammars, we used the EXPRESS grammar engine (Piskorski, 2007). It is a tool for building of cascaded grammars where specific parts of the parsed phrase are assigned semantic roles. We used this last feature of EXPRESS to assign semantic roles of the participating person entities.

For Czech we learned a grammar which detects killings and their victims. For Bulgarian, we learned a grammar, which parses phrases referring to killings, woundings and their victims, arrests and who is arrested, kidnappings and other violent events with their perpetrators and targeted people.

4.1 Learning people-recognition rules

For Czech our entity extraction grammar was relatively simple, since we learned just a dictionary of left modifiers. Therefore, we skipped step 7 in the learning schema, via which more elaborated entity recognition grammars are learned. Thus, the Czech grammar for recognizing phrases, referring to people contains the following rules:

PEOPLE → LeftMod PEOPLE_TERM*

LeftMod → ("mladou" ("young") | "neznámému"("unknown") | "starší" ("old") | ...)

PEOPLE_TERM → ("vojáci" ("soldiers") | "civilisté"("civilians") | "ženu" ("woman") | ...)

This grammar recognizes phrases like "mladou ženu" ("young woman" in Czech). Two dictionaries were acquired in the learning process: A dictionary of nouns, referring to people and left modifiers of people. The dictionary of people-referring nouns contains 268 entries, obtained as a result of the semantic class expansion algorithm. We used as a seed set 17 words like "muži" ("men"), "voiáci" ("soldiers"), etc. The algorithm learned 1009 new words and bigrams, 251 of which were correct (25%), that is refer to people. One problem here was that not all morphological forms were learned by our class expansion algorithm. In a language with rich noun morphology, as Czech is, this influenced on the coverage of our dictionaries.

After manual cleaning of the output from the modifier learning algorithm, we obtained 603 terms; the learning accuracy of the algorithm was found to be **55%** .

For Bulgarian we learned a more elaborated people recognition grammar, which is able to parse more complex phrases like "един от маскираните нападатели" ("one of the masked attackers") and "бойци от българския контингент в Ирак" ("soldiers from the Bulgarian contingent in Iraq"). The most important rules which we learned are shown in Table 1. In these rules *PEOPLE_W* encodes a noun or a bigram which refers to people, *ORG* is an organization; we learned mostly organizations, related to the domain of security, such as different types of military and other armed formations like "силите на реда" ("security forces"), also governmental organizations, etc. $PLACE$ stands for names of places and common nouns, referring to places such as "столицата" ("the capital"). We also learned modifiers for these categories and added them to the grammar. (For simplicity, we do not show the grammar rules for parsing ORG abd $PLACE$; we will just mention that both types of phrases are allowed to have a sequence of left modifiers, one or more nouns from the corresponding class and a sequence of 0 or more right modifiers.) Both categories $PLACE$ and ORG were obtained in step 7 of the learning schema, when exploring the clusters of words which appear as modifiers after the nouns, referring to people, like in the following example "бойци от българския контингент" ("soldiers from the Bulgarian contingent"); then, we applied manual unification of the clusters and their subsequent expansion, using the semantic class expansion algorithm.

Regarding the semantic class expansion, with 20 seed terms we acquired around 2100 terms, from which we manually filtered the wrong ones and we left 1200 correct terms, referring to people; the accuracy of the algorithm was found to be **57%** in this case.

We learned 1723 nouns for organizations and 523 place names and common nouns. We did not track the accuracy of the learning for these two classes. We also learned 319 relevant modifiers for people-referring phrases; the accuracy of the modifier learning algorithm was found to be **67%** for this task.

4.2 Learning of event detection rules

This learning takes place in step 8 and 9 of our learning schema. As it was explained, first linear patterns like *[PEOPLE] "byl zadržen" ([PEOPLE] was arrested*) are learned, then through a semi-automatic generalization process these patterns are transformed into rules like:
ARREST → PEOPLE "byl" ARREST_VERB

In our experiments for Czech we learned grammar rules and a dictionary which recognize different syntactic constructions, expressing killing events and the victims. These rules encode 156 event patterns. The most important of these rules are shown in Table 2. Part of the event rule learning process is expansion of a seed set of verbs, and other words, referring to the considered event (in this case *killing*).For this task the semantic class expansion algorithm showed significantly lower accuracy with respect to expanding sets of nouns - only **5%**. Nevertheless, the algorithm learned 54 Czech words, expressing killing and death.

For Bulgarian we learned rules for detection of killing and its victims, but also rules for parsing of wounding events, arrests, targeting of people in violent events, kidnapping, and perpetrators of violent events. These rules encode 605 event patterns. Some of the rules are shown in Table 3.

4.3 Evaluation of event extraction

In order to evaluate the performance of our grammars, we created two types of corpora: For the precision evaluation we created bigger corpus of randomly picked excerpts of news from Bulgarian and Czech online news sources. More precisely, we used 7'550 news titles for Czech and 12'850 news titles in Bulgarian. We also carried out a preliminary recall evaluation on a very small text collection: We manually chose sentences which report about violent events of the types which our grammars are able to capture. We selected 17 sentences for Czech and 28 for Bulgarian. We parsed the corpora with our EXPRESS grammars and evaluated the correctness of the extracted events. Since each event rule has assigned an event type and a semantic role for the participating people reference, we considered a correct match only when both a correct event type and a correct semantic role are assigned to the matched text fragment. Table 4 shows the results from our evaluation. The low recall in Czech was mostly due to the insufficient lexicon for people and the too simplistic grammar.

Language	Precision	Recall
Bulgarian	93%	39%
Czech	88%	6%

Table 4: Event extraction accuracy

5 Discussion

In this paper we presented a semi-automatic approach for learning of grammar and lexical knowledge from unannotated text corpora. The method is multilingual and relies on distributional approaches for semantic clustering and class expansion.

KILLING → *KILL_VERB* (бяха *(were)* | са *(are)*) *[PEOPLE]*
KILL_VERB → (загинали *(killed)* | убити *(killed)* | застреляните *(shot to death)* | ...)
KILLING → *KILL_PHRASE* на *(of)* *[PEOPLE]*
KILL_PHRASE → (отне живота *(took the life)* | причини смъртта *(caused the death)* | ...)
WOUNDING → *WOUND_VERB* (бяха *(were)* | са *(are)*) *[PEOPLE]*
WOUND_VERB → (ранени *(wounded)* | пострадалите *(injured)* | ...)
ARREST → *[PEOPLE]* *ARREST_VERB*
ARREST_VERB → (арестувани *(arrested)* | задържани *(detained)* | ...)

Table 3: Some event parsing rules for Bulgarian

We are currently developing event extraction grammars for Czech and Bulgarian. Preliminary evaluation shows promising results for the precision, while the recall is still quite low. One of the factors which influences the law recall was the insufficient number of different morphological word variations in the learned dictionaries. The morphological richness of Slavic languages can be considered by adding morphological dictionaries to the system or creating an automatic procedure which detects the most common endings of the nouns and other words and expands the dictionaries with morphological forms.

Another problem in the processing of the Slavic languages is their relatively free order. To cope with that, often the grammar engineer should introduce additional variants of already learned grammar rules. This can be done semi-automatically, where the system may suggest additional rules to the grammar developer. This can be done through development of grammar meta-rules.

With respect to other approaches, grammars provide transparent, easy to expand model of the domain. The automatically learned grammars can be corrected and extended manually with hand-crafted rules and linguistic resources, such as morphological dictionaries. Moreover, one can try to introduce grammar rules from already existing grammars. This, of course, is not trivial because of the different formalisms exploited by each grammar. It is noteworthy that the extracted semantic classes can be used to create an ontology of the domain. In this clue, parallel learning of a domain-specific grammars and ontologies could be an interesting direction for future research.

The manual efforts in the development of the grammars and the lexical resources were mainly cleaning of already generated lists of words and manual selection and unification of word clusters. Although we did not evaluate precisely the invested manual efforts, one can estimate them by the size of the automatically acquired word lists and their accuracy, given in section *Semi-automatic Learning of Lexica and Grammars*.

We plan to expand the Czech grammar with rules for more event types. Also, we think to extend both the Bulgarian and the Czech event extraction grammars and the lexical resources, so that it will be possible to detect also disasters, humanitarian crises and their consequences. This will increase the applicability and usefulness of our event extraction grammars.

Acknowledgments

This work was partially supported by project "NTIS - New Technologies for Information Society", European Center of Excellence, CZ.1.05/1.1.00/02.0090.

References

A. Carlson, J. Betteridge, B. Kisiel, B. Settles, R. Estevam, J. Hruschka, and T. Mitchell. 2010. Toward an architecture for never-ending language learning. In *Proceedings of the Twenty-Fourth AAAI Conference on Artificial Intelligence (AAAI-10).*

A. D'Ulizia, F. Ferri, and P. Grifoni. 2011. A survey of grammatical inference methods for natural language learning. *Artificial Intelligence Review vol. 36 issue 1.*

F. Hogenboom, F. Frasincar, U. Kaymak, and F. Jong. 2011. An overview of event extraction from text. In *Workshop on Detection, Representation, and Exploitation of Events in the Semantic Web (DeRiVE 2011) at ISWC 2011.*

M. Naughton, N. Kushmerick, and J. Carthy. 2006. Event Extraction from Heterogeneous News Sources. In *Proceedings of the AAAI 2006 workshop on Event Extraction and Synthesis*, Menlo Park, California, USA.

J. Piskorski. 2007. ExPRESS – Extraction Pattern Recognition Engine and Specification Suite. In *Proceedings of FSMNLP 2007.*

E. Riloff and R. Jones. 1999. Learning dictionaries for information extraction by multi-level bootstrapping. In *Proceedings of the Sixteenth National Conference on Artificial Intelligence (AAAI 99).*

H. Tanev and V. Zavarella. 2013. Multilingual learning and population of event ontologies. a case study for social media. In P. Buitelaar and P. Cimiano, editors, *Towards Multilingual Semantic Web (in press).* Springer, Berlin & New York.

H. Tanev, J. Piskorski, and M. Atkinson. 2008. Real-Time News Event Extraction for Global Crisis Monitoring. In *Proceedings of NLDB 2008.*, pages 207–218.

H. Tanev, V. Zavarella, J. Linge, M. Kabadjov, J. Piskorski, M. Atkinson, and R. Steinberger. 2009. Exploiting Machine Learning Techniques to Build an Event Extraction System for Portuguese and Spanish. *Linguamática: Revista para o Processamento Automático das Línguas Ibéricas*, 2:550–566.

M. Turchi, V. Zavarella, and H. Tanev. 2011. Pattern learning for event extraction using monolingual statistical machine translation. In *Proceedings of Recent Advances in Natural Language Processing (RANLP 2011), Hissar, Bulgaria.*

R. Yangarber, R. Grishman, P. Tapanainen, and S. Huttunen. 2000. Unsupervised Discovery of Scenario-Level Patterns for Information Extraction. In *Proceedings of ANLP-NAACL 2000, Seattle, USA, 2000.*

V. Zavarella, H. Tanev, and J. Piskorski. 2008. Event Extraction for Italian using a Cascade of Finite-State Grammars. In *Proceedings of FSMNLP 2008.*

Wordnet-Based Cross-Language Identification of Semantic Relations

Ivelina Stoyanova **Svetla Koeva** **Svetlozara Leseva**
Department of Computational Linguistics, IBL, BAS, Sofia, Bulgaria
{iva,svetla,zarka}@dcl.bas.bg

Abstract

We propose a method for cross-language identification of semantic relations based on word similarity measurement and morphosemantic relations in WordNet. We transfer these relations to pairs of derivationally unrelated words and train a model for automatic classification of new instances of (morpho)semantic relations in context based on the existing ones and the general semantic classes of collocated verb and noun senses. Our experiments are based on Bulgarian-English parallel and comparable texts but the method is to a great extent language-independent and particularly suited to less-resourced languages, since it does not need parsed or semantically annotated data. The application of the method leads to an increase in the number of discovered semantic relations by 58.35% and performs relatively consistently, with a small decrease in precision between the baseline (based on morphosemantic relations identified in wordnet) – 0.774, and the extended method (based on the data obtained through machine learning) – 0.721.

1 Introduction

Natural language semantics has begun to receive due attention as many areas of natural language processing have recognized the need for addressing both the syntactic structure and the semantic representation of sentence constituents. Modelling conceptual and syntactic relationships such as semantic roles, semantic and syntactic frames, or semantic and syntactic dependencies is known as semantic role labeling – SRL (Gildea and Jurafsky, 2002), (shallow) semantic parsing (Pradhan et al., 2004), semantic role tagging (Xue and Palmer, 2004), extraction of predicate-argument structures (Moschitti and Bejan, 2004), automatic extraction of semantic relations (Swier and Stevenson, 2005), among others.

We propose a method for automatic semantic labeling based on the morphosemantic relations in Princeton WordNet (PWN). A morphosemantic relation associates a verb synset S_v and a noun synset S_n if there is a derivational relation between a literal L_v in S_v and a literal L_n in S_n. Morphosemantic relations inherit the semantics of the derivation. Consider, for instance, the morphosemantic relations *agent*, *instrument*, *location*, and *vehicle*, which link a verb to its agent (*administrate – administrator*), instrument (*collide – collider*), location (*settle – settlement*), vehicle (*bomb – bomber*).

We apply word and clause similarity measurement to parallel and comparable texts in order to perform partial word sense disambiguation and to identify candidates for labeling with semantic information. We enhance the WordNet morphosemantic relations with semantic generalizations derived from the general semantic word classes of the synsets and use this knowledge to learn and assign different types of semantic information:

- semantic relations associated with the noun collocates of a particular verb sense;
- general semantic noun classes that are eligible to collocate with a particular verb sense.

We apply this method to English and Bulgarian using PWN and the Bulgarian WordNet (BulNet). An advantage of the proposed approach is that it is able to assign semantic labels to unstructured text.

The paper is organised as follows. We outline the background against which we approach the identification of semantic relations in Section 2 where we present in brief groundbreaking and influential recent work in semantic role labeling (SRL). In Section 3 we discuss the linguistic motivation for the proposed approach. In Section 4 we describe the method for wordnet-based identification of semantic information and its implementation. Section 5 presents assessment of the results, followed by conclusions and an outline of directions for future research in Section 6.

2 Related Work

Many applications treat the assignment of semantic roles, semantic frames, and dependencies as a classification problem that involves the training of models on (large) manually annotated corpora, such as FrameNet text annotation (Ruppenhofer et al., 2010), the Prague Dependency Treebank (Hajic, 1998), or PropBank (Palmer et al., 2005), and the subsequent assignment of semantic labels to appropriate sentence constituents.

A number of models have been developed using the FrameNet corpus. Undoubtedly the most influential one has been Gildea and Jurafsky's machine learning method (Gildea and Jurafsky, 2002), which is based on the training of a SRL classifier on a set of lexical, morpho-syntactic, syntactic and word order features extracted from the parsed FrameNet corpus in conjunction with knowledge of the predicates, prior probabilities of various combinations of semantic roles, etc.

PropBank spurred a lot of research in SRL (Pradhan et al., 2004; Pradhan et al., 2008; Toutanova et al., 2008; Surdeanu et al., 2003; Xue and Palmer, 2004), to mention but a few. For instance, Pradhan et al. (2004) and Pradhan et al. (2008) propose SRL algorithms that augment previously developed systems, such as Gildea and Jurafsky's (2002) by replacing earlier classifiers with SVMs. Xue and Palmer (2004) train a Maximum Entropy classifier on the PropBank using linguistic features that can be directly extracted from syntactic parse trees and achieve results comparable to the best performing system at the time (Pradhan et al., 2004).

Semantic role labeling based on (large) annotated corpora need to deal with a number of issues, such as the situation specificity of semantic roles, the manual selection of annotated examples, variability in the sets of roles used across the computational resources, among others (Marquez et al., 2008). Pradhan et al. (2008) have also shown that the transfer of such models to other domains leads to substantial degradation in the results.

Some researchers employ other resources as an alternative. Swier and Stevenson (2005) describe an unsupervised SRL system that combines information from a verb lexicon – VerbNet with a simple probability model. Shi and Mihalcea (2005) propose the integration of VerbNet, WordNet and FrameNet into a knowledge base and use it in the building of a semantic parser. The system identifies the FrameNet frame best corresponding to a parsed sentence either as a direct match, or via VerbNet and/or WordNet relations.

Despite these alternatives the dominant trend has remained the corpus-based SRL, with unsupervised approaches gaining popularity as a way of overcoming the deficiencies of supervised methods (Lang and Lapata, 2011a; Lang and Lapata, 2011b), among others. Syntactic analysis has been considered a prerequisite in SRL, with full parsing winning over partial parsing, as demonstrated by the results in the CoNLL-2004 (Carreras and Marquez, 2004) and the CoNLL-2005 (Carreras and Marquez, 2005) shared tasks. Syntactic analysis and SRL have been dealt with within two general frameworks. In the "pipeline" approach the systems first perform syntactic parsing followed by SRL, while In the joint parsing approach syntactic and semantic parsing are performed together. Joint parsing of syntactic and semantic dependencies has been the focus of the CoNLL-2008 (Surdeanu et al., 2008) and CoNLL-2009 (Hajič et al., 2009) shared tasks.

To sum up, a classical SRL system takes a parsed input and assigns semantic roles on the basis of: i) a language model learnt from a pre-annotated semantically labeled corpus; ii) a frame lexicon; or iii) a combination of different resources. In the systems using annotated corpora the syntactically parsed sentences are usually semantically annotated using classifiers trained on the corpus on the basis of linguistic features derived from the parses. In the case of lexicon-based systems semantic roles are directly or indirectly assigned from the lexicon.

3 Motivation

Morphosemantic relations in WordNet denote relations between (synset members) that are similar in meaning and where one word is derived from the other by means of a morphological affix (Fellbaum et al., 2009). The authors also note that most of the morphosemantic relations connect words from different classes and go on to demonstrate that part of the noun-verb relations correspond to semantic roles. In fact, many of the noun-verb morphosemantic links in WordNet designate typical relations between a participant and a predicate, such as *agent*, *instrument*, *material*, *location*, *undergoer*, *destination*, etc.

For instance the verb literal *send* (cause to be directed or transmitted to another place) is related to the noun *sender* (someone who transmits a message) through the morphosemantic relation *agent* and to the noun *sendee* (the intended recipient of a message) through *destination*; *train* (educate for a future role or function) is connected to *trainer* (one who trains other persons or animals) through *agent* and to *trainee* (someone who is being trained) through *undergoer*. The noun members of these morphosemantic relations can function as arguments of the particular verbs and bear the respective semantic roles, i.e. *agent* for *sender* and *trainer*, *destination* for *sendee*, and *undergoer* for *trainee*.

Further, we assume that if a noun and a verb enter into the same morphosemantic relation individually, they are licensed for it and therefore, when they collocate, they enter into this relation if there is no other appropriate noun candidate for the same relation. As an example, consider the sentence: *The author used the method of cost-effectiveness analysis*. The verb *use* is linked to *user* through the morphosemantic relation *agent*. The noun *author* is connected with the verb *author* (be the author of) by means of the same relation. By virtue of the above assumption we assign the relation *agent* between *use* and *author* in this particular sentence. In such a way the morphosemantic relation identified between the derivationally related verb and noun may be inherited by synonyms, direct hypernyms, hyponyms, sister terms, etc. Thus, given a morphosemantic relation and words in the context that participate in such a relation independently of each other, we are able to discover certain types of semantic relations.

4 Method for Cross-Language Learning of Semantic Relations

The goal of the study is to identify semantic relations between a verb and collocated nouns[1] within similar clauses in Bulgarian and English (often but not necessarily translational equivalents) and to assign a semantic matrix to the verb based on collocational evidence and the WordNet hierarchy.

The method is developed and tested on a Bulgarian-English comparable corpus (Table 1) which is an excerpt from the Bulgarian National Corpus (Koeva et al., 2012).

	Bulgarian	English
Administrative		
Politics	28,148	27,609
Economy	25,800	28,436
Health	26,912	30,721
Ecology	27,886	36,227
News		
Politics	25,016	25,010
Economy	25,010	25,127
Culture	25,319	25,355
Military	25,283	25,328
Fiction		
Adventure	25,053	29,241
Humour	30,003	26,992
Love	32,631	25,459
Fantasy	30,200	32,393
TOTAL	327,261	337,898

Table 1: Distribution of texts (in terms of number of words) in the Bulgarian-English comparable corpus applied in the study

4.1 WordNet Enhancement with Morphosemantic Relations

The interest in morphosemantic relations has been motivated by the fact that they overlap to a great extent across wordnets (Bilgin et al., 2004) and thus improve the internal connectivity of the individual wordnets, as well as by the fact that the derivational subnets reflect certain cognitive structures in natural languages (Pala and Hlavackova, 2007). n approach to wordnet development based on enrichment with morphosemantic relations has been adopted for English (Fellbaum et al., 2009), as well as for a number of other languages – Turkish (Bilgin et al., 2004), Czech (Pala and Hlavackova, 2007), Bulgarian (Koeva et al., 2008), Serbian (Koeva, 2008), Polish (Piasecki et al., 2009), Romanian (Barbu Mititelu, 2012), to mention a few.

Provided there is a mapping algorithm between two or more wordnets, such as the cross-language relation of equivalence between synsets (Vossen, 2004), a morphosemantic relation between a pair of synsets in a given language can be mapped to the corresponding synsets in a different lan-

[1] Collocated here means that nouns are found within the same clause as the verb.

guage, even if the latter language does not exhibit a derivational relation between members of these particular synsets.

We automatically expand BulNet with morphosemantic relations in the following two ways:

(1) Morphosemantic relations are mapped from the morphosemantic database distributed with the PWN[2] to the corresponding Bulgarian synsets. The morphosemantic relations currently encoded in Princeton WordNet 3.0.[3] have relatively limited coverage – 14,876 verb-noun synset pairs, which involve 7,960 verb synsets and 9,704 noun synsets. The automatic transfer of morphosemantic links to BulNet resulted in the association of 5,002 verb-noun pairs involving 3,584 verb synsets and 4,938 noun synsets.

For example, the PWN synset *hammer:2* (beat with or as if with a hammer) is related to the noun synset *hammer:4* (a hand tool with a heavy rigid head and a handle; used to deliver an impulsive force by striking) through the morphosemantic relation *instrument*. We map this relation to the corresponding pair in BulNet – the verb synset *chukam:1; kova:1* and the noun synset *chuk:1*. In the particular case a derivational relation exists in Bulgarian, as well, between *chuk* and *chukam*.

(2) In general, the task of detection and classification of the identified relations includes automatic generation of derivational pairs based on knowledge of language-specific derivational patterns followed by filtering of the results through automatic and/or manual validation. Specific methods are described in more detail in the research cited at the beginning of this subsection, as well as in more recent proposals, such as the machine learning approach to generation and classification of derivational pairs made by Piasecki et al. (2012b) and Piasecki et al. (2012a), respectively.

We identify new pairs of verb-noun literals in BulNet that are potentially derivationally (and thus morphosemantically) related by means of a set of rules that describe the verb-noun and noun-verb derivational patterns in Bulgarian (we focus on patterns affecting the end of the word, thus ignoring prefixation) and assign the respective morphosemantic relations to the synsets that include the related pairs.

We identified 89 derivational noun endings (morphophonemic variants of suffixes) and 183 derivational patterns (verb ending to noun ending correspondences), and associated them with the morphosemantic relation they indicate. Only 39 of the selected derivational endings were found to be unambiguous. Moreover, many of them proved to be highly ambiguous, denoting up to 10 of the 14 morphosemantic relations. In order to disambiguate at least partially the possible morphosemantic relations associated with a particular suffix, we filtered those meanings with the general semantic classes derived from the PWN lexicographer files. The PWN synsets are organized in 45 lexicographer files based on syntactic category and general semantic word classes (26 for nouns and 15 for verbs)[4].

For instance, the Bulgarian noun suffix -*nik* is associated with the following relations *agent*, *instrument*, *location*, *undergoer*, and *event*. By virtue of the fact that the synsets denoting locations are found in the lexicographer file `noun.location`, the synset denoting agents – in `noun.person`, and the instruments – in `noun.artifact`, we were able to disambiguate the suffix at least partially.

Initially, 57,211 new derivational relations were found in BulNet. These relations were evaluated automatically on the basis of the morphosemantic relations transferred from PWN. Each triple `<verb.label, noun.label, relation>`[5] was assigned a probability based on the frequency of occurrence in the set of morphosemantic relations transferred from PWN. Those relations with a probability below 1% were filtered out. As a result 34,677 morphosemantic relations between a noun literal and a verb literal were assigned among 7,456 unique noun-verb synset pairs, which involved 2,537 verb synsets and 1,708 noun synsets.

For example the noun synset *kovach:1* (corresponding to *blacksmith:1*) is derivationally related with the verb literal *kova:1* through the suffix *-ach*, which is associated either with an *agent* or with an *instrument* relation depending on the semantics of the noun – a person or an inanimate object. In this case the meaning of the suffix is disambiguated

[2] `http://wordnetcode.princeton.edu/standoff-files/morphosemantic-links.xls`

[3] `http://wordnet.princeton.edu/wordnet/download/standoff/`

[4] `http://wordnet.princeton.edu/wordnet/man/lexnames.5WN.html`

[5] The `verb.label` and `noun.label` are descriptive labels of the wordnet synsets which are listed in the respective lexicographer files.

by virtue of the fact that *kovach:1* is found in the `noun.person` lexicographer file. We link the literals *kova:1* and *kovach:1* via a derivational relation *suffix* and assign the synsets the morphosemantic relation *agent*.

4.2 Preprocessing and Clause Splitting

The preprocessing of the Bulgarian-English corpus used in the study includes sentence-splitting, tokenization, POS-tagging and lemmatization, using the Bulgarian Language Processing Chain[6] (Koeva and Genov, 2011) for the Bulgarian part and Stanford CoreNLP[7] for the English part.

The clause serves as the minimal context for the realization of verb semantics, and hence – the scope within which we carry out the cross-linguistic analysis and the assignment of relations. Clause splitting is applied using a general method based on POS tagging, lists of clause delimiters (clause linking words, multiword expressions, and punctuation) and a set of language-specific rules. We define the clause as a sequence of words between two potential clause delimiters where exactly one predicate (a simple or a complex verb form, which may be a lexical verb, an auxiliary, a copula, or a combination of a lexical verb or a copula with one or more auxiliaries) occurs. We identify the predicates in each sentence using language-specific rules for Bulgarian and English. Each clause is labeled by a clause opening and a clause end. The clause splitting algorithm marks subordinating and coordinating clause linking words and phrases and punctuation clause delimiters. If no clause boundary has been identified between two predicates, a clause boundary is inserted before the second one. The nested clauses are detected, as well.

4.3 Word-to-Word and Text-to-Text Semantic Similarity

WordNet has inspired the elaboration of metrics for word similarity and relatedness that quantify the degree to which words (concepts) are related using properties of the WordNet structure. The so-called path-length based measures rely on the length of the path between two nodes (synsets), possibly normalized. For instance, the Leacock-Chodorow metric (Leacock and Chodorow, 1998) finds the shortest path between two concepts and scales the path length by the overall depth D of the WordNet taxonomy, while Wu-Palmer (Wu and Palmer, 1994) calculates the depth of the concepts and their least common subsumer in the WordNet taxonomy.

Information content based metrics augment the path information with corpus statistics. Resnik (1995) measures the similarity of two concepts by calculating the information content (IC) of their least common subsumer (LCS). Jiang-Conrath (Jiang and Conrath, 1997) and Lin (Lin, 1998) combine the information content of the LCS with the information content of the individual concepts.

Several relatedness metrics have also been proposed, such as Hirst-St-Onge (Hirst and St-Onge, 1998), which measures semantic relatedness based on the path length and its nature (the changes of direction in the path), and the algorithms proposed by Banerjee and Pederson (2002) and Patwardhan et al. (2003), which rely on information obtained from the synsets glosses.

A number of researchers have addressed WSD based on cross-lingual semantic similarity measurement, such as the application of monolingual WSD graph-based algorithms to multilingual co-occurrence graphs based on WordNet (Silberer and Ponzetto, 2010), or of multilingual WSD algorithms based on multilingual knowledge from BabelNet (Navigli and Ponzetto, 2012).

For the purposes of the extraction of semantic relations we are interested in corresponding pairs of clauses in Bulgarian and English satisfying the following conditions: (a) the verbs in the clauses are similar (with respect to a certain similarity measure and threshold); and (b) the clauses are similar in meaning (with respect to a certain similarity measure and threshold). Similar pairs of verbs and nouns are identified on the basis of the Wu-Palmer word-to-word similarity measure (Wu and Palmer, 1994). Clause similarity is computed by means of the text similarity measurement proposed by Mihalcea et al. (2006).

Measuring semantic similarity cross-linguistically enables us to filter some of the senses of a particular word in one language since potential semantic similarity of words within similar clauses strongly suggests that these words are semantically related – translation equivalents, close synonyms, hypernyms, or hyponyms.

In the application of the method described in Section 4.4, we assign semantic relations to the el-

[6] `http://dcl.bas.bg/services/`
[7] `http://nlp.stanford.edu/software/corenlp.shtml`

ements of similar clauses in a comparable, not necessarily parallel, Bulgarian-English corpus. Moreover, we identify semantically similar rather than parallel clauses, which enables us to experiment with a greater number and diversity of contexts for the identification of semantic relations.

4.4 Method outline

We select corresponding (comparable) pairs of texts from the corpus – T_1 in Bulgarian and T_2 in English on the basis of their detailed metadata description (Koeva et al., 2012), including parameters such as style, domain and genre. For each pair of corresponding texts T_1 and T_2 we apply the following algorithm:

Step 1. We identify semantically similar pairs of verbs and consider similarity between their respective clauses – $v_1 \in \mathrm{cl}_1$ and $v_2 \in \mathrm{cl}_2$, where $\mathrm{cl}_1 \in T_1$ and $\mathrm{cl}_2 \in T_2$ and cl_1 are also semantically similar (cf. Section 4.3 for word-to-word and clause-to-clause similarity).

Step 2. We identify semantically similar pairs of collocated nouns in the bi-clause $(\mathrm{cl}_1, \mathrm{cl}_2)$ in the same way as for verbs.

Step 3. We assign morphosemantic relations to the verb and its collocated nouns using the enhanced set of relations (cf. Section 4.1) and map all matching candidates (v_1, n_1, rel) in $\mathrm{cl}_1(v_1)$ and (v_2, n_2, rel) in $\mathrm{cl}_(v_2)$.

Step 4. Since co-occurrence of members of a single instance of a morphosemantic relation are relatively rare, we transfer the morphosemantic relations to non-derivationally related words, provided a noun and a verb participate in the same type of morphosemantic relation independently of each other. In Example 1 the noun *director* enters into a morphosemantic relation (*agent*) with the verb *direct*, while the verb *send* enters independently into the same type of relation with the noun *sender*. Since both *director* and *send* are licensed for *agent*, we assign the relation.

Example 1.
Croatian director Zrinko Ogresta sent an invitation for the international film festival.
send, 01437254-v, verb.contact
{to cause or order to be taken directed or transmitted to another place}
director, 10015215-n, noun.person
VERB *send*: agent, NOUN *director*: agent_inv

Step 5. We hierarchize the candidates for a particular morphosemantic relation and select the most probable one based on the general semantic word classes (`verb.label` and `noun.label`) and the relations they participate in. Where two or more morphosemantic relations are assigned between a pair of words, priority is given to the relation which is most compatible with the general semantic class of the noun in the relation.

Some relations, such as *event*, are very general and therefore are not considered even if their probability is higher, provided a more meaningful relation is available. Moreover, we incorporate some syntactic and word-order dependencies. For instance, a noun which is a complement of a prepositional phrase and is thus found in the following configurations: $p(A)N$ (with any number of adjectives preceding the noun) is not licensed for the morphosemantic relation *agent* if the verb is active.

Step 6. Based on the general semantic class of the noun and/or the verb, some additional potential relations are added to the respective synsets in the model (Example 2). For example, a noun belonging to the class `noun.location` can potentially enter into a *location* relation with the verb, although the respective noun synset might not enter into this morphosemantic relation.

Example 2. Newly added relations

`verb.label`	**role**
contact	agent
motion	location

`noun.label`	**role**
person	agent_inv
location	location_inv
attribute	property_inv

Step 7. We extend the number of relations by learning from previous occurrences. Learning is performed on the News subcorpus (see Table 1), and further experiments extend the information acquired in the learning phase with data from the entire corpus.

Given a verb is licensed to enter into a particular morphosemantic relation, we assign this relation to a co-occurring verb-noun pair, even if the noun in this pair does not enter into this type of relation, provided other nouns belonging to the same general semantic class have been observed to cooccur with this verb. This assumption is generalized over all the members of the verb synset and the noun synset to which the respective verb and noun belong.

Example 3 shows how learning is applied: based on the occurrences of verbs from the same synset (ID: 00974367-v, *announce:2; declare:2*) in a morphosemantic relation of type *agent* with nouns belonging to the semantic class `noun.group` (in 60.4% of the cases), we associate the verb *announce* with the noun *Ministry* (`noun.group`) through the *agent* relation despite the fact that *Ministry* is not linked to any verb through a morphosemantic relation.

Example 3.

Learned:

Verb ID	relation	noun.label	freq
00974367-v	by-means-of	noun.artifact	5
00974367-v	by-means-of	noun.act	14
00974367-v	agent	noun.person	9
00974367-v	agent	noun.group	16

The Ministry of Defense announced on Wednesday its new plans.
announce, 00974367-v, verb.communication
{make known, make an announcement}
Ministry, 08114004-n, noun.group
VERB *announce*: agent
NOUN *Ministry*: agent_inv

At a next stage of generalization we consider only the general semantic classes of a verb and a noun which are candidates to enter in a morphosemantic relation. This step relies on the assumption that verbs from the same semantic class (e.g. perception verbs) show preference to similar semantic patterns. The learned information is in a generalized form, as presented in Example 4.

Example 4. A sample of semantic compatibility information learned from the News subcorpus.

verb.label	relation	noun.label	freq
verb.perception	undergoer	noun.person	15
verb.perception	undergoer	noun.group	3
verb.perception	state	noun.state	12
verb.perception	by-means-of	noun.state	12
verb.perception	by-means-of	noun.act	6
verb.perception	uses	noun.group	3
verb.perception	agent	noun.person	3

4.5 Implementation

We implement the word-to-word similarities with the *ws4j* package for Java[8], which is based on the original Perl package `Wordnet::Similarity` (Pedersen et al., 2007).

We use the Princeton WordNet 3.0 and access it through Java libraries such as JAWS[9] and JWI[10]. We also employ a list of morphosemantic relations available for WordNet 3.0. The access to BulNet is modeled roughly on PWN. The corresponding synsets in the two wordnets are linked by means of synset IDs.

5 Results and Evaluation

Evaluation was performed with respect to the coverage of the morphosemantic relations, the precision of the assigned relations, and the informativeness of the extracted semantic patterns. Testing was carried out on the News subcorpus (Table 1) totaling 100,628 tokens distributed in four subdomains: Politics, Economy, Culture, and Military. The corpus comprises 3,362 sentences and 7,535 clauses for Bulgarian and 3,678 sentences and 8,624 clauses for English.

	Method	# clauses	# relations
1	Baseline_0	920	1,183
2	Baseline	951	1,246
3	Learned and transferred to synsets	1,032	1,353
4	Learned and transferred to semantic classes	1,395	1,973

Table 2: Coverage of relations in the News subcorpus using the baseline method (2) and the extended method (4)

Table 2 presents: (1) the number of morphosemantic relations covered by the baseline_0 method, i.e. applying only the Princeton WordNet morphosemantic relations; (2) the number of morphosemantic relations after adding those specific to Bulgarian; and (3, 4) the number of morphosemantic relations learnt with the method described in Step 7 (Section 4.4). The results show that the extended method leads to an increase in coverage by 58.35% (compare the extended method (4) with the baseline (2)).

To assess the precision of the automatic relation assignment, we performed evaluation on five relations: *agent*, *undergoer*, *location*, *result*, and *state* (Table 3). The overall precision based on these relations is 0.774 for the baseline and 0.721 for the extended method, which shows that the performance of the method is relatively consistent.

We also obtained two types of generalizations based on WordNet and confirmed by the corpus

[8]`https://code.google.com/p/ws4j/`

[9]`http://lyle.smu.edu/~tspell/jaws/`

[10]`http://projects.csail.mit.edu/jwi/api/`

Relation	Precision (baseline)	Precision (extended method)
Agent	0.963	0.950
Undergoer	0.575	0.577
Location	0.857	0.750
Result	0.303	0.316
State	0.750	0.667

Table 3: Precision of the results for five semantic relations – baseline (Princeton and Bulgarian morphosemantic relations) and extended method (transfer of morphosemantic relations to pairs of nouns and verbs one of which does not participate in morphosemantic relations)

data that can be used for further classification. The first one represents the combinatorial properties of general semantic verb classes with particular (morpho)semantic relations. For example a verb of communication is more likely linked to an *agent* rather than to a *result* (Example 5).

Example 5. Frequency of relations in WordNet and the entire corpus.

verb.label	relation	fr wn	fr cor
verb.com	agent	744	555
verb.com	undergoer	306	362
verb.com	by-means-of	244	560
verb.com	result	192	283

Moreover, the nouns that are eligible to collocate as agents with a communication verb belong to a limited set of classes – `noun.person` or `noun.group` (Example 6).

Example 6. Frequency of relations in WordNet and the entire corpus.

verb.label	relation	noun label	fr wn	fr cor
verb.com	agent	noun.person	473	333
verb.com	agent	noun.group	271	220

The second generalization refers to the probability of the association of a given verb sense with a particular set of semantic relations and the general noun classes eligible for these relations. For instance, the communication verb *order* (Example 7) in the sense of *give instructions to or direct somebody to do something with authority* connects with the highest probability with an *undergoer* (`noun.person`) and an *agent* (`noun.person`).

Example 7. Relations of the verb *order* in WordNet and the entire corpus.

verb.label	relation	noun label	fr wn	fr cor
verb.com	undergoer	noun.person	33	8
verb.com	agent	noun.person	12	6
verb.com	by-means-of	noun.phen	9	7

6 Conclusions and Future Work

In this paper we have explored the applicability of the morphosemantic relations in WordNet for cross-language identification of semantic and in some cases syntactic dependencies between collocated verbs and nouns. As morphosemantic relations are valid cross-linguistically, the method is applicable for any language or a pair of languages.

The limitations of the proposed method lie in the insufficient connectivity of the nodes (synsets and literals). We have described an approach to automatic wordnet enhancement, which has resulted in a substantial increase in the number of morphosemantic relations. Another inherent weakness is that some of the relations are very general or vaguely defined. We have addressed this problem by considering relations jointly with the general semantic classes associated with the synsets in WordNet.

The method has the advantage of using limited linguistic annotation. It does not require text alignment, syntactic parsing or word-sense disambiguation. The cross-linguistic similarity partially disambiguates the target words, so that the senses for which the clauses are not similar are discarded; the semantic restrictions imposed by the general semantic classes and their compatibility also contribute to semantic disambiguation. The method is thus to a large extent language-independent and well suited to less-resourced languages.

In order to improve the performance and overcome the limitations of the method, we plan to explore deeper into the possibilities of predicting the roles of the verb participants from their general semantic class and the semantic compatibility of verb and noun classes, as well as from the compatibility of the different types of morphosemantic relations with the general semantic classes.

Another line of research to pursue in the future is the application of the proposed method and its subtasks to other NLP tasks, such as clause splitting, alignment based on wordnet relations, extraction of patterns from comparable corpora, and augmentation and enhancement of training data for MT.

References

Satanjeev Banerjee and Ted Pedersen. 2002. An adapted lesk algorithm for word sense disambiguation using wordnet. *Lecture Notes In Computer Science*, 2276:136–145.

Verginica Barbu Mititelu. 2012. Adding Morpho-Semantic Relations to the Romanian Wordnet. In *Proceedings of the Eight International Conference on Language Resources and Evaluation (LREC'12)*, pages 2596–2601.

Orhan Bilgin, Özlem Cetinouğlu, , and Kemal Oflazer. 2004. Morphosemantic Relations In and Across Wordnets – A Study Based on Turkish. In P. Sojka, K. Pala, P. Smrz, C. Fellbaum, and P. Vossen, editors, *Proceedings of the Global Wordnet Conference*, pages 60–66.

Xavier Carreras and Lluis Marquez. 2004. Introduction to the CoNLL-2004 Shared Task: Semantic Role Labeling. In *Proceedings of CoNLL-2004*.

Xavier Carreras and Lluis Marquez. 2005. Introduction to the CoNLL-2005 Shared Task: Semantic Role Labeling. In *Proceedings of CoNLL-2005*.

Christine Fellbaum, Anne Osherson, and Peter E. Clark. 2009. Putting Semantics into WordNet's "Morphosemantic" Links. In Z. Vetulani and H. Uszkoreit, editors, *Proceedings of the Third Language and Technology Conference, Poznan, Poland. Reprinted in: Responding to Information Society Challenges: New Advances in Human Language Technologies*, volume 5603 of *Springer Lecture Notes in Informatics*, pages 350–358.

Daniel Gildea and Daniel Jurafsky. 2002. Automatic labeling of semantic roles. *Computational Linguistics*, 28(3):245–288, September.

Jan Hajic. 1998. Building a syntactically annotated corpus: The prague dependency treebank. *Issues of Valency and Meaning*, pages 106–132.

Jan Hajič, Massimiliano Ciaramita, Richard Johansson, Daisuke Kawahara, Maria Antnia Martí, Lluís Márquez, Adam Meyers, Joakim Nivre, Sebastian Padó, Jan Štěpánek, Pavel Straňák, Mihai Surdeanu, Nianwen Xue, and Yi Zhang. 2009. The CoNLL-2009 Shared Task: Syntactic and Semantic Dependencies in Multiple Languages. In *Proceedings of the Thirteenth Conference on Computational Natural Language Learning (CoNLL 2009): Shared Task*, pages 1–18.

Graeme Hirst and David St-Onge. 1998. Lexical chains as representations of context for the detection and correction of malapropisms. In Christiane Fellbaum, editor, *WordNet: An electronic lexical database*, page 305332. MIT Press.

Jay J. Jiang and David W. Conrath. 1997. Semantic similarity based on corpus statistics and lexical taxonomy. In *Proceedings on International Conference on Research in Computational Linguistics*, page 1933.

S. Koeva and A. Genov. 2011. Bulgarian language processing chain. In *Proceedings of Integration of multilingual resources and tools in Web applications. Workshop in conjunction with GSCL 2011, University of Hamburg*.

Svetla Koeva, Cvetana Krstev, and Dusko Vitas. 2008. Morpho-semantic relations in wordnet - a case study for two slavic langages. In *Proceedings of the Fourth Global WordNet Conference*, pages 239–254.

Svetla Koeva, Ivelina Stoyanova, Svetlozara Leseva, Tsvetana Dimitrova, Rositsa Dekova, and Ekaterina Tarpomanova. 2012. The Bulgarian National Corpus: Theory and Practice in Corpus Design. *Journal of Language Modelling*, 0(1):65–110.

Svetla Koeva. 2008. Derivational and morphosemantic relations in bulgarian wordnet. *Intelligent Information Systems*, XVI:359–369.

Joel Lang and Mirella Lapata. 2011a. Unsupervised Semantic Role Induction via Split-Merge Clustering. In *Proceedings of ACL 2011*, pages 1117–1126.

Joel Lang and Mirella Lapata. 2011b. Unsupervised Semantic Role Induction with Graph Partitioning. In *Proceedings of EMNLP 2011*, pages 1320–1331.

Claudia Leacock and Michael Chodorow. 1998. Combining local context and WordNet similarity for word sense identification. In C. Fellbaum, editor, *WordNet: An electronic lexical database*, pages 265–283. MIT Press.

Dekang Lin. 1998. An information-theoretic definition of similarity. In *Proceedings of the International Conference on Machine Learning*.

Lluis Marquez, Xavier Carreras, Kenneth C. Litkowski, and Suzanne Stevenson. 2008. Semantic role labeling: An introduction to the special issue. *Computational Linguistics*, 34(2):145–159.

Rada Mihalcea, Courtney Corley, and Carlo Strapparava. 2006. Corpus-based and Knowledge-based Measures of Text Semantic Similarity. In *Proceedings of the American Association for Artificial Intelligence (AAAI 2006), Boston*.

Alessandro Moschitti and Cosmin Adrian Bejan. 2004. A semantic kernel for predicate argument classication. In *In Proceedings of CONLL 2004*, pages 17–24.

Roberto Navigli and Simone Paolo Ponzetto. 2012. Joining Forces Pays Off: Multilingual Joint Word Sense Disambiguation. In *Proceedings of the 2012 Joint Conference on Empirical Methods in Natural Language Processing and Computational Natural Language Learning, Jeju Island, Korea*, pages 1399–1410.

K. Pala and D. Hlavackova. 2007. Derivational relations in Czech Wordnet. In *Proceedings of the Workshop on Balto-Slavonic Natural Language Processing*, pages 75–81.

Martha Palmer, Paul Kingsbury, and Daniel Gildea. 2005. The proposition bank: An annotated corpus of semantic roles. *Computational Linguistics*, 31(1):71–106.

Siddharth Patwardhan, Satanjeev Banerjee, and Ted Pedersen. 2003. Using measures of semantic relatedness for word sense disambiguation. In *Proceedings of the Fourth International Conference on Intelligent Text Processing and Computational Linguistics*, pages 241–257.

Ted Pedersen, Serguei Pakhomov, Siddharth Patwardhan, and Christopher G. Chute. 2007. Measures of semantic similarity and relatedness in the biomedical domain. *Journal of Biomedical Informatics*, 40(3):288–299.

Maciej Piasecki, Stanisaw Szpakowicz, and Bartosz Broda. 2009. A wordnet from the ground up. In *Wroclaw: Oficyna Wydawnicza Politechniki Wroclawskiej*.

Maciej Piasecki, Radoslaw Ramocki, and Pawel Minda. 2012a. Corpus-based semantic filtering in discovering derivational relations. In *AIMSA*, pages 14–22.

Maciej Piasecki, Radosaw Ramocki, and Marek Maziarz. 2012b. Automated Generation of Derivative Relations in the Wordnet Expansion Perspective. In *Proceedings of the 6th Global Wordnet Conference*, Matsue, Japan, January.

Sameer Pradhan, Wayne Ward, Kadri Hacioglu, James Martin, and Daniel Jurafsky. 2004. Shallow Semantic Parsing Using Support Vector Machines. In *Proceedings of NAACL-HLT 2004*.

Sameer Pradhan, Wayne Ward, and James Martin. 2008. Towards Robust Semantic Role Labeling. *Computational Linguistics*, (34):289–310.

Philip Resnik. 1995. Using information content to evaluate semantic similarity in a taxonomy. In *Proceedings of the 14th International Joint Conference on Artificial Intelligence*, pages 448–453.

Josef Ruppenhofer, Michael Ellsworth, Miriam R. L. Petruck, Christopher R. Johnson, and Jan Scheczyk. 2010. Framenet ii: Extended theory and practice. Web Publication. `http://framenet.icsi.berkeley.edu`.

Lei Shi and Rada Mihalcea. 2005. Putting Pieces Together: Combining FrameNet, VerbNet and WordNet for Robust Semantic Parsing. In A. Gelbukh, editor, *CICLing 2005, LNCS 3406*, page 100111.

Carina Silberer and Simone Paolo Ponzetto. 2010. UHD: Cross-lingual Word Sense Disambiguation using multilingual co-occurrence graphs. In *Proceedings of the 5th International Workshop on Semantic Evaluations (SemEval-2010)*, pages 134–137.

Mihai Surdeanu, Sanda Harabagiu, John Williams, and Paul Aarseth. 2003. Using predicate-argument structures for information extraction. In *Proceedings of ACL-2003*, pages 8–15.

Mihai Surdeanu, Richard Johansson, Adam Meyers, Lluís Márquez, and Joakim Nivre. 2008. The CoNLL-2008 Shared Task on Joint Parsing of Syntactic and Semantic Dependencies. In *CoNLL 2008: Proceedings of the Twelfth Conference on Natural Language Learning*, pages 159–177.

Robert Swier and Suzanne Stevenson. 2005. Exploiting a Verb Lexicon in Automatic Semantic Role Labelling. In *In Proceedings of Human Language Technology Conference and Conference on Empirical Methods in Natural Language Processing 2005*, pages 883–890.

Kristina Toutanova, Aria Haghighi, and Christopher Manning. 2008. A global joint model for semantic role labeling. *Computational Linguistics*.

Piek Vossen. 2004. EuroWordNet: A Multilingual Database of Autonomous and Language-Specific Wordnets Connected via an Inter-Lingual Index. *International Journal of Lexicography*, 17(1):161–173, June.

Zhibiao Wu and Martha Palmer. 1994. Verb semantics and lexical selection. In *Proceedings of the 32nd Annual Meeting of the Association for Computational Linguistics*, pages 133–138.

Nianwen Xue and Martha Palmer. 2004. Calibrating features for semantic role labeling. In Dekang Lin and Dekai Wu, editors, *Proceedings of EMNLP04, Barcelona, Spain*, July.

Author Index